DarkMarket

Also by Misha Glenny

McMafia

DarkMarket

Cyberthieves,
Cybercops
and You

Misha Glenny

Alfred A. Knopf   New York   2011

THIS IS A BORZOI BOOK
PUBLISHED BY ALFRED A. KNOPF

www.aaknopf.com

Knopf, Borzoi Books, and the colophon are registered trademarks
of Random House, Inc.

Originally published in England by The Bodley Head, The
Random House Group Limited, London.

Library of Congress Cataloging-in-Publication Data
Glenny, Misha.
DarkMarket : cyberthieves, cybercops and you / by Misha Glenny.
p. cm.
title: Dark market
Includes bibliographical references and index.
ISBN 978-0-307-59293-4 (alk. paper)
1. Computer crimes. 2. Computer crimes—Prevention.
3. Organized crime—Government policy. I. Title.
II. Title: Dark market.
HV6773.G54 2011
364.16'8—dc23
2011013882

Jacket illustration by Thomas Hubben
Jacket design by Barbara de Wilde

Manufactured in the United States of America
First United States Edition

For Miljan, Alexandra and Callum

CONTENTS

PROLOGUE

crime@21stcentury.com

In humanity's relentless drive for convenience and economic growth, we have developed a dangerous level of dependency on networked systems in a very short space of time: in less than two decades, huge parts of the so-called 'critical national infrastructure' (CNI in geekish) in most countries have come under the control of ever more complex computer systems.

Computers guide large parts of our lives as they regulate our communications, our vehicles, our interaction with commerce and the state, our work, our leisure, our everything. At one of several cybercrime trials I have attended in recent years, Britain's Crown Prosecution Service demanded the imposition of a so-called Prevention of Crime Order on a hacker, which would come into force after his release from prison. The Order would block him from accessing the Internet except for one hour a week under the supervision of a police officer. 'By the time my client completes his sentence,' the defendant's lawyer remarked at the hearing, 'there will barely be a single human activity that will not somehow be mediated by the Internet. How is my client supposed to live a normal life under such circumstances?' he asked rhetorically.

How indeed. Those who have left their mobile phone at home even for a few hours usually notice an intense irritation and a sense of loss, akin to cold turkey among more dependent users. Interestingly, when deprived of the device for three days, this corrosive feeling of unease is often replaced by a rush of liberation as one is transported back to a world, not so far away, where we neither had nor needed mobile phones and we arranged our lives accordingly. Today most people feel they cannot live without these tiny portable computers.

Perhaps the nearest comparison to computers is the motor vehicle. As cars became a standard family item from the 1940s onwards, only a minority of drivers really understood what was going on under the bonnet. Nonetheless that was still quite a number who could fix their vehicle whatever the cause of breakdown, still more who could tweak the carburettor in order to limp home, and most could at least change a flat tyre.

These days if it's only a flat tyre, you can still probably reach your destination. But a growing number of breakdowns are now the result of a computer failure in the control box – the black plastic housing usually located behind the engine. If it is a control-box issue, then even if you are an experienced tank mechanic you won't be able to get the car moving. If you are lucky, a computer engineer will be able to fix it. But in most cases you will need to replace the unit.

Computer systems are so much more complex and fragile than internal combustion engines that only the very tiniest group of people can begin to deal with a problem beyond the familiar mantra, 'Have you tried rebooting it?'

We now find ourselves in a situation where this minuscule elite (call them geeks, technos, hackers, coders, securocrats, or what you will) has a profound understanding of a technology that every day directs our lives more intensively and extensively, while most of the rest of us understand absolutely zip about it. I had first begun to appreciate the significance of this when researching my previous book on global organised crime, *McMafia*. I travelled to Brazil in order to investigate cybercrime because this absorbing country is, among its many positive qualities, a major centre of bad stuff on the Web – though this was little known at the time.

Here I met cyber thieves who had engineered a spectacularly successful phishing scam. Phishing remains one of the most dependable pillars of criminality on the Internet. There are two simple variants. The victim opens a spam email. The attachment may contain a virus, which enables a computer somewhere else in the world to monitor all activity on the affected computer, including the input of bank passwords. The other trick lies in designing an email that appears to have been sent by a bank or other institution, requesting confirmation of login and password details. If the recipient falls for the ruse, then the spammer can use these to access some or all of your Internet accounts. The Brazilian hackers demonstrated step-by-step how they secured tens of millions of dollars for themselves from bank accounts in Brazil, Spain, Portugal, the United Kingdom and the United States.

I then visited the cybercops in Brasilia who had busted four other members of their criminal group (although at least twice that number were never tracked down by the police), and then I interviewed the chief of X-Force, the covert-operations department of the American computer security company, ISS. In the space of about a week I realised that conventional or traditional organised crime, colourful and varied though it was, carried with it significantly greater risks for the perpetrators than for those engaged in cybercrime.

Old-fashioned organised-crime groups, attached to the technology and means of the twentieth century, need to overcome two daunting hurdles if they are to make a success of their chosen profession. The police represent their primary business risk. The efficacy of law enforcement varies both geographically and in time. Organised-crime groups adapt themselves to these changing conditions and choose one of a number of methods of dealing with the forces of law and order. They can attempt to outmuscle them; they can corrupt them; they can corrupt politicians exercising authority over the police; or they can evade detection.

Then they face a second problem: threats posed by the competition, other bad guys trawling for prey in the same waters. Here again they can attempt to outmuscle them; they can suggest forming an alliance; or they might agree to be absorbed by them.

In neither case, however, can the criminal syndicate simply ignore them – that way lies failure, with sometimes fatal results. Key to survival and prosperity is the ability to communicate with your fellow criminals and with the police – and, indeed, to send the correct messages to both groups.

In Brazil, I learned very quickly that twenty-first-century crime is different.

Most importantly, it is much much harder to identify when people are up to no good on the Web. Laws governing the Internet vary greatly from country to country. This matters because in general a criminal act over the Web will be perpetrated from an IP (Internet Protocol) address in one country against an individual or corporation in a second country, before being realised (or cashed out) in a third. A police officer in Colombia, for example, may be able to identify that the IP address coordinating an assault on a Colombian bank emanates from Kazakhstan. But then he discovers that this is not considered a crime in Kazakhstan, and so his opposite number in the Kazakh capital will have no reason to investigate the crime.

Many cyber criminals have the intelligence to research and exploit such discrepancies. 'I never use American credit or debit cards,' one of Sweden's most successful 'carders' told me, 'because that would put me under the legal jurisdiction of the United States wherever I am on the planet. So I just do European and Canadian cards, and I feel both happy and safe with that – they will never catch me.'

The divide separating the United States from Europe and Canada is most important, as these are the areas where the highest concentration of cybercrime victims live. The latter territories have much stronger laws in force to protect individual liberties and rights on the Web. Successive US governments have granted greater powers to law enforcement than most European governments would contemplate, allowing officers easier access to data from private companies, in the name of fighting crime and terrorism.

The implications of this are both profound and, for the moment, impenetrable. Concerns about crime, surveillance, privacy, the accumulation of data by both private and state institutions, freedom of speech (step forward WikiLeaks), ease of access to websites (the so-called net neutrality debate), social networking as a political tool, and national-security interests constantly bump up against one another in cyberspace.

One might argue, for example, that Google's multi-platform, multitasking omnipresence violates the principles of America's anti-trust legislation and that the agglomeration of all that personal data is both an opportunity for criminals and a threat to civil liberties. Yet Google might well respond that the very essence of its genius and success lies in its multi-platform, multitasking omnipresence and that this in itself promotes America's commercial and security interests. If it wishes, the US government can access Google's data using legal procedures within hours and, because Google gathers data from all over the world, this gives Washington an immense strategic advantage. Other governments should be so lucky. Unlike its Chinese, Russian or Middle Eastern counterparts, the American government does not need to hack Google to explore its secrets. It can get a court order instead. Would you really give that up in the name of anti-trust legislation?

The Internet is one big-bubble theory – you solve one problem affecting it, but another, seemingly intractable, pops up elsewhere.

And the biggest problem of all for law enforcement is anonymity. For the moment, it remains perfectly possible for anybody accessing the Internet with the requisite and learnable knowledge to mask the physical location of a computer.

There are two primary ways of doing this – the first cyber wall is the VPN or Virtual Private Network, whereby a group of computers can share a single IP address. Usually the IP address relates to a single machine, but with a VPN several computers in entirely different places around the world can appear to be situated in Botswana, for example.

For those who are not satisfied with the VPN as protection, they may also build a second cyber wall by using so-called proxy servers. A computer that is located in the Seychelles could be using a proxy in, say, China or Guatemala. The proxy does not reveal that the original IP is transmitting from the Seychelles, and in any event that computer is part of a VPN based in Greenland.

Setting all this up does require advanced computer skills and so these techniques tend to be used by only two groups involved in cyber-crime – real hackers and real criminals. But these high-end operators who represent a new type of serious organised crime are a small minority of those involved in computer crime.

That leaves the small-time players who deal individually with relatively trivial sums of cash, effectively petty thieves who are barely worth hunting down, given the paucity of resources available to law enforcement. Even if these characters cannot be bothered to set up VPNs, proxies and a host of other masking techniques, they can still make life very difficult for police officers by encrypting their communications.

Software that guarantees the encryption of your written (and even voice and video) communications is widely available on the Web for free, most notably PGP, an acronym for the cheerfully colloquial Pretty Good Privacy.

Encryption is a powerful tool that plays an important role in cyber security. It is a way of scrambling language using digitally generated keys, the permutations of which are so astronomical mathematically that it can only be revealed if you know the password. For the moment, encrypted documents are effectively secure, although Washington's National Security Agency (NSA), the most powerful digital spy agency in the world, is always working on ways to crack them. Among the cyber-criminal fraternity, rumours already abound that the NSA and its intelligence-gathering partners in Canada, Britain, Australia and New Zealand possess the ability to break these public encryption systems using its Orwellian Echelon system. Echelon, it has been reported, can access phone, email and satellite communications anywhere in the world.

The political implications of digital encryption are so immense that the government of the United States started to classify encryption software in the 1990s as 'munitions', while in Russia should the police or KGB ever find a single encrypted file on your computer, you could be liable for several years in jail, even if the document only contains your weekly shopping list. As governments and corporations amass ever more personal information about their citizens or clients, encryption is one of the few defences left to individuals to secure their privacy. It is also an invaluable instrument for those involved in criminal activity on the Web.

Just as traditional criminals have to develop ways of talking to each other to identify friends, foes, cops or rivals, so the cyber villains face the permanent challenge of trying to establish the bona-fide credentials of anybody they chat to online. Part of the story of this book tells how they developed methods to identify one another, and how police forces around the world have attempted to counter the hackers' ability to spot law-enforcement agents and so-called Confidential Informants (CIs) on the Web.

During the 1990s, the simplest way of preventing unwanted guests prying into criminal activity lay in the introduction of a strict vetting and membership system for websites devoted to discussing malfeasance on the Internet. Notwithstanding these security measures, it was only a matter of months before law enforcement like the US Secret Service or intelligence agencies such as the KGB's successor, the FSB, were crawling all over the sites, having gained access by patiently posing as criminals or by persuading informants to work on their behalf.

The performance of some agents was so convincing that some law-enforcement agencies have even devoted resources to chasing undercover cops from their sister organisations, on the assumption that they were real criminals.

As a result of their efforts, police forces and spies have, over the last decade, built up a large database of criminal hackers: their nicknames, their actual or presumed locations, the type of activity they engage in and whom they communicate with most frequently. The lowest level of cyber criminals have had their data crunched down to a pulp. Yet despite all this information, it remains extremely hard to prosecute cyber criminals.

This is where the very nature of the Web – in particular its interconnectedness – creates an enormous headache for the forces of law and order: nobody is ever 100 per cent certain whom they are communicating with on the Web. Are you dealing with a common-or-garden criminal hacker? Or are you dealing with somebody who has friends in higher places? Are you talking to a criminal? Or a spook? Or a military researcher assessing the value of criminal hacking techniques? Are you watching your interlocutor or is he watching you? Is he trying to make money for himself? Or for al-Qaeda?

'This is like a game of seven-dimensional chess,' the futurologist Bruno Guissani has remarked, 'in which you are never certain of who your opponent is at any one time.'

Arriving at Google's headquarters in Mountain View, California, was not quite like clapping eyes on the Taj Mahal for the first time, but I nonetheless felt a spasm of awe as I parked on Charleston Avenue in front of the multicoloured sign proclaiming one of the wonders of the post-industrial world.

The speed with which Google has melted into our consciousness, with all the highs and lows associated with a controlled narcotic substance, has no precedent. Its only rivals are cousins in the family of digital behemoths, like Facebook, Microsoft and Amazon. But not even these three are quite able to boast the success that Google can, in assisting, guiding and monitoring our lives as its cavernous servers spit out gazillions of bytes of requested information while slurping up and storing individual and collective data profiles of billions of humans. This data, of course, reveals much more about us than we know ourselves. One shudders to think what might happen if the information fell into the wrong hands. Maybe it already has . . .

The jolly pastel mix of primary and secondary colours, familiar from Google's logo, is replicated throughout the 'campus'. Often they use soft, rounded edges to define the large objects scattered around the place with precision higgledy-pigglediness. The sculptures are designed for sitting on, looking at or playing with, so that the entire complex resembles either a vast kindergarten or, depending on your anxiety and paranoia levels, the bizarre toytown village from the 1960s TV show *The Prisoner*, whither national-security risks were sent and whence there was no escape. Is it my imagination or does everyone I see on the campus, from cleaners to senior management, sport a trance-like smile? This both strengthens the paranoid interpretation of Google's essence and gives the impression that they are all working a little too hard on not being evil. I cannot quite gauge whether this is a dream or a nightmare.

It is almost a relief when I meet Corey Louie, Google's Trust and Safety Manager, because people involved in security have a no-nonsense air and a penchant for secrecy, regardless of who they are working for. His demeanour is a welcome contrast to Google's vibe of Buddhist oneness. A smart Asian American in his thirties, with a brisk but warm manner, Louie cut his cyber teeth not among the lotus eaters in Silicon Valley, but in the much more abrasive and masculine world of the United States Secret Service. He had been recruited to Google two and a half years before my visit, in late 2006. And by the time he left law enforcement Corey Louie was in charge of the Secret Service's E-Crimes Unit. There was little he did not know about attacks on networks (so-called intrusion or penetration), credit-card fraud, the pervasive Distributed Denial of Service or DDoS attacks (capable of disabling websites and networks) and the malware that soon after the millennium began multiplying like rats in a sewer. And he knew a great deal about carding, the daily bread of cybercrime. This is the practice of buying or selling stolen or hacked credit-card details, hundreds of thousands of which are exchanged around the world before being used to buy goods or withdraw cash from ATMs.

How could Google resist a strategic asset like Corey Louie? Well, they couldn't. And how could Louie resist a strategic career move to Google – the balmy weather of the United States' southern Pacific rim versus DC's humidity, the winter freeze and just one week of cherry blossom; the West Coast's casual dress code or the stiff collars of the

Beltway; the money and the sense that you were involved in a dynamic project or US government service? Hardly a fair fight, really.

As you drive down Freeway 101 from San Francisco, Google is not the only cyber icon that you pass – Sun Microsystems, Yahoo! and McAfee are among the many famous names whose headquarters drift past the window as you head south. The more companies you visit to discuss security, the more ex-government agents you meet from the FBI, the US SS, the CIA, the Drug Enforcement Administration (DEA) and the US Postal Inspection Service. An entire phalanx of erstwhile spooks and undercover cops have migrated from the clinical surroundings of DC to live the good life in Silicon Valley, attracted by the same gorgeous conditions that lured the movies to Hollywood.

This flow from state agencies into the private sector results in a distinct disadvantage for the government. The Treasury ploughs money into educating cyber investigators who, with a few years' experience under their belt, then leave for more pleasant climes. Yet the investment is not entirely dead because this has led to the consolidation of powerful links between the public and private sectors. Google is not just a private corporation; it is a strategic national asset, in the eyes of the White House. The message from DC is quite clear – attack Google and you are attacking the US. Within that context, the ability of somebody like Corey Louie to pick up the phone and chat to his old pals at the Secret Service, alerting them, say, to a major attack on gmail, makes the critical cooperation between public and private sector in Internet security a lot easier.

I don't know, but I'll wager Corey's standard of living has improved since he headed out west, but then he has to work extremely hard for it. Google is among the two largest depositories of data in the world – the other being Facebook. This is what makes them lucrative businesses (advertisers are happy to pay for the secrets about personal habits that this data reveals) and it is what makes them the holy grail for hackers working on behalf of themselves, of the underground, of industry and of rival states.

Towards the end of my conversation with Corey, he told me about a friend, a cop, who had invested much time in developing friendships with hackers. He had been so successful that he had taken over the administration of a vast criminal website. 'He'll probably be happy to talk to you,' he said. 'He ran a site called DarkMarket.' It was the first time I had ever heard either of the website or the name of the FBI Special Agent Keith J. Mularski. It was the beginning of a strange journey.

I set out to meet and interview as many of the central characters in DarkMarket's history as I could, spread out in a dozen countries: thieves, cops, double agents, lawyers, hackers, crackers and more prosaic criminals. I also consulted a large volume of court documents relating to DarkMarket and those involved in it. Former and current cyber criminals and police officers supplied me with additional documents and information. I was never able to access a full archive of the website itself, but managed to forage for significant chunks of it. Agent Mularski, with an almost full archive of DarkMarket, is the only person involved that I met who had complete documentary oversight.

Beyond the elusive archive, some of the documentary evidence – while helpful – was inaccurate; this especially relates to material that prosecutors presented at many of the trials. In my assessment, these inaccuracies were not the result of carelessness or vindictiveness, nor were they intentional. Rather they reflected the highly technical and often confusing nature of the evidence in cyber-related trials. Judges and attorneys were struggling to come to terms with this peculiar culture as anyone else does, when confronted with malfeasance on the Web for the first time.

So the core of the story lies in the personalities involved and their actions. This testimony is of course largely based on their personal memories stretching back over a decade. Beneath the well-established fallibility of recall, all players involved were pursuing their own agendas, seeking to highlight some parts of their DarkMarket activity and conceal others. In this they were assisted by the duplicitous nature of communication over the Internet, by a culture in which there are few sanctions against lying and dissembling.

My attempts to assess when an interviewee was lying, embellishing or fantasising and when an interviewee was earnestly telling the truth were only partially successful. Everybody I interviewed was brimming with intelligence, even if some lacked the firm hand on the moral rudder necessary to negotiate the troubled waters of cyber criminality. But as I delved deeper and deeper into DarkMarket's weird world, I realised that the different versions of the same stories at the heart of the website's history were contradictory and unreconcilable. It has been impossible to establish fully what was really going on between the players, and with whom they were ultimately working.

The Internet has generated unfathomable stores of data and information, a large percentage of which is valueless, a large percentage of which remains uninterpreted, and a small percentage of which is dangerous in its falsity. Our growing dependence on networked systems and the interconnectedness that sees highly specialised groups like hackers and intelligence agents migrate between crime, industrial espionage and cyber warfare means that documenting and trying to understand the history of phenomena like DarkMarket has become a vital intellectual and social exercise, even if the evidence is partial, tendentious and scattered both in the virtual and the real world.

BOOK ONE

Part I

I

AN INSPECTOR CALLS

Yorkshire, England, March 2008

The Reverend Andrew Arun John was in a minor state of shock one morning in early March 2008. Hard to blame him. Not only had he just survived the long journey from Delhi in cattle class, but it was two weeks before the opening of Heathrow's new Terminal 5, and the world's busiest international airport was exploring new standards in passenger misery. His flight had left India around three o'clock in the morning and, after negotiating passport control and the baggage mayhem, he still had to face a four-hour drive north to Yorkshire.

Switching on his mobile phone, Reverend John saw he had an inordinate number of missed calls from his wife. And before he'd had time to call back to ask her what the fuss was about, she was ringing again. She told him that the police had telephoned several times and were desperate to get in touch with him.

Taken aback and confused, the Reverend replied sharply to his wife, saying that she was talking nonsense – though he regretted his tone almost immediately.

His wife, happily, chose to ignore his grumpiness. Clearly and calmly, she explained that the police had wanted to alert him to the fact that somebody had broken into his bank account, that this was a matter of urgency and that he should ring the number she had for the officer in charge as soon as possible.

His wife's call unsettled the Reverend still further and his weary brain went into overdrive. 'Who has broken into my account?' he wondered. 'What account? My Barclays here?' he speculated. 'My

Standard Bank account in South Africa? Or my ICICI one in India? Or maybe all three?' Even more puzzling: what did she actually mean? '*How* have they broken into my account?'

Coming so soon after his exhausting flight, the whole affair made the Reverend anxious and edgy. 'I'll deal with this later when I get to Bradford and after I've rested,' he muttered to himself.

Bradford is 200 miles north of Heathrow Airport. Sixty miles due east of the city lies Scunthorpe, where Detective Sergeant Chris Dawson's small team was nervously awaiting the Reverend John's phone call. The officer began to feel he was sinking in the quicksand of a case that he suspected was very big, and which presented him with one seemingly insuperable problem – he couldn't get his head round it. The evidence gathered so far included hundreds of thousands of computer files, some of which were large enough to hold the complete works of Shakespeare 350 times over. Inside these documents lay a planetary library of numbers and messages in a language that was effectively indecipherable to all but a tiny elite around the world who are trained in the arcane terminology of cybercrime.

DS Dawson may have known nothing about that novel and particularly rarefied branch of criminal investigation, but he was a first-class homicide officer with many years of service behind him. He could detect among the endless lists and number strings an agglomeration of sensitive data, which should not be in the possession of a single individual.

Yet as police officers in many parts of the world were discovering in the first decade of the twenty-first century, it was one thing to stumble across an information trove like this. It was quite another attempting to link it to a specific crime.

If DS Dawson were to persuade a magistrate in the sleepy town of Scunthorpe on the Humber estuary to place his suspect on remand, then he needed to show crystal-clear evidence of a specific crime. Furthermore, there was always a fair chance that he would be presenting said evidence to a doddery old circuit judge who might have difficulty using a TV remote, let alone accessing email. Convincing wasn't sufficient – the case had to be watertight and simple enough for anyone to understand.

Time was dribbling away. The suspect could only be held for three days and two of those had already passed. Among the files, figures, weblogs, chatlogs and who-knows-what-else, Dawson had only one tiny scrap of evidence.

He stared at the fifty words on a sheet of A4. These included an account number, 75377983; the date the account was opened, 24/02/2006, along with the account balance, £4,022.81. But there was also a name on it: Mr A A John; an email address: STPAULS@LEGEND. CO.UK; a physical address: 63 St Paul's Road, Manningham, Bradford; a corporate sign-on ID and, crucially, a corporate sign-on password: 252931.

If he could just confirm the account holder's identity, and if that man were to state that he had never knowingly divulged his password, then Dawson would probably be able to persuade the judge to send the accused for trial and refuse bail. And that might just buy enough time for the Detective Sergeant to comprehend exactly what he was dealing with.

When Dawson had tried to contact Mr A.A. John he had learned that he was a minister of the Church of England who was taking a group of underprivileged children on holiday around India. He was also told that he would not be contactable until his return from Delhi. The Reverend was scheduled to arrive a few hours before the suspect had to be released. If he failed to come through, then the quicksand of this case would swallow up the ocean of data upon which Dawson had stumbled. Along with the data, the suspect would doubtless fade back into the anonymity of his virtual alter ego.

It was Dawson's misfortune that the Reverend John was sufficiently unsettled by the telephone conversation with his wife that he resolved to deal with the matter only once he had arrived in his parish, Manningham. Indeed, he had turned off his mobile phone and concentrated instead on his long drive from the airport.

So why was he so upset?

Short and compact, the Reverend John was by temperament a jovial man. Born on the edge of the Thar Desert in Rajasthan, his slightly hexagonal face was usually all sunshine, radiating from behind his professorial glasses. He was born into the minority-faith community of India's Christians and joined the priesthood to work for the Anglican Church of India in Delhi for fifteen years.

But in 1996 he was approached by the Church of the Province of South Africa to take charge of a parish in the Indian township of

Lenasia, three miles south of Soweto, during the transition from apart-heid to multi-party rule.

It was a challenging move for anybody, as these were testing times for his new home. The joy that greeted the end of the racist regime was tempered by the knowledge of how deep the resentments ran that had accumulated over the previous 200 years. Outsiders like the Reverend John required sophisticated political and social skills to under-stand the meaning of those tensions and how he might help to reduce them.

His successful work in South Africa was noticed further up the Anglican Church's hierarchy and, after eight years, the Bishop of Brad-ford in the English county of West Yorkshire urged him to consider an equally challenging post in Manningham, a residential district on the edge of Bradford city centre. The Reverend John was reluctant – England had always struck him as a rather gloomy place, with its miserable weather and urban sprawl.

Equally, he knew that Manningham was no bed of roses. Many Britons regarded Bradford, and Manningham in particular, as a symbol of their country's failing attempts to integrate its many ethnic and confessional groups. More malignant types saw in Manningham an opportunity to ratchet up the mistrust between those communities.

In July 2001 this district exploded into brief but violent riots that reflected a deepening division between the city's large Asian constitu-ency and its white population. Even earlier, Manningham had experi-enced the phenomenon of white flight and, by the time the Reverend John arrived, three years after the riots, 75 per cent of the population were Muslims whose origins lay largely in the rural districts of north-eastern Pakistan. 'The remaining twenty-five per cent are Christians, although only about five per cent of those are church-going. The white community here looks and feels like the minority it is,' said the Reverend John. Although its climate, architecture and culture bore no resemblance to the townships of Jo'burg, in other ways Manningham felt uncannily like South Africa.

This was a hardship posting. When the clouds gathered or the snow fell, there was little that appealed in streets lined by sombre neo-Gothic buildings. Yet a little more than a century ago Manningham had been a most desirable area in which to live. This was during the period, now forgotten to the outside world, when Bradford was hailed as 'the wool capital of the world', acting as a mighty engine of Britain's Industrial Revolution.

By the beginning of the twenty-first century, however, Manningham had been in a state of decay for many years. Employment and prosperity, once flourishing, had moved away long before. Drug abuse, domestic violence, property crime and prostitution had taken their place. The Reverend John cared for more people in his drop-in centre, all trying to escape the traps of poverty and criminality, than attended his church on Sundays.

With the ever-present threat that latent violence could break through the surface, the Reverend John's work was on the front line of Britain's class, cultural and social wars. Not easily scared, he maintained a readiness to chuckle in most circumstances. Given the challenges of his daily work, he wondered why the news of his compromised bank account unsettled him to such a degree. Above all, he wanted to talk to his sons, who understood about computer things. And then he decided that he needed to talk to the police quickly, to find out exactly what was going on. 'Above all,' he resolved, 'I want this thing to be sorted out and put to bed as soon as possible.'

The Reverend's nervous reaction is not uncommon. The psychological response on learning that one has become a victim of cybercrime is similar to that experienced on being burgled. Even though the act is confined to cyberspace, a world of accumulated tiny electronic impulses, it still feels like a physical violation. For if one's bank account has been hacked into, what else might the thieves have discovered in the privacy of your computer?

Have they, perhaps, stolen your passport details, which some criminal or intelligence agent is now using as a fake travel document? Could they even, as you read this, be examining your emails, with confidential information about a colleague or employee? Might they have stumbled across some dangerously flirtatious emails or other indiscretion that you wrote or received? Is there any part of your life they could not explore, with access to your computer?

Now quite determined, the Reverend John called the police officer in the neighbouring county of Lincolnshire as soon as he arrived at the pleasant little cottage next to the imposing spire of his church in Manningham.

That this case should fall into the lap of Chris Dawson, a

Scunthorpe-based policeman in early middle age, was especially unusual. Most cases of cybercrime in Britain are picked up by specialist units allied to three forces – the Metropolitan Police, the City of London Police and the Serious Organised Crime Agency (SOCA), also based in the capital. Untrained officers would mostly miss such cases because of their esoteric nature. But Dawson was unusual: he was an instinctive copper with a sharp eye. He also possessed a quiet charm, but was frank in a typical northern English fashion that contributed to his methodical and precise approach to policing. This attention to detail would serve him well in the coming months.

If Manningham was associated with ethnic tension and precipitous economic decline, nearby Scunthorpe (population 75,000), lying south of the Humber estuary, was more often regarded either as an English nowheresville or as the butt of jokes provoked both by its name and the perennially poor performances of its soccer team. (In fairness, one should add that at least it did not inherit its original Scandinavian name, Skumtorp, and until its relegation in May 2011 Scunthorpe United FC had been punching above its weight in the second tier of English football.) As far as one can establish, the town has never been cited in connection with large-scale organised criminal activity.

A mere four days before the Reverend John's return from his charitable work in India, DS Dawson had been working happily at Scunthorpe's central police station. He was watching the Command and Control log, a computer screen that relays information and crime reports phoned in by the public. The standard fare would include drunken fracas, the occasional domestic, and a kitten getting stuck up a tree. But on that Wednesday afternoon at 1.30 p.m. a message ran across the log that aroused the Detective Sergeant's curiosity. It was very much out of the ordinary. He turned to his colleague and in his lilting Lincolnshire brogue said gently, 'Come on then. We'd best go take a look. Seems like there's something rather fishy going on at Grimley Smith.'

2

MIRANDA SPEAKS OF
A BRAVE NEW WORLD

Grimley Smith Associates' website displays a sepia photograph of their head office in Edwardian times when it functioned as one of Scunthorpe's first ever car showrooms. Bizarrely the business proudly advertises the Belsize, an early symbol of vehicular chic in Britain whose manufacturer went into liquidation soon after the First World War. But this venerable antecedent and Grimley Smith's Dickensian name deceive. For GSA, as it is also known, was established as recently as 1992 by a Mr Grimley and a Mr Smith.

The company offers far more complex technical services than the sale and repair of old jalopies. It specialises in chemical-engineering applications for the energy and pharmaceutical industries, and is recognised as one of Scunthorpe's most successful young companies that now boasts a worldwide presence.

GSA's two founders comprised the total original workforce, which has since expanded to include several dozen highly skilled engineers. Like all businesses where success drives expansion, GSA grew in an exciting but haphazard fashion. Its engineers would be contracted to mammoth projects in places as far apart as Iran, China and Venezuela. The specialist nature of their work and the zero room for error in their calculations required some powerful computer programs. In particular, they ran so-called CAD (Computer-Aided Design) software that offered intricate 2D and 3D simulation of projects.

By the middle of 2007 the company had reached a stage where it desperately needed to manage its computer infrastructure. Outsourcing its maintenance and security was proving an expensive option, and the company found the management of all its various cyber needs ever more taxing. The directors decided they would commission a fresh approach to the whole system.

In Darryl Leaning, an easygoing local lad, they found just the right person to take on the job. Apart from his technical competence, he was young, scrupulously honest, but perhaps most importantly his relaxed, friendly manner disguised an unusually sharp wit. For it is a little-appreciated fact that the very best computer managers are as talented in managing social and psychological expectations as they are in fixing widgets.

The minute he walked into the office for the first time, Darryl realised that Grimley Smith's computers needed urgent attention. His overriding concern was that all staff members had 'administrator rights' at their workstations. They could install any program they wanted and use any online services they selected (except for pornographic material, which the previous IT regime had centrally blocked).

On a family computer, a single individual (usually a parent) will act as 'administrator'. He or she can choose, for example, to limit electronically the amount of time other family members spend on the computer, or can restrict the type of website that the rest of the family is permitted to visit.

One of the most important 'privileges' that family PCs will confer upon the administrator concerns the installation of new software programs. In this way, parents can prevent children playing games that they consider unsuitable. But they may also exercise this privilege to stop software of dubious origin being downloaded, because the program could contain a virus or other malicious material that would leave the family's entire digital world vulnerable to attack.

The same principles obtain in a business environment, except usually on a larger and more complicated scale. The first problem Darryl identified when he started work at Grimley Smith was the absence of a central administrator. It was insupportable in a modern business, he argued to the directors, that the staff could upload, download or install anything they desired.

He told them that central control was essential to prevent people from unwittingly allowing viruses to breach the network's defences. He explained that the employees were, in all likelihood, entirely trustworthy – you don't put anti-virus software on your system because you suspect your colleagues of wanting to infect it, because on the whole they don't. The same applied, he continued, to the issue of software installation – and everything else, for that matter. The value of data in a highly specialised company like GSA is effectively incalculable. If it fell into the wrong hands, it might destroy the company.

Certain problems confronted Darryl in his crusade to purge Grimley Smith's computer system of harmful vulnerabilities: those invisible digital holes through which worms, trojans and viruses could slip unnoticed. First, he understood that people resist surrendering privileges they already enjoy – and, apart from viewing writhing naked bodies, the GSA staff enjoyed a lot. For a young techie, Darryl demonstrated a firm grasp of the psychology associated with computer use. Somehow he had to wean staff off their local administrator rights. He decided the best way to do this was incrementally. He knew that people don't like losing things they already have, but he further reasoned that equally they like receiving new toys.

So he used the next computer upgrade as an opportunity to introduce the first restrictions. Thrilled with their sparkly and ever more powerful new machines, the GSA employees were prepared to accept that they could no longer download their favourite games or pastimes whenever they chose.

Again demonstrating an innate grasp of psychology, Darryl avoided overtly draconian methods. Facebook was a problem. A lot of employees were draining resources, using the social networking site when they should have been working. But increasingly this was also what the security industry calls an attack 'vector', an instrument that virus-makers can hijack in order to spread their wares.

Darryl figured that banning Facebook altogether might lead to rebellion in the workplace, so instead he allowed access to the site between 12 and 2 p.m., when most people took their lunch. By setting the Facebook time himself, he was also able to increase his monitoring of malware and hacking attempts, to ensure that the site did not compromise company security.

Gently he introduced a system of relatively powerful central control, without alienating any of the computer users at Grimley Smith. At the heart of the new order was a complex program called Virtual Network Computing or VNC. This was Grimley Smith's very own version of Big Brother. If Darryl identified any unusual or threatening behaviour on the network, he could release the VNC from its virtual hibernation to swoop down and investigate in detail what was happening on any of the dozens of computers he now managed.

One morning, when staff logged onto their computers, Darryl sent a message warning everyone from the Managing Director downwards that henceforth anyone might be subject to screening by the Computer Manager. Unbeknownst to most, Darryl's newly installed VNC was humming away merrily in the background. If he received an alert that somebody had downloaded a virus or was trying to install some unrecognised software, the VNC would be activated.

The VNC is a mighty powerful tool. To some, its use will appear like a straightforward business practice, but in the global Internet, deployment of VNC software is fiercely contested. In much of continental Europe, governments and companies are strictly forbidden from accessing any information on their employees' computers that is not related to work (and even that is not easy). The monitoring of emails is strictly illegal.

Crime detection and civil liberties have always been uneasy bedfellows, but their coexistence has become significantly more troubled since the spread of the Internet, and this will continue in the future. In Germany, if a police officer is tracking a suspect anonymously over the Internet, he or she is legally bound to identify themselves as belonging to law enforcement, if asked by an online interlocutor. This makes very difficult the practice widespread in Britain and the United States of officers posing as underage girls and boys in order to entrap paedophiles who appear to be grooming children online. The deployment of a VNC is politically charged and circumscribed by important data-protection laws. So Darryl Leaning had to handle his pet with great care.

One day in early February 2008 an alert that warned of suspect software flashed up on Darryl's screen. *Unauthorised Application: Messenger.* Darryl's systems were looking out for several different types of unauthorised application. The word 'Messenger' suggested that someone was trying to install or operate some form of communications package like Skype. Within minutes Darryl had traced its origin to one of the chemical engineers who represent the backbone of GSA's business. Walking over to the workstation in question, Darryl decided simply to ask him outright whether he was running any new instant messenger on his machine.

'And he turned to me quite cooly and said "No!" He flatly denied it. So I replied, "Oh, okay. That's weird, though, because I just had a warning saying that this computer was running an unauthorised messenger application."'

Darryl shrugged his shoulders. He wasn't unduly surprised by the engineer's reply, because security systems are sensitive devices and, by his own admission, he was running various scanning tools, which look like hacking devices to his own anti-malware software. In any event, Darryl figured, even if the engineer was running the program, he was probably just chatting to his mates in company time. Now at least he would realise that it was the wrong thing to do and that, if he did use it again, Darryl would be watching. So he just forgot about it.

Two weeks later, however, the same thing happened. This time, Darryl decided, he would wake the mighty VNC beast. Diving into the engineer's computer, he started to search for the communications program – which he quickly identified as Miranda Instant Messaging. Many people now use instant messaging, which enables them to talk in real time to friends by sending a few words or sentences in little text boxes. In most cases Windows Instant Messenger (IM) can only talk to someone else who has the same software. Miranda's advantage lies in the fact that you can communicate with a variety of different IM programs. It is especially beloved of some obsessional computer users.

Before unleashing the VNC, Darryl checked the engineer's hard drive to see if he could spot anything peculiar, but the search proved fruitless. It was about 12.15, lunchtime. Just the time, Darryl thought, to run a little VNC session on his machine to ascertain once and for all whether this unauthorised program really was running on the engineer's computer.

Miranda IM was as nothing compared to what Darryl saw when the VNC began to explore the secrets of the employee's computer. The engineer had opened ten text documents at the same time and was scrolling through them at unnatural speed. Darryl was open-mouthed. Never had he come across anyone able to work with documents so quickly. All he could see as he watched the engineer's screen was a blur of numbers, symbols and words. Slowly he realised that the engineer was copying parts of the document and then pasting them into a separate wordpad file.

He could not yet grasp what was happening, or from where all these documents were coming, but as far as he could establish, this did not resemble anything like company work. The name of the file into which he was pasting the text was confusing. It was called 'Sierra Leone'. The engineer was indeed working on an oil-refinery project in Sierra Leone. Darryl breathed a sigh of relief – perhaps it was legitimate business after all. It was later on that it dawned on Darryl why the engineer had chosen this name. If anyone walked past his computer, he would just minimise the file and all they would see on the task bar was a tab named 'Sierra Leone': the very project he was working on.

It would have fooled Darryl, too, had the VNC not then spotted an unregistered drive – F: – which indicated that the engineer was using a portable disk of some type. Darryl sent the VNC into the mystery drive and ordered it to copy the tens of thousands of documents that he found there.

Still unsure how to proceed, and not yet in a position to establish what on earth was going on, Darryl ordered his faithful VNC to explore the innards of the suspect computer one more time. He programmed it to start taking screenshots of the engineer's PC every thirty seconds. Looking at the computer in real time was baffling. It was impossible to identify what the data actually represented. But when he saw the screenshots – frozen images of the engineer's activity – he gleaned a pretty good idea of what was going on: these were hundreds upon hundreds of credit-card numbers, bank accounts, personal details, PIN numbers and email addresses. This had absolutely nothing to do with the development of Sierra Leone's nascent oil-refining capacity.

Darryl then printed one particularly dense page from Bank of America Online, and took it to his MD, Mike Smith. Within minutes Smith had picked up the phone and called the police in Scunthorpe.

When DS Dawson arrived at Grimley Smith, the MD presented him with the printouts. There was a mind-boggling array of data: information on banks, estate agents, insurance companies, theme parks, cinemas, charities and more, including what looked like some information extracted from the US military. He immediately suspected that he was dealing with some form of fraud, but he could not know what the material signified or how he could begin to confirm these suspicions. These were difficult questions.

'Right,' said Dawson 'Let's get him in the office for a chat, shall we?'

The Grimley Smith managers looked at each other nervously.

'What is it?' asked Dawson.

'He's a big lad,' came the reply, 'and I'm sure he can kick off.'

'Well, we'll address that issue when we come to it,' said Dawson, mustering as much authority as he could.

But when the tall, imposing man walked into the office, he looked shocked rather than angry. He asked the detective who he was and what he was doing there, with a hint of disdain. Dawson explained why he had been called into GSA and asked the man directly what all the documentation signified. With unexpected nonchalance, the man explained that it was part of a report he was compiling for one of the managers in the room. There was a moment's silence before the manager piped up defiantly, 'No, it isn't!'

'Right,' said Dawson, 'put your hands out, sir.' And he nodded to his colleague: 'Put the cuffs on him!'

Far from 'kicking off', as the managers had feared, the man remained quite calm, if a touch bewildered, throughout. Two hours after seeing the Command and Control report, Dawson had a suspect under arrest in a police cell. But now he had to build a case quickly. If he was unable to come up with prima-facie evidence of conspiracy or fraud within three days, he would have to let his man go, and that would be the end of it.

Dawson returned to Grimley Smith with an officer from the high-tech recovery unit and the two of them got to work with Darryl Leaning. As Darryl had predicted, the portable disks were packed with hundreds of thousands of documents, most crammed full with details of hacked credit cards and bank accounts. But there were also email exchanges, one of which related to a Yahoo! newsgroup, which was prosaically called *bankfraud@yahoogroups.com*. The postings and various messages from this group amounted less to an online tutorial and more to a university degree in how to perpetrate fraud on the Internet.

Dawson next drove to the flat on Plimsoll Way in neighbouring Hull, where the suspect lived. The address was on an estate, seemingly part of a dockside regeneration scheme that was showing the first signs of wear. Grimy water marks stained the cream stone façade, which was pockmarked by rust emerging from the rendering. It was an apt physical symbol of New Labour's Britain – shiny and bright on the outside, but unable any longer to prevent the rotten interior from punching through the surface.

Inside, the rooms bore the mark of a bachelor. It was by no means a pigsty, but there were items strewn about. 'Lacks a woman's touch,' mused Dawson to himself. Then, in the bedroom, the detective hit paydirt. Sitting on the bed were two laptops, one of which was still running. On top of it there was a large pile of documentation. This included countless Western Union receipts confirming transfers to and from the whole world: New Zealand, Mexico, the United Arab Emirates, Ukraine – wherever.

It was all very well having all these files and documents, but, as we know, Dawson needed evidence of a specific crime to bring a charge. As he picked up a huge bundle of papers, a single sheet fell out and floated to the floor. In the months to come, Dawson would often reflect on the serendipity of that moment. For on that sheet were the details of a gentleman somewhere in West Yorkshire with all his bank-account numbers on it. After studying it, Dawson realised this could be the vital smoking gun, because it included a password. If only he could prove that this person had never handed his password out to anyone, then he might just have a case. And that is why DS Dawson was so keen to talk to the Reverend Andrew Arun John. If John confirmed this, then Dawson could charge the suspect with a specific crime of online fraud, and a judge would almost certainly refuse bail. Dawson could then embark on the Herculean task of wading through this ocean of documentation.

3

MR HYDE OF LAGOS

2003 was the year that Adewale Taiwo received his BSc in chemical engineering from the University of Lagos. The son of a university lecturer and a civil servant, Adewale, who was tall and striking, had grown into an articulate and measured young man with a promising future in industry or academia. By Nigerian standards, the family was comfortably off and they had relatives in London able to assist Adewale when he explored the possibility of continuing his education in the United Kingdom.

This was also the year that he created his alter ego, Fred Brown of Oldham in Lancashire. Although Adewale had never yet been to England, he decided in advance to create this veritable Mr Hyde of the cyber world. It was Fred Brown who established the yahoo newsgroup on bank fraud.

Before long Fred Brown was also posting adverts on the Internet, using such sites as the *Hacker Magazine, Alt 2600* or *UK Finance*:

OPPORTUNITY: A business opportunity has arisen for people employed in High Street banks or people who have family or friends working for banks to go into partnership. Banks include HSBC, Royal Bank of Scotland but others will be considered. Please reply to Fred B Brown on yahoo, icq or Safemail.

The messaging programs icq (derived from I Seek You) and the older IRC (Internet Relay Chat) are tools beloved of hackers and crackers, as criminal hackers are sometimes known. They are instant messaging services on which you can chat to one or more people.

Importantly for hackers, they are 'dynamic', which means that they do not leave a trace of the conversations conducted on them unless somebody consciously saves their exchanges. 'Safemail' is an encrypted email system that cannot be cracked. Unless, that is, you can persuade an Israeli court to subpoena the information you are looking for, as a company in Tel Aviv owns and runs it.

Respondents to Fred Brown's adverts were then invited to join *bankfraud@yahoogroups.com*, whose aims and ethos were explicit: 'This group is for people who don't want to work legit but for cash and are willing to bend the rules. This group will teach you how to defraud banks and identity theft.' It is a measure of the pervasiveness of fraudulent activity on the Web that Fred felt able to promote his business so openly. It would be several years before law enforcement noticed him, and that was only because he eventually made an uncharacteristically crass error.

Fred's adverts were designed to skin a cat in that most traditional fashion – the inside job. If you can persuade a bank employee to filch and then hand over customer details, you save yourself the sweat of having to crack the accounts or credit cards. Perpetrators of fraud on the Internet invest considerable effort in trying to find disgruntled or distressed bank employees, because having a reliable insider working with you can increase your earnings dramatically. Armed with the account details, the criminal is free to enter the account over the Internet as he would his own, before transferring cash into a designated account of his choosing. Unless the infiltrator needs a significant sum in a hurry, the preferred method of theft involves sucking out small amounts over a long period, so that neither bank nor customer notices.

But Fred Brown was also developing some more advanced methods of fraud. He was able to enter deeper into a bank's system, where he could engage in such practices as increasing an account's overdraft facility. He seemingly had the know-how to change names and addresses and, of course, fish out passwords.

By laying the foundations of his trade long before he came to the United Kingdom, Fred demonstrated his systematic approach to business. He was considered; he was not socially insecure; and he did not waste much time playing computer games. Fred Brown (aka Freddy Brown, Fred B. Brown, Freddy B, FredB and Freddybb) regarded the Internet as a simple and easy way of defrauding countless people of large sums of money.

But before Fred was let loose on the Web, his Dr Jekyll – Adewale Taiwo – had other matters to attend to, namely the year spent studying for an MSc in chemical engineering at Manchester University, where he arrived in October 2005. A month before receiving his Masters in May 2006, he opened an account with the London Gold Exchange (LGE), into which he could transfer money from any high-street bank.

The LGE buys gold with the money you deposit and gives you 'digital currency' credits. With its headquarters in Belize and its gold stored in Switzerland, the misnamed London Gold Exchange was one of several institutions that expanded during the 1990s and were favoured by fraudsters and money-launderers. Once Taiwo had shifted his funds into the London Gold Exchange, he then sent it on to an account he held at a similar institution, E-Gold, from where he would distribute cash around the world via Western Union, either to launder it or pay off his collaborators.

As with all his work, he proved meticulous and efficient: an excellent student and an excellent criminal. Grimley Smith snapped him up as a first-class prospect soon after Manchester awarded him the Masters degree – at the same time as the Internet fraud fraternity welcomed him as a serious player.

Adewale Taiwo was a gifted chemical engineer. Still in his twenties, he was regarded as one of the high-flyers at Grimley Smith and before long he was travelling as far afield as China and Venezuela for his work. He dressed well, but never ostentatiously, and his BMW was appropriate to his salary and his lifestyle. He took both his lives very seriously and, of course, his legitimate work acted as a credible disguise protecting his underground activity. A respected and successful company in the energy sector is one of the last places one would look for a major cyber criminal, especially not among the firm's industrious and highly skilled engineers.

When DS Chris Dawson started looking at the extent of Fred Brown's fraud, he was flabbergasted. Even after narrowing the evidence down, he was still looking at some 34,000 files, some of which were 100–150 pages long. Early on, he spotted a single file that had 100 pages jam-packed with American credit-card numbers, along with their security codes and all the requisite passwords.

DS Dawson was a homicide officer – nobody in Humberside had ever worked a high-end Internet fraud before, and he and his colleague on the case had to attend to their day jobs. He simply didn't know where to start. Along with the files, there was the software for an MSR206. This device is probably the most important weapon in the arsenal of the credit-card fraudsters, who are known by the generic term 'carders'. With this, the carder can 'clone' a credit card. This means copying all the information on the magnetic strip at the back and pasting it onto a piece of blank white plastic with an empty magnetic strip. The MSR206 is a personal mint.

Dawson also found key logging trojans on the files. These are to the criminal hacker what a jemmy is to the safe-cracker. The early viruses were very different creatures from the key loggers. When viruses first circulated in large numbers in the 1990s, they were designed by adolescents and students, so-called script kiddies, who wanted to demonstrate their prowess as anarchic programmers. Irritatingly, they chose to do this by inconveniencing as many computer users around the world as they could.

Once your computer was infected, it might behave in any number of ways: it could slow down; if you requested one application, say Microsoft Word, an Internet browser might open instead; it would automatically shut the computer down; and, worst of all, it could destroy your files and data. There are tales of authors losing entire manuscripts to some mischievous virus, and of statisticians who saw months of data input being gobbled up in front of their eyes by a naughty digital worm.*

But after the millennium hackers, crackers and criminals began to appreciate that viruses, trojans and worms could be put to more lucrative use. The key logger was born, and it multiplied over the Internet at great speed. Once this little chap nestles inside your computer, its job is to track every stroke of your keyboard. So when you type *www. hsbc.co.uk* into your browser, it sends that information back to its Creator or Owner, who could be anywhere in the world. If you were then to type in your password as, say, Robinhood, the virus Commander in

---

* The simplest, albeit incomplete, distinction between viruses, worms and trojans, known collectively as 'malware', lies in their method of transmission – viruses through infected email attachments, trojans through downloads, while worms have an ability to self-replicate on a host computer and then use that computer's communications programs to spread themselves to other machines. But, basically, they all do bad things to your computer.

New Jersey, Rostock, Lilongwe or deepest Ruritania would immediately log it. Bingo! *Mi casa es su casa!* Or, more to the point, *Mi cuenta bancaria es su cuenta bancaria!**

Just as having thousands of credit-card details and bank-account numbers sitting on your computer is not a crime, nor is storing a key-logger virus. It may be a strong indication of criminal activity, but it does not amount to a case. Ploughing through the endless files, Dawson and another colleague had to untangle the hundreds of jumbled threads.

After manually inputting several thousand account details onto an Excel spreadsheet, the police then decided to approach the banks. Eminently sensible, one might think, for after all it is the banks' security systems that Fred Brown had breached so successfully.

Think again.

Many of Dawson's enquiries ran into a brick wall because the banks simply did not bother to respond to his requests. The detective was pushed for time throughout the investigation, and much was wasted on futile attempts to persuade banks to cooperate.

The attitude of most banks to cybercrime is ambiguous. While writing this book, a gentleman from my bank, NatWest, called me and asked if I had made any recent purchase at a jewellers in Sofia, the capital of Bulgaria. Furthermore, he enquired whether I had spent 4,000 francs settling a bill with Swiss Telecom. I said that I had not. I was then told that my NatWest Visa card had been compromised, that I would need a new one, but that I could be safe in the knowledge that NatWest had cancelled the £3,000 for which the card had been fraudulently used. Like everyone else who goes through that experience, I was hugely relieved when the bank gently reassured me that I was not liable.

But who is actually paying for that? The bank? No, they are insured against such losses. The insurance company? No, because they set the premiums at a level that ensures they don't lose out. So maybe it is the bank after all, given that they're paying the premiums? Yes. But they recoup the money by levelling extra charges on all consumers. Essentially, bank fraud is paid for by all bank customers.

This is something that banks understandably do not wish to have widely advertised. Similarly, they do not like the public to learn how

---

* 'My bank account is your bank account.'

often their systems have been compromised by cyber criminals. Journalists find it impossible to get any information out of banks about the cyber attacks that rain down on them daily. That is understandable. What is less excusable is their frequent reluctance to work with police, in case the information be revealed in open court. By refusing to admit that their customers are victims of cybercrime, for fear of losing an edge against their competitors, banks are indirectly assisting the work of criminals.

Of course, the banks have a problem: their customers are the most vulnerable part of the networked financial system. Even the finest hackers would find cracking the computer systems of the major retail and investment banks a challenge these days. But getting into most customers' computers and then watching them access their accounts and, indeed, playing around with the money in those accounts, is child's play for any hacker worth his or her (although usually his) salt. How can one improve one's customers' online habits when the great draw of Internet banking (as with so much of our activity on the Web) is convenience? People are in general put off by elaborate security measures needed to access their accounts, because they're so tedious.

Banks like to keep the extent of fraud quiet partly for competitive reasons and partly because they do not want their customers to demand a return to the old ways. Electronic banking saves them huge sums of money because the customer is carrying out tasks that were once the preserve of branches and their staff. If we were all to refuse to manage our finances via the Internet, banks would be compelled to reinvent the extensive network of branches through which they used to serve us. That would cost an awful lot of money and, as we now know, the banks have spent everything they have, along with hundreds of billions of taxpayers' cash, underwriting egregious speculative ventures and their obscenely inflated bonus payments.

So DS Dawson was obliged slowly to piece together the puzzle with only limited assistance from the banking fraternity. In his favour, however, was the fact that Fred Brown had made a couple of significant errors in constructing his network of fraud: although his *bankfraud@ yahoogroups.com* was registered with yahoo in America, the email address attached to it was *yahoo.co.uk*. Because it was a British domain name, Dawson was able to subpoena the material from yahoo immediately. He was less fortunate with the Safemail account. He had to request a British court to request from an Israeli court that Safemail allow him access to Fred Brown's encrypted account. That took months and all the time he was under pressure from the courts to disclose its evidence to defence lawyers and to speed up the proceedings.

Dawson's bosses were unhappy: he could feel the pressure building. None of the victims of the crimes he was investigating came from Humberside – the credit-card holders were spread all over the world. One, the Reverend John, was in neighbouring West Yorkshire, but that was about it. 'I can't afford to have one of my best homicide officers working on a fraud case which has nothing to do with this area!' Dawson was warned on more than one occasion. Something in the detective drove him on, though. He wouldn't let go and so, to assuage his superiors, he started working in his own time, sometimes late into the night, poring over the dancing numbers.

In despair at how the investigation of Adewale Taiwo was starting to consume his life, Dawson requested assistance from the regional intelligence unit. They were unable to help, but suggested that Dawson ask the City of London High-Tech Unit if they had information that might assist him. No, came the reply, but why don't you approach the Serious Organised Crime Agency?

Finally, Dawson contacted SOCA at their secret operational head-quarters in London, which is like something out of Len Deighton's *The Ipcress File* or *Funeral in Berlin*: brass plates with the name of a ficti-tious company, and everyone pretending not to work for the agency that Tony Blair described as Britain's answer to the FBI (much to its officers' irritation).

Dawson asked for assistance in a complex fraud case that involved a mysterious man named Fred Brown. He received a curt call back from the big boys in the metropolis: 'What do you know about Freddie Brown?' After all, the tone implied, you're just a local plod from Humberside.

'Nothing,' DS Dawson replied, 'except that I've got him on remand up here in Scunthorpe.'

There was silence down the end of the line. 'Have you ever heard of something called DarkMarket, DS Dawson?' the voice continued.

'No, never. Why?'

Dawson's fish was even bigger than he realised.

But the news also came as some surprise to SOCA. Freddybb had been on their radar for several years, but the DarkMarket investigation had gone quiet for a while after a series of arrests the previous summer. They had not envisaged that a copper from Scunthorpe would revitalise it. But Britain's largest online crime unit had learned one thing above all else since a group of Ukrainian cyber thieves set up the first website dedicated to global crime in 2001 – expect the unexpected.

Part II

4

THE ODESSA FILES

Odessa, Ukraine, June 2002

They came from as far north as St Petersburg and from Latvia on the Baltic Sea; one delegate arrived from Belarus, a country created in 1990, seemingly as a living memorial to communism. The Russians were there in force and Ukraine provided a host of delegates, whether from Ternopil in the west, Kiev in the centre, Kharkov in the north or Donetsk in the east.

But the First Worldwide Carders' Conference (FWCC) was truly international. Some attendees had arrived from Western Europe while others had flown in from as far away as the Persian Gulf, Canada and South America. The FWCC's press release lamented how delegates from Australia and South-East Asia hadn't made it, due to travel difficulties.

The organisers hand-picked three dozen or so delegates from the 400 applications they had received. Those lucky enough to be given the thumbs-up knew that the invitation alone would provide a huge boost to their reputation within the fiercely hierarchical world of online criminals.

In order to throw police off the scent, the organisers originally announced that they were holding the event on several luxury yachts moored off Turkey's Black Sea coast. But this was just a feint. After all, where else could you possibly hold the world's first ever conference for cyber criminals than in Odessa – Ukraine's fabled city of rogues?

Using their well-tested methods, the Tsar, Stalin and Hitler all had a crack at taming this wild beast, but none of them could crush Eastern Europe's most enduring criminal fraternity. 'Without an understanding of Odessa's gangsters and their lives,' one chronicler wrote about his home town, 'the city's history is simply unintelligible.'

For most of Eastern Europe the bare-knuckled gangster capitalism that followed the collapse of communism in the 1990s came as a genuine shock. But Odessa knew what was coming. The Odessites had no option but to embrace the new era – and, it should be said, they did so with a certain brio. Red lights extinguished red stars overnight. Dingy casinos sprouted like weeds behind the Primorskaya Boulevard and it was not long after 1989 that the restaurants and saunas became the scenes of gluttony and bloodshed.

Further out from the centre, in the housing estates, drugs became the currency of choice. Penniless youngsters took to shooting up *boltushka*, a home-made amphetamine mix, leaving them scarred, mentally damaged or dead.

Gunmen and clans from as far away as Chechnya and Moscow battled with local Robin Hoods for control of the city – because although Odessa was theoretically part of a new independent Ukraine, it was entirely Russian-speaking and, even more important, was the only warm-water port able to handle Russia's gas and oil exports.

Hyperinflation and nationalism destroyed the value of the ruble, the karbovanets, the hryvnia or whatever else the government claimed at any time was 'real' money. Only the Yankee dollar provided any real stability.

For most ordinary people, Odessa in the 1990s was about two things: survival and dollars. Nobody cared or disapproved of how you managed the first or acquired the second. In fact, they admired those that achieved either, although sudden wealth was no guarantee of a long life.

In this atmosphere, who could blame thirteen-year-old Dimitry Golubov for selling vehicle registration documents and driver's licences with the forged signature of the head of the Municipal Transportation Bureau? If businessmen were prepared to pay for this, surely the trade must have a real value?

So far, so Odessa. But young Dimitry had something that placed him in a different world from the traditional city gangland of protection rackets, brothels, oil and caviar. Instead of packing a knife, he could drop down from the streets into smoky dark cellars where computer games like Street Fighter, Pacman and that Russian classic, Tetris, were busily turning teenage brains into mush. In this subterranean culture the only light emanated from soft-coloured neon shapes and flickering PC screens. Cigarettes and Coca-Cola were so ubiquitous it was as though they were the only kosher nutrition tolerated by some ancient Lore of the Geek.

Dimitry liked games as much as anyone, though his preference was for exploring the world from the comfort of Odessa's Internet cafés. But young Golubov did not only enjoy surfing the sites of distant lands, he wanted to penetrate them and explore their innards.

By the time he was sixteen in 1999, Visa and MasterCard had blocked the use of their cards on the websites registered in the former Soviet Union. When Russian Internet companies submitted invoices to the two credit giants, they were ignored. But Golubov and his fellow pioneers soon worked out that if you could somehow extract the information held on a credit card and reproduce it, then you could use the data to take cash out of ATMs or to buy goods on the Internet and then send them to a third party somewhere else in the world. One option was to copy that information from the physical credit card itself, although at first that involved the laborious and hence wholly unsatisfactory act of conventional robbery. Much better by far, you could simply sniff out the information stored in the gold mines that were company databanks!

And even if some American websites would not deliver to the former Soviet Union, they were happy to send goods to places like the United Arab Emirates or Cyprus, two countries that had rapidly become favoured destinations of the new Russian moneyed elite. This was one of the first truly globalised crimes. Money was stolen by a Russian in Ukraine from an American company and paid out in Dubai – and the whole transaction need last no longer than ten minutes!

The other great breakthrough that moulded the new profession of 'carding' was the skimming device. 'Skimmers' are machines that read and store the magnetic strip on a credit card. They come in several shapes and sizes. Some are small rectangles that can be affixed to ATMs so that when a customer's card is read by the bank's machine, it is also read by the 'skimmer'. Others are identical to the point-of-sale devices through which a waiter or petrol-station cashier will swipe a card for payment. At both the ATM or the rogue point-of-sale device there may well be a tiny camera hidden somewhere that is secretly recording the customer inputting their PIN (note to self: *always* cover the keypad when tapping in your PIN).

The machines are only referred to as 'skimmers' if they are being used for nefarious purposes, otherwise they are identical in function to those commercially available. Some 'skimmers' are commercially produced and then acquired by criminals, others are home-made. The 'skimmer' was the carding equivalent of James Watt's steam engine at the outset of the Industrial Revolution. Over the next decade the great majority of credit-card and PIN numbers ('dumps' and 'wholes', as they are known) used fraudulently were 'skimmed' from ATMs and businesses around the world.

As a talented hacker, Dimitry also quickly noticed that the security systems developed by the nascent e-commerce community in the United States were primitive and easily cracked. How successful he was initially is entirely unclear. Dima liked to put it about that he had attained the gold standard of dollar millionaire before celebrating his seventeenth birthday. But never forget: lies are the most common currency of the Internet, and some of his cyber pals tell a different story.

'He was greedy, deceitful and always drawn to the criminal milieu,' blogged another Odessa hacker. 'But the image of a successful millionaire was a far cry from reality.'

At this point, Dimitry disappeared, along with some of his more outrageous money-making schemes. Some months later he emerged from a chrysalis conferring anonymity as Script, a gloriously adept creature that flitted excitedly between two new websites, *carder.org* and *carder.ru*. These were little more than discussion forums where Russian hackers chewed the digital cud about how it might be possible to access the gazillions of dollars, pounds, yen and euros locked away behind credit cards. One of the original members of these sites remembered them as 'desultory, unstable' and ultimately 'unrewarding'.

Script, however, thought long and hard. If you had websites for all other manner of commerce, why not develop one for the inchoate trade in stolen credit-card numbers, bank accounts and other valuable data? He had a compelling motive for wanting to establish such a presence on the Web. For Script himself had begun to accumulate large amounts of these data, which he had neither the time nor the resources to exploit. He wanted to turn all his numbers into cash. He wanted to sell.

The timing was perfect. In the preceding five years, the Internet had hosted a furious growth in commercial activity. Nobody had fully anticipated this, because its originators had envisaged the Web as a tool to improve and accelerate communication, an arena where ideas and gossip could be exchanged.

Amazon, eBay, *lastminute.com* and other first movers of the cyber enterprise world came out of left field. But their success did not go unnoticed. Thousands upon thousands of people tried their hand at setting up websites. This being one of those historical moments that emerge once in a generation, and where human greed and fantasy coincide, it was not long before banks and venture capitalists convinced themselves that e-commerce was a guarantee of quick riches. They began pouring money into these companies, the great majority of which were intrinsically worthless entities despite having been capitalised to the tune of millions, if not tens of millions, of dollars. The first major bubble of the globalised age had begun, and how fitting that the bubble was in high-tech stocks.

But while most dot.com companies were indeed commercial Potemkin villages, firms already well established in the real world found that there were distinct advantages to conducting part of their business on the Web.

Banks were swift out of the traps in this regard because, as already noted, it dawned on them that if they could persuade their clients to make payments and manage their accounts online, then they would not have to pay employees to do so. Those customers who felt comfortable with the Web were almost certain to prefer the close control over their finances that Internet banking enabled.

At this time the Masters of the Universe, the new class of financial capitalist, were casting off the fetters that had in the past restricted their speculative activity on derivative markets. Essentially, politicians in Washington and London had issued them with a licence to gamble (the dot.com boom was a fine example) and, as the price of assets that were worth very little rose to great heights, money was lent on the supposed value of those assets. For a decade the Western world was bathed in cheap credit. The Ages of Empire and Capital morphed into the Age of Plastic.

Personal credit-card debt in the four biggest users of plastic – the US, the UK, Japan and Canada – started rising manically in the mid-1990s. In the space of ten years from 1997, the number of cards in circulation worldwide rose from just under 1.5 billion to 3 billion, and average individual debt among the most addicted users, the Americans, doubled from $5,000 to $10,000. Banks adored our new-found affection for credit cards because at a time of virtually o per cent interest rates, they were still gaily charging anywhere between 5 and 30 per cent. In Britain the head of Barclaycard confessed to a parliamentary Select Committee that he did not 'borrow on credit cards because it is too expensive.'

Other parts of the globe were less inclined to be moulded by plastic. Western Europe had traditionally eschewed the buccaneer economics that had so bewitched America and Britain. As a consequence, credit-card ownership was much lower, along with the level of personal debt. In Eastern Europe there was neither sufficient capital spread across the population nor a secure banking industry to administer credit cards. Plastic was a rarity in the former communist world, an executive toy for the New Russians – that tiny proportion of the population who had made breathtaking fortunes by ripping off their countries and compatriots during the transition from communism to capitalism.

But in the Anglo-Saxon casino economics of the 1990s and 2000s, plastic was the closest invention to printing money ever devised by financial institutions and they were not slow to excavate this rich lode of capital. Tons of leaflets were sent daily to addresses in the Western world exhorting people to sign up for credit cards or to exchange an existing debt for a new account that would not charge interest for six months. For three or four years more diligent consumers were able to secure interest-free credit as they transferred their outstanding balance from one card to the next, while the banks became ever more frantic in their attempts to secure new customers.

So many cards. So much money with which to play. Since large electronic wads of the stuff were sloshing around on the Web, it was perhaps no surprise that it began to attract the attention of cyber men from the East who were short on cash, but brimming with technical ingenuity. One of them was Script, eighteen-year-old Dimitry Golubov from Odessa.

And so it was that CarderPlanet was born.

5

CARDERPLANET

A question fades up in flickering *Star Wars* script:

LOOKING FOR PROFESSIONAL SOLUTION?

The shot zooms in on a rapidly spinning Earth that explodes into a metallic psychedelic pattern, accompanied by an aggressive electro-dance number, followed by a series of messages:

DISCOVER THE POWER OF TECHNOLOGY

FEEL TIRED OF EVERYDAY ROUTINE?

WANT TO CHANGE YOUR LIFESTYLE?

BECOME ONE OF US!

DUMPS — CREDIT CARDS

CAN MAKE YOU RICH!

The screen fades to black, before three more messages appear underscored by a militaristic bass drum:

THE TEAM YOU CAN RELY ON

Boom!

EVERYTHING YOU NEED FOR BUSINESS

Boom!

CARDERPLANET IS INEVITABLE

Boom!

A year after CarderPlanet was founded in 2001, Script invited his hacker friends to the First Worldwide Carders' Conference in Odessa – the world's first ever cybercrime convention – to celebrate the trailblazing website. This group could boast the same incredible cyber ability as the members of the Hacker Republic, the secret group to which heroine Lisbeth Salander belonged under her nickname, Wasp, in Stieg Larsson's best-selling *The Girl with the Dragon Tattoo*.

But there was nothing fictional about Script and his friends. CarderPlanet was for real.

6

A FAMILY AFFAIR

The First Worldwide Carders' Conference celebrated CarderPlanet's first birthday. It was unique and remarkable. By 2002 Odessa had calmed down: there were even signs of normality. Its iconic boulevard, Deribasovskaya, was brimming with street vendors, shops and fancy restaurants. Surrounded by the four-leaved clover and Gaelic inscriptions of Mick O'Neill's, one of post-communist Ukraine's first fake Oirish pubs, an inner core of Ukraine's top hackers, known as The Family, discussed the goals of the conference. Among them were top figures such as Auditor, Rayden and Bigbuyer, along with the moving spirits of the event: Boa, a communications and security boffin with a distinctive white beard, and the energetic if slightly juvenile Script.

Over the next three days in several different locations around the city they drank and sang, but above all they discussed the short- and long-term development of their nascent website, CarderPlanet, which was already changing the nature of cybercrime around the world.

General discussions were held in The Odessa Hotel, the most expensive in the city at the time. A fine example of ugly post-communist chic, the tall building did at least stand on a pier right opposite the Potemkin Steps, made famous in Eisenstein's masterpiece of early Soviet film, *Battleship Potemkin*. Those topics in which all delegates took part at The Odessa included the need to understand the technical details of the lesser credit cards, such as JCB and Diners, which, it was felt, had been neglected in favour of the more lucrative Visa and MasterCard franchises. It was also agreed to develop or strengthen new networks of people who could 'cash out' stolen credit cards in regions such as South America, Oceania and Africa. After all, somebody had to undertake the actual criminal transaction of taking money from ATMs – outsourcing this riskiest part of the chain was a no-brainer.

The more secretive discussions, where only about fifteen leading 'carders' were present, took place in a small, dingy restaurant down by the sea. The aim of this group was to persuade delegates to establish their own regional networks of CarderPlanet franchises so that its owners could continue to make money, but for less work.

As the meeting started, one of the lesser-known delegates sent an inconspicuous signal to Boa. The man had performed an electronic sweep of the restaurant and detected that hidden video cameras and digital recording devices were active inside the room. In all probability, the SBU, Ukraine's secret police, were carrying out the surveillance. And if the SBU were monitoring the event, so was Russia's KGB, who at the time were able freely to exercise the intelligence equivalent of *droit de seigneur* over the SBU – the right to trawl over pristine data before the collector had even examined it.

The Family, CarderPlanet's Politburo or Cupola, did not especially fear American and European intelligence and policing operations. But the KGB was another matter, and it was no coincidence that the most important resolution of the conference warned against hostile activities inside Russia and Ukraine. 'One more time, we stressed the absolute inadmissibility of any action in relations to our billing systems, banks or financial institutions,' it thundered. If Russian-speaking cyber criminals had turned on Russian banks or businesses, the entire project would have been shut down within five minutes.

Instead, CarderPlanet proved more durable. The website existed for nearly four years. It is no exaggeration to say that its creators were responsible for the emergence and consolidation of an entirely new method of engaging in major criminal activity: fraud that could be perpetrated on a huge scale with minimal resources and minimal risk.

CarderPlanet's primary role (later adopted by its many successors) was to act as a bazaar for stolen data – credit-card numbers and PINs, bank accounts and their passwords – along with other goodies such as viruses and fake documents. Until this point, the exchange of such information generally took place in laborious one-to-one transactions over icq and IRC (the two messaging systems favoured by hackers).

Cybercrime's perpetrators – so-called carders, spammers, skimmers and virus-makers – already looked like a breed apart from criminals attached to traditional mafia structures. Script called them 'lone wolves' in an interview with *Hacker* (*Xakep.ru*), the great chronicler of Russia's cyber underworld. 'They don't huddle together in groups or form their own distinctive networks; everyone works by himself, for himself.'

The Russians were not the only hackers developing the techniques of cybercrime, but CarderPlanet gave them a structure, hitherto elusive, enabling those lone wolves to form opportunistic packs in order to commit crime (or mere mischief) before evaporating back into a desolate cyber wilderness, brilliantly camouflaged in the clicking and whirring environment of the Web, resisting all attempts to identify who on earth they might be.

Very quickly, its members came to adore CarderPlanet. 'You must understand,' said a former *consigliere* from the website's inner circle, 'CarderPlanet was not just a source of information. People lived on CarderPlanet – we referred to it simply as The Planet as though it were our home.'

While theft, spamming and other forms of electronic malfeasance played a very important role, these were by no means the only activities attracting Russian speakers to land on the Planet and make their home there. The average user was gifted with a fascination for electronics, computing, games, network systems and hacking as sport.

These were not mere criminals who identified CarderPlanet as a vehicle through which they might ply their trade. Instead, they created a community of men largely in their teens and early twenties who were struggling to get by in a chaotic, ruthless historical moment and who possessed unique abilities. In Odessa, everybody was compelled to behave in a certain criminal fashion as a matter of course. But most were naturally confined by their location. The Planeteers armed themselves with the survivor's logic, from an Odessa in political and economic turmoil, and replicated these behavioural patterns in cyberspace. They were not natural-born killers, but natural-born survivors.

The new site was divided into categories, each devoted to a specific aspect of Internet crime or hacking. The first time one of Odessa's young hackers logged onto CarderPlanet, he was overwhelmed. 'I swear it was the same feeling that Ali Baba must have experienced when he first opened the cave and saw it stuffed full of treasure. Each section had heaps of information, which you could use to make yourself stinking rich without ever getting up from your computer!'

In the first year, hundreds upon hundreds of Russian-speaking hackers began exploring the site, attracted by its entertaining graphics and efficient organisation. The visual logo for CarderPlanet was a cigar-smoking gent with a twinkle in his eye – a dead ringer for Flash Harry, the cheeky spiv played by George Cole in Britain's post-war comedy classic, *The Belles of St Trinian's*.

'For innocent lads from the provinces like me who could at best expect to earn one hundred dollars a month,' the young Odessa hacker continued, 'the financial promise of this unknown language – including words like Dumps, Drops, Wires, COBs – was mesmerising.'

The website was not open to all-comers. To access its walled-off areas one had to become a member, and that meant being vetted by the administrators. Along with Script, four others assumed this privileged role in the first year of CP's activity, including Script's most influential collaborator, Boa.

Among other tasks, the administrators' job was to decide who should be granted membership and who not. In the first instance, these security measures were designed to ward off the interest of law-enforcement and intelligence agencies from around the globe. The US Secret Service and Britain's MI6 were well acquainted with CP's predecessors, *carder. org* and *carder.ru*. Script was determined to keep them at bay this time round. He was confident that the local Ukrainian police would present no great threat to the website. 'They're equipped with nothing, neither personnel nor resources,' he argued. 'No one in the Ukrainian agencies has fluent English and they hardly understand anything in any case. So even if they do get information from the "enemy", i.e. from us, they're not going to read it (and they don't get funds for it), so, essentially, they have nothing to read at all.'

More assiduous than the Ukrainian police were their Russian counterparts in Department R of the Interior Ministry, which was later reorganised, eventually re-emerging as Department K, dealing with all high-tech crime. CarderPlanet was penetrated and compromised by the Russian Secret Police almost as soon as it was set up. But as the Belorussian carder, Police Dog, has pointed out, 'If we didn't make a mess on our own doorstop then our local cops and intelligence services didn't have a problem with us.' Why would the KGB waste resources on investigating networks that are ripping off American and European credit cards? A complete waste of time. So for the moment Moscow was content to observe and store information. They knew exactly who was who in the Odessa carding community.

Ironically, given that CarderPlanet and cyber criminals boasted a very different social, cultural and psychological profile from traditional crime syndicates, Script and his collaborators nonetheless chose to designate their membership structure by borrowing the terminology of the Sicilian mafia. Later, carders reflected that it was unwise to use such an obvious criminal metaphor, although in these early days the language also hinted at Script's specific psychological profile and his future ambition to lead a powerful social movement.

The most senior members (never more than six) belonged, then, to 'The Family', whose highest representatives or administrators were each entitled to the honorific 'Godfather'. Once these Family chiefs granted somebody admission into CarderPlanet, the member could explore the website's various sections. In one part, for example, he could browse through a whole raft of viruses on sale, which he could later use to launch a specific type of attack against other computer users. Virus writers also offered to write a piece of customised malware, for payment, that could infiltrate specific systems or programs.

Most activity took place on the Carders' Forum. In this department you could buy and sell stolen credit-card and bank-account data. 'In the course of his work,' Script explained, 'a carder can specialise in one or more areas of carding. But there's nobody who does everything. Sooner or later that carder will need someone else's services. That's why there's a place for the networks and groups – people exchange numbers and information. That could be bank accounts, complete information on card owners, sometimes even including passport details. Carders can also be part-time hackers, since sometimes you can't come up with the necessary information (without paying for it) unless you break into a server.'

In another department you could purchase a Western passport or, say, an American driver's licence. In most instances, the counterfeit documents were of the highest quality. But, as purchaser, how could you be certain of the quality of these fakes? And furthermore how could you be confident that the seller was not going to rip you off? After all, you already knew that the person you were buying from was a criminal! 'Rippers' – criminals who rip off criminals – were already an established presence on the Internet.

This was CarderPlanet's trump card. The Family members were monitoring all the comings and goings. After introducing the vetting system, they further strengthened security by making this a pay site to keep out mischief-makers. There was initially 'a big influx of amateurs who just cluttered up the forum', whom Script wanted rid of, but even more damaging was the presence of the rippers, 'who offer low-quality services or fail to deliver services in exchange for the money they take'.

But CarderPlanet was not just a department store for cyber thieves, for the vetting system enabled administrators to act as guarantors for the business conducted via their website. In exchange, they received adulation, cash and a much bigger and more efficient market for their own products, all in one go.

While a genuine hacker, Script was unusual inasmuch as he was driven primarily by a desire to make money. Although young, he well appreciated the oceans of cash in which the Western world and particularly America was floating. Profit is indubitably a powerful force, but the creative genius behind CarderPlanet was not Script, but his senior collaborator, Boa, for whom money was a secondary consideration.

Boa was a very different character from the rest of the Planet's inhabitants. In his late thirties when Script first created the Planet, he was a good two decades older than most of his colleagues and vastly more experienced in the ways of the world.

In the 1980s when the Soviet Union still existed, Boa had proved himself a gifted student of electronics, completing two university degrees. He developed a particular interest in the world of amateur short-wave radio. In those days that was a sensitive hobby to pursue, as Soviet intelligence (and, in the case of short-wave radio, *military* intelligence) was intent on maintaining control of all communication flowing in and out of the country.

Boa was hugely popular, with an easy manner that could mutate into charisma at a moment's notice. Even though some friends assumed he was working with the signals section of military intelligence, he nonetheless became a poster-boy for the ham-radio fraternity around the world, which, as one might imagine, includes a high percentage of rather shy, geeky characters.

Boa attained a worldwide reputation for becoming the first amateur radio operator to broadcast from the military-restricted area of the Vietnamese Spratly Islands, following this up with an even more astonishing achievement: sending the first ever amateur signals from North Korea. He was fêted from America across Europe to Australia for this ham-radio first, drawing large crowds of fans when he appeared at their conventions in the 1990s. Good-looking and exceptionally articulate, he was instinctively liked by people, and everyone wanted to be his friend.

Boa came across CarderPlanet while surfing the Web in the autumn of 1999 and was immediately impressed by its entrepreneurial, if chaotic spirit. Living on Malta, he already had a successful global business that sold high-end surveillance, counter-surveillance and anti-terrorist technology to politicians and businessmen in more than sixty countries around the world.

Aware of Boa's professional experience and organisational ability, Script invited him to join 'The Family' after a few months. Struck by Script's drive and energy after he first spotted the website in early 2002, Boa agreed to join CarderPlanet. 'When Boa came on board, he completely reanimated the Planet,' remembered one of the youngsters who had moved to the Planet. 'He was responsible for the slick design and introduced a number of new sections. He became a local celebrity.'

At the same time, Boa agreed with Script that he would set up a second website, Boa Factory, whose activities would complement the work of CarderPlanet while emphasising different sectors of the trade – Boa Factory was known, amongst other things, as a specialist producer of counterfeit passports and ID cards, as well as developing a larger wholesale trade in cloned credit cards and dumps. Whereas Boa was exclusively a business site, CarderPlanet emphasised the social aspect of the underground where individual carders could meet, chat, buy and sell on the Web.

Boa Factory developed a revolutionary tool, subsequently adopted by CarderPlanet, that enabled the growth of cybercrime on an industrial scale. The greatest challenge facing cyber thieves lay in the knowledge that the person they were doing business with was also a criminal and, *ipso facto*, untrustworthy. Boa devised the escrow system, known initially as the Warrant Service, to solve the problem. A vendor would provide the escrow officer with a sample of his wares (a dozen or so credit card numbers and PINs) while the potential buyer would send the money to him at the same time. The escrow officer would then test the wares and, if they delivered the cash as promised, he would release the money to the vendor and the dumps and PINs to the buyer. This simple device proved to be a touch of genius. From now on, the trade was protected and it boomed accordingly.

It was Boa's idea to bring the Family together to the First Worldwide Carders' Conference in the summer of 2002. So when his invitation to visit Odessa dropped on electronic doormats across the former Soviet Union, the recipients were only too willing to pay the airfare south (though naturally enough they were almost certainly charging it to someone else's credit card). Would a Catholic turn down the chance to visit Lourdes? Or a Muslim an opportunity to see Mecca? Well, no self-respecting criminal would pass up the offer of a week in Odessa.

The Planet was on top of the world. Its users raved about its money-making properties while hundreds of hackers, crackers and spammers waited nervously to see if the Cupola would grant them the precious privilege of membership.

Script prefaced the gathering by giving the first ever public interview by a major carder. *Xakep.ru* (*Hacker* magazine), which still publishes today, is the bible of the Russian underground, but even its readers were shocked to see Script reveal the secrets of the Planet in March 2002. 'What motivates someone to become a carder?' the magazine asked Script, pointing out that Russia's notorious Department R was created to hunt down carders and their ilk.

> *Script:* They're motivated by what their hearts and minds tell them. Science has shown that people who take risks experience a rush of the so-called happiness hormone. That hormone, multiplied by whatever quantity of rustling dollar bills, plays the fundamental, decisive part in motivating someone to keep working in this not entirely honest industry.

> *Hacker:* Guilt-free?

> *Script:* Guilt-free. Not only because anyone can cancel any payment even after a long period of time has elapsed just by sending the bank a statement to that effect, but also because carding isn't as heinous an occupation as it might seem. It's a lot less shameful than robbery. We

don't cause card owners any problems; they'll get back
everything from the banks, right down to the last
penny if they ask for it. Instead, our government
should feel guilty about the fact that teenagers are
becoming embezzlers at such a young age.

Golubov was rationalising the trade as most carders do: the banks
will always pick up the tab, and so ordinary people remain unaffected.
Such sentimental, populist twaddle conveniently overlooks how banks
pass on the costs of fraud to their customers, and so the carders are
having a direct and negative effect on the ordinary people for whom
Script showed apparent concern.

Nonetheless, his point regarding the government not giving a damn
about how large numbers of teenagers were turning to crime is near
the mark. Ukraine was little more than a mafia state and its leading
politicians and businessmen were setting an appalling example, one
that Script proved adept at following.

Set against this backdrop, Script believed that CarderPlanet would
be able to furnish him with sufficient funds to enter into the bigger
league of Ukrainian business. He was nothing if not ambitious.

What could possibly go wrong?

7

BOA CONSTRICTED

Around the time that Script was launching CarderPlanet in Odessa, researchers at the software giant Autodesk in San Rafael, California, decided it was time to contact the FBI. The largest global manufacturer of 2D and 3D modelling software, Autodesk sell its products across the world to architects, designers, town planners, model-makers, mortgage brokers, vehicle manufacturers – well, they are even the chosen suppliers of software to Scunthorpe's firm of chemical engineers, Grimley Smith Associates.

Specialist software like this does not come cheap. Single licences for Autodesk's professional CAD programs range between $3,000 and $7,000, reflecting the huge amounts invested in the research and development of the product.

In 2002 the company's Piracy Protection Unit noticed that a seller in the Ukraine was offering brand-new versions of one of Autodesk's design programs on eBay for a bargain $200, when in the shops exactly the same product was retailing at $3,500. 'Hmm,' they thought, 'something's not right here!'

Silicon Valley suffers from the same problem as the Hollywood studios. The making of motion pictures often involves resources comparable to those required in the development of complex software programs. As production costs rise, the emergence of a global network of counterfeit DVD manufacturers, frequently linked to organised-crime syndicates, has reduced revenues from movies. This is especially true in a recession – if you have a choice between spending $15 to watch a film in a theatre or seeing it on a perfect DVD copy for $1, two months before it is even released to cinemas, the latter course is hard to resist.

Likewise, you might run a company in a competitive field where you must have access to, say, an Autodesk product. To buy the requisite software and licences for your needs from the company might weigh in at almost $20,000, but if you bought them from this Ukrainian chap on eBay, your total outlay would be $800. Let us be frank: it may be illegal, but it's tempting!

Since the 1970s, when software started to become commercially available for the first time, manufacturers have tried in vain to develop technology that can prevent it from being copied (as they have also attempted with CDs and DVDs). No such technology has ever lasted more than a few days before being cracked by one of the tens of thousands of hackers and crackers around the world. It has proved to be one of the most quixotic branches of the high-tech industry over the past three decades.

The hackers of Eastern Europe played a particularly important role in cracking security devices placed on software. In the 1980s, before the fall of communism, the Soviet Union had tasked various allies in its trading bloc, COMECON, to develop a personal computer and a software industry – notably Bulgaria and East Germany. The defining characteristics of communist computers were common to all Eastern Bloc consumer products: they were ugly and constantly breaking down. The challenges posed to the region's nascent computer engineers were so considerable that they developed an exceptional ingenuity in overcoming glitches and bugs.

Furthermore, the software factories that the East Europeans built in the 1980s could not compete with Silicon Valley during the 1990s after the fall of the Berlin Wall – there was no money to invest in research or equipment. But the powerful new organised-crime syndicates that exerted such a huge influence over the economies of the former communist countries saw the factories as a genuine opportunity. First, they acquired these facilities (usually by foul means rather than fair), then they employed those talented engineers to produce counterfeit software on an industrial scale. Bulgaria, Ukraine and Russia set the pace, with the Romanians not far behind.

So when Autodesk spotted that a single seller on eBay was shifting significant numbers of a counterfeited version of their product from Ukraine to buyers in the United States, they naturally felt obliged to do something about it. After some deliberation they called the FBI, who in turn alerted the US Attorney's Office in San Jose, California. And because the fraud involved eBay, the Attorney's Office called up one particular investigator: Greg Crabb of the US Postal Inspection Service (USPIS), who at the time was based in San Francisco.

There are three main American law-enforcement agencies that claim authority in cases of cybercrime: the FBI (because its job is to stop crime); the Secret Service (because its brief includes protection of the US currency and credit-card fraud); and the USPIS (because its job is to monitor any illegal activity related to the federal mail service). The last-named became involved in the cyber game primarily because scams perpetrated through eBay and similar services often involve sending goods by post (whether illegally purchased or as part of a money-laundering scam).

Over the past fifteen years the USPIS has built up a dedicated team that investigates high-tech crime, and Greg Crabb was so successful that he eventually moved from San Francisco to head up its Global Cyber Investigations unit, out of a large anonymous building in Washington DC's large anonymous complex called the Federal Center (remember to strike it off your 'must do' list when visiting the US capital).

Crabb's Teutonic looks and slightly gravelly drawl are simultaneously attractive and intimidating. He qualified as a chartered accountant and it is hard to dispel the feeling that if he were to have a look at your finances, it would not take him long to turn up evidence of major wrongdoing, even if you are squeaky clean. This quality confers a real professional advantage on Crabb, as the ability to study long lists of numbers, short messages and seemingly incomprehensible data is a *sine qua non* for a good cybercop. The job may sound exciting, but like so much to do with computing, most of the work is grindingly tedious.

Once detailed to the Autodesk case, Crabb traced the fraud by checking where customers of the counterfeit programs were sending their money. It turned out they would make payments into bank accounts belonging to fifteen 'mules', US citizens dotted around the country. Money-laundering and scams depend upon these (largely) unwitting characters, who respond to advertisements offering good returns on work carried out from your home computer. Successful candidates are then required to place their bank accounts at the disposal of their new employer. In the Autodesk case, the mules would receive

$200 and then forward $180, holding back $20 as their commission. They sent the money to a bank in Latvia, one of the three Baltic states whose role in both cybercrime and the broader issue of cyber security is out of all proportion to their combined population of seven million.

With the help of the Latvian police, Crabb discovered that the final destination of the monies was a set of bank accounts in Ternopil, western Ukraine. The accounts all belonged to a certain Maksym Kovalchuk or his wife.

Crabb realised that Kovalchuk by himself was not going to bring down the US economy. By the standards of major organised-crime groups, he was earning peanuts from this particular scam, galling though it was for Autodesk. Instead, Crabb worked on cracking open Kovalchuk's email account to discover if there were any other secrets there, and at some point he hit upon a 'unique capability' to monitor Kovalchuk's communications – which one can only interpret to mean that Crabb either hacked into his target's computer or persuaded Koval-chuk's email host to give him access. Whatever the truth, the 'unique capability' was to have a far-reaching impact on the real world, because almost as soon as he had started reading the emails, Crabb realised that Kovalchuk was involved in a project that was much bigger than the Autodesk scam: the development of a website called CarderPlanet.

Although the primary focus of his investigation remained Kovalchuk and his connection with the scam, Crabb began to map CarderPlanet's Family tree, almost as a sideline. Unaware that he was being monitored by a US agency, Kovalchuk was fairly free with his conversation and so a combination of luck and diligent investigative work had put Crabb in an enviable position. Not only was he ahead of the game with Koval-chuk himself, but the inspector had even stolen a march on Western intelligence agencies as well. By partially penetrating the most dynamic cyber-criminal community in the world, he had succeeded where the Western spooks had so far failed.

Yet while Crabb was able to learn a great deal about what was going on in Ukraine's hacking community, there was not much he could do about it. He couldn't even bust Kovalchuk. Not only did the United States have no extradition treaty with Ukraine, but the political circum-stances prevailing in this enormous East European country were most infelicitous. Leonid Kuchma was President of this country, which embodied a vast network of corrupt relationships between oligarchs and organised crime. Furthermore, the United States was competing with Europe and Russia for influence over the country, and at this time the prevailing wind was blowing from Moscow with some force. As long as he stayed in Ukraine, Kovalchuk was safe.

In the midst of this, in late 2002 while Inspector Crabb was still in San Francisco, he was called in by the security department of Visa, whose headquarters happen to be located there, too. Their people were frustrated by the inordinate success of a hacker named Boa, who had successfully stolen or assisted others in stealing tens of thousands of credit cards through his notorious website the Boa Factory. Crabb's ears pricked up – he knew that name, Boa, from various conversations he had seen on Kovalchuk's account. Hadn't Kovalchuk been buying a lot from Boa Factory and learning the tricks of the trade from it, as well as discussing the development of CarderPlanet? The postal inspector was rapidly homing in on Boa and Script as the two key figures behind CarderPlanet. Discreetly, through Interpol, he put out a note to other law-enforcement agencies requesting that they be in touch should they pick up any Ukrainians suspected of high-tech crime.

In late February 2003 Roman Vega was returning from a business trip to his home in Malta when one of his friends asked him to drop off and see him in Nicosia, Cyprus. He spent an evening drinking and reminiscing with his pal about their adventures in Burma in 1991 when they were part of the team that sent the first ham-radio broadcast from the military-run state.

On returning to his room at the Hotel Castelli, Vega had an unpleasant surprise awaiting him in the form of Modesto Poyiadjis, a local police inspector, who promptly arrested the Ukrainian as an accessory to a credit-card fraud perpetrated by another Ukrainian guest whom Vega had allowed to stay in his room (a bad move, as it turned out). For Vega, it was the beginning of a relationship with law enforcement in Cyprus and the United States that can only be described as Kafkaesque.

After Poyiadjis had checked through the Interpol records, he made contact with Greg Crabb, the lead officer in the US investigation of Boa. He told the man from the US Postal Inspectorate that he believed Roman Vega was none other than Boa. Crabb could barely contain his excitement. Even before the call was over, in his mind he was booking the first flight to Nicosia. It was not just the prospect of attempting to extradite one of the masterminds behind CarderPlanet . . . *they had his laptop!* If the Cypriots had managed to work out who his alter ego was without really knowing what they were dealing with, just imagine what an investigator like Crabb could extract from that hard disk.

'Boa's arrest came as a huge shock,' said the CarderPlanet member Xhora, echoing what many of his cyber compatriots on the Planet felt at the time. Boa had been the man who had made CarderPlanet fun, as well as interesting and lucrative. Because he was that much older and more experienced than the rest of the Planet's inhabitants, many assumed that he would be invulnerable to inconveniences like law enforcement.

At the same time, Script was accumulating ever greater power and cash as a result of his control over CarderPlanet. 'His interviews were designed to make the site more popular and to increase his business,' said another CP devotee, Null _ Name, 'and in this he succeeded. There was a flood of new members into the site. And the atmosphere changed. It was not the same.'

The cosy camaraderie of CarderPlanet's early days was, it is true, fast disappearing. Nonetheless the website was generating more money than ever. The English section of the forum was now up and running, and before long carders from all over the world were signing into the site. But in far-away San Francisco, Greg Crabb was feasting on Boa's hard disk, mining it for the thousand secrets that had passed back and forth between Boa and Script. 'I never needed to interview Boa,' said Crabb, 'I'm not even interested in what the guy has to say because I had his hard disk – there was nothing new he could tell me!'

In fact, Crabb may not have mined the computer for everything he wanted. It seems that at some point, US law enforcement cracked one of the encryption systems on the VAIO laptop, but its owner had also reinforced it with a powerful system, Handy Bits EasyCrypto (downloadable for free), which would have prevented access to about 80 per cent of the computer files.

On the carder forums, bitterness lingers to this day because members assumed that Roman Vega had ratted on Golubov. This is untrue – any intelligence on Golubov was extracted from the VAIO computer. Not only did Vega himself remain silent, at considerable personal cost, but he has now spent almost a decade in various Cypriot and American jails, even though he has never been convicted of a single crime.

Despite all the new information, there was still nothing Crabb could do about Script. He was in the Ukraine – unlike Maksym Kovalchuk, who was arrested with his wife for the Autodesk fraud in a Bangkok milk-bar three months after Roman Vega had been picked up in Nicosia. Just as Vega was extradited to California from Cyprus, so Kovalchuk headed to the West Coast from Thailand.

Script had no intention of leaving his home country and, to protect himself further, he announced on CarderPlanet in early 2004 that he was resigning his authority and would be leaving the site for good.

As always, Script had a plan. He had made sufficient money from those carding activities, which he had memorably described as 'guilt-free', and now he wanted to invest in legitimate businesses. Perhaps he was hoping to head off future unpleasantness. Perhaps he had ambitions beyond the cybersphere. He made his dramatic announcement on CarderPlanet – he would be handing over the administration of the website to a trusted *consigliere* and would no longer tread the Planet's boards.

Script, it seems, was going straight. But there was one thing he hadn't bargained for.

Revolution.

8

SCRIPT REWRITE

Boris Borisovich Popov called his office to say that he was feeling under the weather. The doctor had told him he would have to take it easy for a few days, he explained. Some colleagues were surprised. Boris Borisovich's slight build and adolescent features occasionally resembled those of a sickly child, but he was probably the most industrious and most disciplined man among them. 'Working with him was a pleasure,' one of them remarked later, 'you couldn't find anyone better in the whole service.'

Despite crying off work, Popov did not take to his bed, but – fit as a fiddle – walked out of his apartment, hailed a cab and made his way to Kiev's Borispol airport, where he checked in for a flight to Odessa. Originally from Donetsk in eastern Ukraine and with Russian as his mother-tongue, his presence down south would not arouse suspicion provided he kept his wits about him.

On arrival in Odessa, he took a bus into town. It was a hot July day. The temperature was in the low eighties, but was made pleasant by a cheerful breeze coming off the Black Sea. Before long, Popov had found the private apartment he had rented. Within hours his three teammates had turned up – Natasha Obrizan and Messrs Grishko and Baranets. 'We couldn't stay in a hotel,' explained Boris, 'because we didn't trust the local police.' Only one other person in the whole country knew they were in Odessa: the Minister of the Interior.

Six months earlier Ukraine had undergone a dramatic convulsion – the Orange Revolution. This exceptionally fertile country, with the potential to provide the continent of Europe with more or less all the food it needs, was no stranger to drama. Twentieth-century regimes included extreme nationalism, autocracy, communism and fascism, each responsible for visiting their own brand of terrifying violence on the country's population: civil war, mass starvation, genocide, deportation and widespread poverty.

The most enduring domestic legacy of this chaotic history has been the division of Ukraine into two geographic and two Slavic language camps: west and east; Ukrainian and Russian. The capital Kiev sits between the two like a wobbly bridge, hoping to reconcile the sometimes hostile traditions. In the darkest days of the twentieth century the west of the country became linked in some people's minds with fascism and Germany, while the east was regarded a bulwark of communism and Muscovy.

This split is not always so clear – pockets of Ukrainian speakers are found in the east, while pro-Russian candidates often pick up unexpected votes in parts of the west. Nonetheless, it is a useful rule of thumb. Since independence, Kiev and the western provinces have striven for closer ties with the European Union and NATO, while the east has sought to strengthen its links with Russia. Indeed, many eastern Ukrainians still feel they belong in every sense to their giant neighbour.

Until 2004 successive Ukrainian governments and presidents had supported a pro-Russian line, much to the satisfaction of the east and the unhappiness of the Ukrainian nationalists in the west. As a consequence, relations with the EU, NATO and the USA were frosty – Ukrainian government officials were hosted as often in US jails, convicted of money-laundering and other McMafia activities, as they were in the White House.

But as civil servants, politicians and oligarchs lined their pockets at the expense of ordinary citizens, whose living standards collapsed before and after the turn of the millennium, a fresh political movement coalesced around two 'new-style' politicians, Viktor Yushchenko and Yulia Tymoshenko. Only later did it emerge that they were cut from similar cloth to their opponents. Yushchenko hit the headlines in September 2004 after somebody tried to poison him with dioxin (almost certainly the work of Russia's KGB). He survived the assassination attempt, albeit with severe facial disfigurement, and announced that he would continue to stand for election as President.

The campaign to oust the old guard caught the imagination of young

Ukrainians, who transformed it into a festival of politics dubbed the Orange Revolution. Student activists from Serbia in the Balkans who had helped bring down their own dictator, Slobodan Milošević, arrived in Kiev to school the budding street-politicians of their near-neighbours. Neo-con proselytisers from the US poured into the country, sensing a real opportunity to give Moscow a bloody nose and drag Ukraine closer into NATO's orbit.

From the start there were international implications to the sudden surge in political activity. By the time Yushchenko was finally declared President and Tymoshenko Prime Minister in January 2005, Ukraine had become a very live testbed for Russian–US relations that were steadily deteriorating. Both the new leaders not only affirmed Ukraine's commitment to join the EU, but also announced their hope that the country would become a NATO member before too long. Even though this was destined to fail (it was, after all, only supported by 30 per cent of Ukrainian voters), Moscow interpreted their action as all but a declaration of war.

In the four years since he had first stumbled across Maksym Koval-chuk, the man who sold fake Autodesk products, Inspector Gregg Crabb had been patiently developing relationships with his colleagues from Ukrainian law enforcement's baffling array of agencies. But while he had made important contacts, they politely turned down his requests for the arrest of Dimitry Golubov, aka Script.

The dramatic events of December 2004 and January 2005, when Yushchenko and Tymoshenko came to power, changed all that. Crabb realised that the Orange Revolution represented an opportunity that could not be missed. Early after the tumultuous events he received a call from the US Embassy in Kiev. Ukraine's Interior Ministry, he learned, had already been purged of the old hardliners and a new team, more inclined to work with the West, had been installed. 'Get over here quick!' the embassy told him. The man from the Postal Inspection Service didn't need a second invitation.

He made it to Kiev in June 2005 and presented his evidence on the Golubov case to Interior Ministry officials. Two weeks later Inspector Popov of the Anti-Organised Crime Department was on his way to Odessa with instructions to track down and arrest the elusive Script.

Popov knew this was a tough assignment. Above all he was worried about any leaks, because if news of the raid were to arrive in Odessa before he did, the whole operation would collapse before it began. As an accomplished carder who by this stage had finally achieved the status of 'dollar millionaire' many times over, Golubov would have bought himself the protection of local law-enforcement agencies. Among his own, he was invincible.

Dovzhenko Street lies two miles south of Odessa's city centre. The streets are lined with trees and it is counted among the city's more fashionable addresses. Golubov was living at his grandmother's apartment, so when Popov and his team pitched up they were surprised to find a thick steel door blocking their access. After moving into position, Popov signalled to his colleagues. 'Open up! Police,' they shouted while banging on the immovable door. Greeted by silence, they strained to hear anything behind the steel barrier – one of them thought they detected some shuffling, but despite their efforts, the door remained firmly barred.

As Popov was wondering whether to call in some heavy equipment, the sharp smell of burning paper hit their nostrils. 'Christ!' he thought, 'he's started destroying evidence!' Popov lost no time in alerting the emergency services, and before long a fire engine was on its way. With the heat intensifying, the firemen smashed open a hole in the apartment wall and started to spray foam through it. When it looked as if his grandma's apartment was about to be flooded by industrial chemicals, Golubov finally decided the game was up and at last opened the door.

It was a bizarre scene. Not only did Popov discover Golubov's records on fire, but the hacker was feeding computer disks through a Raskat. Had Golubov merely deleted files from his various computers, this would have presented little challenge to anyone with rudimentary skills in computer forensics seeking to reconstruct them. You can burn paper – it is much harder to burn computer files. But the Russian-designed Raskat could deploy powerful electromagnetic waves in order to obliterate data completely. Golubov had been caught red-handed, and Popov accompanied him to Kiev where he was incarcerated.

Vega and Golubov were now both under lock and key (as were several other vital members of CarderPlanet's family). Both strenuously denied that they are Boa and Script. Neither has yet been convicted of a crime – indeed, the former has spent seven years in American jails without ever having gone to full trial, raising serious questions about the efficacy of the US criminal justice system.

Whatever the precise cause, the stuffing had been knocked out of CarderPlanet. The visionary website for hackers and crackers may have disappeared but its legacy was immense – it has revolutionised criminality on the web.

Furthermore, large-scale cybercrime had already broken out of its Ukrainian origins. In the final two years of CarderPlanet the administrators had encouraged the development of an English-language forum that had been running alongside the Russian discussion boards. This forum spread the Spirit of Odessa to hackers and carders the world over. Two of its members were novices, but they were intrigued by the new world of professional carding. One had adopted a jolly pirate as his avatar and the other an image from many geeks' favourite film: enter JiLsi and Matrix001.

Part III

9

TIGER, TIGER

Colombo, Sri Lanka, 1988

Bang! Bang! Bang!

'Open up! Open up!'

Soldiers in this mood rarely wait for an answer, particularly not at half-past five in the morning. They smashed against the door with their rifles and poured into the house. Searching from room to room, they ordered family members to lie on the floor before ransacking the place.

Three youngsters woke in terror as their home filled with noise and light. 'Out of bed! Out of bed!' Sweating in the tropical heat with nothing but their underwear on, the children found that their teeth started chattering with fear. The soldiers pulled out the eldest, just eleven years old, and pointed to a patch of white skin the size of a hand on his stomach. 'What's this? What is this?' they shouted almost triumphantly. 'He's been using explosives!'

'It's a birthmark,' he replied, 'it's just a birthmark.'

They pulled the boy away and sat him on a chair in the living room before beginning the interrogation. His parents and his grandmother pleaded with the soldier who appeared to be in charge, and finally they agreed that the frail youngster, who had yet to embark on his adolescence, seemed an unlikely bomb-manufacturer for the Tamil Tigers.

Little Renu was used to turbulence like this. It had punctuated his life from an early age. Five years earlier, in July 1983, he was evacuated from Colombo when still only six years old. Tamil militants had murdered thirteen soldiers of the Sri Lankan army. Taking revenge, a Singhalese mob slaughtered hundreds of innocent Tamils in Colombo, the capital, triggering a sustained civil war, which only came to an end twenty-six years later.

Sitting tight in Colombo as Singhalese gangs marauded through the city was no longer an option, and so Renu's parents packed up and took their three children to Jaffna, the main centre of the Tamil community in Sri Lanka. Lying at the northern tip of the country, Jaffna was separated by only fifty miles from the south-eastern coast of India. It was also the stronghold of militant Tamil guerrillas. Resistance to the Singhalese-dominated government in Colombo was growing.

It was not long after Renu's move that the unpredictable violence of civil war and insurgency started to creep ever closer to his new home. By 1987 government troops were laying siege to Jaffna, battling with various armed groups, notably the LTTE, the infamous Tamil Tigers. The number of refugees streaming from the city into southern India across the Palk Strait reached a critical mass, persuading the government in New Delhi that it had to act. In a deal reached with the Sri Lankan government, the Indians sent a large peace-keeping force into Jaffna to oversee a peace agreement.

Before long, relations between the Indian peace-keepers and the Tamil Tigers had broken down and once more Jaffna became one of the most dangerous cities on Earth. In October 1987 Indian troops were responsible for the massacre of several dozen innocent civilians in the city's main hospital, the only incident during a quarter of a century of civil war that united the Colombo government and the Tigers in their outrage. For Renu and his family, the risks of staying in Jaffna were too high and so they trekked back down south to Colombo.

One afternoon, Renu's father asked the young boy to buy some groceries. Renu had never seen so many rupees and he stuffed them in his pocket, along with the list of things to get. On the way to the shops, he spotted a man by the side of the road playing a game. There were three pots and underneath one of them was a pebble. Renu watched as people placed their money against one or other of the pots after the deft entertainer switched them around at lightning speed. Renu was mesmerised and shocked that the players consistently failed to find the pebble, and yet he had guessed right every time. He wriggled his way to the front of the queue and pulled out his father's crumpled banknotes. One by one they were scooped into the man's pocket as Renu failed to guess the right pot, just like those before him.

The more he lost, though, the more frenziedly he placed his bet. Oblivious to his losses, he just couldn't stop himself – until there were no more notes and his little body, woozy with adrenalin, was suddenly overcome by a cold sweat and a vision of his father's hand raised high above his head. He never gambled again.

In the years since they had left for Jaffna the capital had calmed down somewhat, although the safety of Tamil residents was never fully assured, as the raid on their house by the military made clear. But the options for Renu's family were running out.

Not yet in his teens, Renu had spent much of his life toing and froing between the frying pan and the fire, sometimes literally avoiding the crossfire. Soon after the army's raid on the house, when a birthmark almost made a terrorist of the young lad, Renu's grandmother decided that his situation as a Tamil coming of age in Sri Lanka's capital was too perilous. He might either be tempted to join the Tigers or fall foul of the nationalist Singhalese groups on a prowl across the capital.

By 1992 the family had scraped enough money together to send Renu to London, where his aunt and uncle lived.

His new life on the other side of the world, in a most unfamiliar setting, contained its own dangers. At the Langdon School – one of the biggest and most unruly in east London – Renu, stick-thin and small, found himself caught between two large communities, one white and one Bengali. He performed well in maths, outstripping all his peers, but was barely able to express himself in English. A complete outsider, he was bullied relentlessly and after six months simply refused to attend classes any more, despite the entreaties of his despairing aunt and uncle.

For two years Renu locked himself inside the house, sometimes not emerging into the fresh air for weeks on end. Watching television from morning till night was his sole activity.

Renukanth Subramaniam learned how to be alone.

And he might have stayed alone, had his uncle not finally forced him back into the outside world, specifically to Newham College of Further Education. Here he learned some new skills: how to socialise with his peers; how to smoke marijuana; how to drink Martell brandy; and how to programme a computer.

Down at the local pub, stoned and drunk, Renu would hammer his virtual opponents on the arcade machine, Street Fighter. How many young men were drawn obsessively to this mesmerically repetitive challenge, which pitched their avatar in a fight to the death against a string of equally aggressive fighters? Did this tame aggression or encourage it? Did the flood of dopamine around the brain's frontal lobe, which these games trigger, lead to intense addiction in all young men or just in some of them?

Renu pounded away at the machine, drenching his body in adrenalin and his brain in endorphins. When he finished, his body still wired, he hit the Martell to sustain a feeling of well-being and to calm himself down. Slowly, this dual habit began to take its toll on his paltry allowance. Street Fighter became ever more central to his life. As he lay down to sleep, the game's violent images would appear in technicolour in his mind's eye.

As he had once stopped gambling, so he now resolved to stop playing and he never touched the machine again. Unfortunately, his decision at the time only applied to Street Fighter, and not to his burgeoning predilection for drink and drugs.

His break with the game did not mean an end to his fascination with computers in general. He had loved them ever since he had first played with one as a nine-year-old in Sri Lanka. Lack of money had ensured he never had regular access, but he overcame that problem in his early twenties by accepting a place to study computer science at London's Westminster University.

Soon afterwards Renu had discovered warez, pirated software programs whose security systems had been cracked and distributed among devotees known collectively as The Scene.

It was a world where he could be with friends and alone, at one and the same time.

GAME THEORY

Eislingen, Baden-Württemberg, 2001

Just as Renu was exploring The Scene for the first time, 500 miles away in southern Germany another young computer user had stumbled across the same mysterious community.

Fifteen-year-old Matrix001 had fallen in love. Not with a girl. Matrix was infatuated with computer games. At first, they were just one aspect in a balanced and normal adolescence, competing for his spare time with gymnastics and the school orchestra in which he played the clarinet. There was nothing outwardly unusual about him. His secret obsession with games was easily hidden. Nobody knew – not his friends, not his parents or his siblings – except perhaps for his younger brother.

Not only did he adore games, but he was a skilled practitioner too, and as his final high-school exams approached, his sessions at the keyboard began to extend deep into the night. Keeping up with the latest games proved an expensive affair, especially if (as among Matrix's gaming peer group) there was kudos in announcing that you had played and beaten those games which had only just been released.

By the year 2000 new games with dazzling graphics were cascading onto the market. The Pokémon series rolled out thick and fast, while at the more extreme end, WWF Smackdown 2: Know Your Role was proving a big hit, along with Grand Theft Auto, whose storylines were forging their violent and pornographic hallmarks. Matrix was always desperate to get his hands on the latest game, but he just couldn't afford them all.

In respect of gaming, his life mirrored Renu's. Otherwise the two had nothing in common.

Determined to satisfy his driving passion, Matrix discovered an Internet community known as the fXp scene. This phenomenon was an important moment, not just in Matrix's life, but in the rapidly changing parameters of Internet culture.

Over two decades since the introduction of the personal computer, its usage had become the subject of a passionate if arcane debate – among its developers, prophets and most committed users – about its role in society. Many of the criminal skills on the Web have emerged from an essential division in the philosophical debate generated by the Internet.

In simple terms the debate is between those, on the one hand, who believe its commercial role is paramount and those, on the other, who argue that it is in the first instance a social and intellectual tool, whose very nature changes the fundamental moral code of mass communication. For the former, any copying of computer 'code' (shorthand for the computer language in which software or a program is written) that is not explicitly sanctioned is regarded as a criminal violation. The latter, however, are convinced that by releasing software you are also relinquishing copyright.

The heart of the matter was revealed as long ago as February 1976 when Bill Gates addressed an open letter to 'the hobbyists', an inchoate cluster of computer users who would variously evolve into geeks, hackers and crackers. In the letter Gates bemoaned the fact that 90 per cent of those using Microsoft's first programming language, Altair BASIC, had never bought it. Instead they had copied it, which meant that Gates was not getting the return on the huge amount of work and cash he had invested in developing it. Although Gates's language bore the hallmark of inelegance common to many geeks, the message was clear: he accused the hobbyists of theft.

The hobbyists, geeks, hackers – 'crackers' as they later became known – disagreed. As far as they were concerned, once 'code' was out there, it was fair game. Both on the West Coast and at MIT in Cambridge, MA, some of the world's most important computer developers and early users were infected by a strong dosage of a 'kumbaya' ideology, which held that this particular technology was one for bringing the world together and that for some (unspecified) reason it was not subject to the rules of copyright that had traditionally applied to books, music and other creative output.

It was clear *why* this could happen: in the past the public was not in a position to print an unlicensed copy of a book or produce pirated pressings of an LP, as it did not have the machinery to do it. And if it did, this machinery was cumbersome, stationary and easy for law enforcement to track down, in the name of intellectual copyright.

Code or software was different. After graduating from the cassette machines on which the first computer games for domestic use were written in the early 1980s, it was produced on floppy disks, CDs, DVDs and ever-shrinking hard disks. By this time, the Empire of Commerical Software Producers attempted its first strike-back by inserting pieces of additional code onto their product, which sought to prevent unauthorised copying of their material. CDs and cassettes routinely included digital locks.

While understandable as a tactic, it backfired. As far back as 1982 another German teenager, who later went under the enigmatic hacker's moniker of MiCe!, finally persuaded his parents – against their better judgement – to buy him a computer for Christmas. But having spent all that money, they refused to give him a penny more for games, not understanding that without the games' software, which was written on cassettes at the time, the computer was useless as far as their son was concerned.

He found that the only way he could use the computer was to borrow software from friends and then copy it. On one occasion he discovered that the cassette would not copy. He tried everything imaginable, but his computer crashed every time. After days and nights of frustration, he finally spotted a bit of code at a specific point on the tape, which had no apparent function. And then it dawned on him: it was blocking the process! Once he had understood this, MiCe! was able to experiment by rewriting the code in different sequences until one night – bingo! – he cracked it.

Early gamers like MiCe! were inspired to crack the locks because they were addicted to gaming, not because they wanted to make money. The copies were passed from gamer to gamer, giving birth to The Scene.

It was still a laborious and time-consuming process as it involved physically copying the code onto a new cassette. Nonetheless, the gamers had taken up with gusto the challenge laid down by software manufacturers, and before long a significant subculture of cracker groups had flowered. Its members' sole aim was to crack games and other software the minute they came onto the market and then parade their cracking skills to their peers.

The cyber underworld was born, although it would quickly start fracturing into very different communities – some good, some bad.

II

NO TURNING BACK

Almost two decades after MiCe! had cracked his first cassette, young Matrix was faced with an identical dilemma. He was addicted to games, but he could not afford them. The dilemma was the same, but the technology had advanced almost beyond recognition. Games now boasted breathtakingly sophisticated graphics, intricate storylines and mind-bending challenges.

For many gamers, their obsession had intensified correspondingly. Cassettes and floppy disks were already museum pieces and time was running out for CD-Roms, DVDs and memory sticks (before they were even invented). Increasingly games could exist merely as code on the Internet. However, you could not store very many on your domestic PC. Furthermore, these were the days of dial-up modems, when hooking up to the Internet meant keeping the phone line busy for hours. But if, with your home computer, you could access a much bigger computer, then you could store and share all the games you liked . . .

fXp stands for File Exchange Protocol, but all you need to know about fXp is that it enables the very swift transfer of data between two computers. It is especially useful for exchanging data between servers. It is important to spell out that a server is simply a computer that has been adapted to function as a communications hub. Thus a large company, for example, will have its own server that provides Internet access for all employees. Many servers are big and powerful and not dependent on telephone lines for their access to the Web.

The fXp message boards united a fraternity whose members hacked into servers and then used them to store and play games. Matrix was a quick learner and before long his computer was scanning for servers on the Internet.

Using an automatic program, his computer would send myriad messages onto the Web that would effectively knock on the door of servers whose physical location could have been anywhere in the world. When the server answered the door, Matrix's computer would ask, 'Can I come in?' Most servers would then reply to his computer, 'What's the password?' But he found a sufficient number of servers whose administrators had not bothered to set a password, in which case the server replied to Matrix's machine, 'Sure, come on in. I'm yours to do with as you please, you naughty master computer!'

For Matrix, administrators who left their computers vulnerable like this were beneath contempt. Anyone could walk in and steal a company's secrets. It's no different, he thought, from me taking my wallet stuffed full of notes to a shopping centre and then placing it in the middle of the mall before walking away.

Then there were other servers whose passwords could be easily guessed, such as those that retained the default password from the manufacturer, usually something like 'admin' or – the most crushingly stupid password of all – 'password'.

With other computers, he found a vulnerability in their security system (perhaps a little-used 'port' or point of entry that failed to ask for a password), which he could exploit to gain access to the inner workings of the server. It might have looked like rocket science to most computer users, but to Matrix it was like pushing at an open door and he could teach anyone how to do it in half an hour.

The first task Matrix had to undertake, once he had taken control of the server, was to fix the vulnerability that he himself had exploited to gain entry: he had to ensure that nobody else could attack it as he had done.

Having entered a server, he was then in a position to control it. If he wished, he could watch all the email and Internet traffic going in and out. But he didn't wish: all he wanted to do was use these servers to receive, store and distribute games using fXp technology.

Matrix was just fifteen years old, but he could at will come and go in huge parts of the Internet that most adults did not even appreciate existed. His parents had no idea of the secret world he was exploring from his bedroom. Nor were they likely to find out – downloading games and software was patently illegal and an infringement of copyright laws, but the practice was at this time restricted to a very small number of users. It was regarded by manufacturers as an irritation, but not a terminal problem. The overwhelming majority of games were bought perfectly legally in stores or from sites like Amazon.

Matrix did not conceal his activity from his parents out of concern that he might be infringing intellectual property laws. No – the most wonderful thing about the Internet for teenagers, he realised, was that your parents would never (and in most cases can never) have the slightest notion of what you are doing. It was tough enough for parents to keep track of which DVDs were entering or leaving a house. But at least DVDs were physical objects that a mother or father could confiscate, should they find their thirteen-year-old watching an X-rated movie (always at the risk, of course, of provoking a tedious temper tantrum).

The Internet was changing all that. Children were growing up in a cyber environment which to them was self-explanatory and normal, but which parents found increasingly mystifying and treacherous to navigate. Teenagers were perfectly aware that their parents were at cybersea in this same environment. This in turn started to reinforce a sense that the Web was an area of their young lives from which parents could legitimately be banned. How many mothers and fathers have walked into a room and observed their teens minimising their Internet browser as their cheeks flush briefly? And if parents so much as glance at a Facebook page, even when the kids are accessing it in a public room, the child is transformed into a human-rights activist, accusing the beleaguered carer of acting like a Gestapo officer.

What many children and teenagers were less aware of was how, while they were able to pull the wool over their parents' eyes, there were all sorts of people less easily fooled – and whose numbers were growing. These might include stalkers, advertisers, bullies, groomers, police, teachers and criminals. Only the most sophisticated users are able to cover up what they are actually doing on the Web.

In contrast to long-suffering parents, these other interested parties with a modicum of computer literacy were starting to track digital footprints that children and teenagers were beginning to leave over many years. Such records habitually included admissions of drug-taking and alcoholic binges, the insulting of teachers, the bullying of classmates and, increasingly, the posting of pornographic self-portraits.

Parents may have known nothing about this, but other people did. Even really smart kids like Matrix could become complacent.

In taking over poorly protected servers, then storing and playing games on them, Matrix was not actually doing anything wrong. At the turn of the millennium this was not a crime in Germany, and the issue of copyright in the digital age was opaque – already teenagers and young adults had started sharing music files using Audiogalaxy and Napster. These were websites where, if you wanted to download Queen's 'Bohemian Rhapsody', for example, they would direct you to a PC somewhere in the world on which the song was stored. Using the website as a bridge, you could then download a copy onto your computer.

In a very short space of time, millions of people figured out that they no longer had to purchase recorded music – everything was available for free! While file-sharing was a mere inconvenience to the computer-games business, it was a huge challenge to the music industry. To combat the problem they would need lawyers to redefine copyright for the digital age; then they would have to persuade legislators to pass laws in that spirit; finally, they had to convince the cops that apprehending digital pirates was part of their job. Furthermore, the music trade would have to develop new technical devices to prevent the practice (something they have signally failed to do).

The practice of sharing music files that are small and easy to transfer from computer to computer spread like wildfire. Music sales in the United States peaked in 1999 at just over $14.5 billion, but started to fall the following year, and that is what they have been doing ever since.

By contrast, the unauthorised downloading of games that were much more unwieldy made barely a dent on physical CD-Rom and DVD sales, which kept growing year-on-year. If anything, the downloaders helped to advertise games. So the worst thing that could be said about Matrix's cyber activity was that it deprived him of sleep and led to his homework being neglected.

But then Matrix, almost without noticing it himself, shuffled one little step further down a spiral of mischief.

The advertising industry had discovered the Internet and, like everyone else, it was trying to work out how best to exploit it. The Web offered distinct advantages for advertisers – first, you could target your potential audience with much greater accuracy. If you want to sell nappies, then avoid websites that cater for skydivers and concentrate on message boards for young parents. If you are paying for adverts on the television, radio or billboards, you are hitting the skydivers as well, but to no real purpose (unless, of course, the skydivers happen also to be young parents).

Second, you can calibrate the success and the cost of advertising. Each time a young mum or dad clicked on the nappy ad, this would register with both the nappy manufacturer and the advertiser. The advertising company then got paid according to the number of clicks. Advertisers and sellers were then able to analyse the so-called Click Through Rate (CTR), so that our nappy manufacturer could see how, out of 100 visitors to the skydiving site, none of them clicked on the advert. But on the young parents' message board, ten out of 100 visitors clicked on the site, giving a 10 per cent CTR – and the advertising firm would be paid accordingly. Before long the CTR had spawned Click Fraud.

An administrator on one of the forums that Matrix visited was involved in a scam. He encouraged Matrix to use the servers he controlled to set up a program that would click automatically on banner ads at intervals. Each time he did it, he earned a cent. He didn't even know it was illegal. The administrator then told him that there was another forum that he should look at where similar matters were discussed, and it was on this forum, CarderPlanet, that he learned about credit-card fraud for the first time.

Matrix crossed the Rubicon in a psychological trance, unable to perceive the waters swirling around him. He was a kid and he was sliding into crime, slowly, incrementally. Somewhere at the back of his mind, he maybe knew that something was wrong, but the boundaries in cyberspace are very blurred, if indeed they are visible at all.

12

A PASSAGE TO INDIA

Chennai, Tamil Nadu, 2001

By the year 2001 Renu had not seen his parents and siblings in nine years. Yet even young men like Renu, who have taught themselves to survive with the loosest familial links, are occasionally obliged to respond to the entreaties of a mother. After much cajoling, he promised her he would find the funds to fly to Tamil Nadu in the south of India to visit the whole family.

Funds, however, were hard to come by. While at Westminster University, Renu had taken a job with Pizza Hut as a delivery man. He worked until about midnight or one o'clock in the morning and then had to get up early to attend his first lecture (although his punctuality slipped steadily as the year went on). The job had given him some extra cash for the first time in his life. But it wasn't sufficient to allow him to save: what he had left over was being absorbed by his drug habit, which now included cocaine and before long would embrace that most devastating narcotic, crack cocaine.

Unable to muster the fare, Renu borrowed it from friends, and for safety purchased £3,000 worth of American Express traveller's cheques before setting off on the long flight to Chennai.

Nobody knew what to expect from the encounter: when he had left his mother, he was still a boy. Now he was a young adult whose life was punctuated by bouts of intense solitude. His social life had picked up since college, but he was given neither to easy talk nor to any great expression of emotion. And, although youthful, he was also rapidly creating a patchy past. There was much that he would not be sharing with his family.

The trip began inauspiciously. From Chennai, he had to take one of India's overstuffed, clammy buses into the countryside, sharing his space with too many people, too many chickens and too much luggage. Halfway through the journey, his eyelids drooping after the long plane ride from London, he felt a slight tug that woke him momentarily. He thought nothing of it. But the joy of being reunited with his mother was tempered when he left the bus – his little purse had been slit open and the £3,000 of traveller's cheques were gone.

There was worse to come. When he visited the Amex office in Chennai, the staff refused to reimburse him (which he had understood was the whole point of taking cheques rather than cash in the first place). Before they would stump up the replacements, he would have to provide written confirmation from the local police that the money was gone. He was also told that Amex did not guarantee to return the money, but would pay it back 'at their discretion'.

Once back in England, the bureaucrats at Amex were similarly stony-faced. Renu, they adamantly maintained, had failed to provide the requisite documentation that would prove the cheques had been stolen or lost. There would be no payout.

The people he had borrowed money from were friends. But only up to a point. They sympathised with Renu's plight, but they still wanted their cash back. The only way that Renu could stump up the money was by taking out credit cards – this was after all the Age of Plastic, and the banks and credit companies were as keen for Renu's custom as they were for anyone else's.

The lousy job at Pizza Hut could not cover his increasing financial demands: the debt; the drink and drugs; the college costs; the rent. Renu's world began to wobble. College assignments were the first to suffer. Having passed the first-year exams at the Harrow campus of Westminster University, he started turning up to ever fewer classes. He failed the second-year exams and failed the retakes.

To escape the despair, he started obsessively downloading songs from Napster, before discovering the sites where members of The Scene would share the games and programs they had cracked. The nights became ever longer as Renu sank into the safe and distant world of the flickering screen, far from the circling dogs of reality.

One evening, he told the tale of his lost Amex money to one of the many itinerant surfers he met on the Net and his IRC channel. 'Go check *amexsux.com*,' his contact said, 'it'll make you feel better, if nothing else!'

Renu loved the new site (logo: *DO leave home without it*), where former clients of American Express poured out their anger at perceived wrongs. The animus felt towards this particular company is fairly extensive, as a Google search testifies: there are hundreds of sites dedicated to bitching about Amex, many of which post a fairly impressive set of links to negative news stories featuring the company.

One poster on the message board offered an original idea to those who felt they had grievances against the company. 'Take your revenge! Go to *CarderPlanet.com!*'

As Renu set sail in search of CarderPlanet, he felt it was time to bid farewell to his own personality. He became JiLsi, whose avatar was the face of a mischievous cartoon pirate with a red hat and a black patch over his left eye. A veritable Captain Jack Sparrow amidst the cyber Caribbean, he soon felt at home among the scurrilous crew of hackers, crackers and fraudsters when at last he weighed anchor on Carder-Planet. Somewhere among this group of misfits wandered Matrix, and although it was a few months before they exchanged the vows of virtual friendship, the two became familiar figures floating between the myriad sites that sought to emulate CarderPlanet.

Where else might you find a drug-addicted refugee from Sri Lanka hanging out with a strait-laced middle-class German teenager, hosted by a charismatic Odessite with a vision for a new Ukraine? Only on the Web.

13

SHADOWLANDS

New York, New York, 2003–4

RedBrigade decided that the time had come to hit Washington Mutual – in his eyes, nothing more and nothing less than a purveyor of free money. The bank had actually lost its mutual status in 1983, and now its CEO had announced that he intended this venerable institution from Seattle to become the 'Wal-Mart of banking'. Strip it down wherever you could was the boss's philosophy. Shift those loans and don't look too closely at the customers' assets, liabilities and wages. Move those sub-prime mortgages, package 'em up. Invest as little as possible in staff and equipment. This was low-cost banking with all the frills cut out. Fortunately for RedBrigade and his pals, the frills included elementary security systems.

He left the Four Seasons Hotel on 57th and 5th Streets at around eleven in the morning. His head was still groggy from the previous night's partying, but as it was vintage champagne and almost uncut cocaine, he felt fully combat-operational.

On reaching the bank, he casually strolled up to the untrained teller ('they didn't have to pay 'em as much') and passed over the WaMu debit card.

'How much would you like today, sir?'

'Ten thousand, please.'

'Alrighty!'

Tip-tap, tip-tap. Here at WaMu, RedBrigade had to hand over his card to the teller, who would then swipe it through a point-of-sale device. In any other bank this is the moment when the teller might be reading a coded message on their screen telling them to 'call in immediately'. RedBrigade would have to scrutinise the teller's face. Is she rumbling me this minute? Should I run? Or do I just stand here like an imbecile and wait for the cops to turn up? Maybe there's nothing wrong at all and I'm being paranoid?

Not at WaMu. Those cheapskates didn't want to waste money on computer screens and coded security messages. So if the card was rejected in this establishment, RedBrigade would just look slightly surprised, apologise and walk off. Nobody called in the cops at WaMu.

But his cards never were turned down. On this December day in 2003 the lady swiped his card and it was approved straight away. He then signed a printed-out receipt with a transactional code on it, before walking to the machine at the front of the bank. In went the code. A momentary wait and then, like a fantasy one-armed bandit in a Las Vegas casino, it spewed out the cash in fifties: 1,000, 2,000, 3,000 . . . on and on, until RedBrigade stuffed 200 fresh fifty-dollar bills in his pocket.

Sometimes it seemed as though the banks had left their ATMs open to him and his friends on purpose. It was so easy, he thought, it was as if we were the chosen ones. He particularly enjoyed siphoning funds from Citibank. Of all the banks, Citi deserved it. First of all, they were the most immoral of all those bastard bankers. Second, their security sucked.

Phishing was, from an early stage, critical to all manner of cyber-crime. Even if a company's digital defences were sealed tight, a relatively inexperienced hacker could breach them with a phishing attack. This is the mass dispatch of emails to addresses that are sometimes targeted as belonging to a specific company – a bank, for example – and some-times chosen at random. Many spam messages contain either an infected attachment or a link which, if pressed, would direct a browser to a site that can automatically download malware. If a hacker sends out several million spam emails, he does not need a high response rate in order for it to be worthwhile – each compromised computer promises access to bank accounts and other personal or financial information.

Banks have always been faced with one overwhelming security head-ache: their customers (although this did not excuse the banks' appall-ingly weak security systems during the first fifteen years of Internet banking). The best networked system was only as good as it weakest element – and we, their hundreds of millions of customers, were as vulnerable as it gets.

So if a bank is unbreachable, the cyber thief would ask its clients for help. Send out millions of emails to account holders, which look as if they have been sent from their bank, and then wait for the replies: the account numbers and passwords arrived like an avalanche.

Phishing Citibank customers was a breeze:

Buy bulk freshly hacked emails. Check.
Buy Dark Mailer, the spammer's wet dream. Check.
Buy proxies. Check.
Buy hosting. Check.
Design new Citibank page. Check.
Put in pop-up box that never goes away until a card number and pin are entered. Check.
Set up email address for the account numbers and passwords to roll into. Check.

Every day RedBrigade would go phish. He looked at the account details of one Dr H.M. Hebeurt from upstate New York. 'Hmmm . . . she lives close by. Fuck me, she's making 50k a month and her fucking husband is pulling in more than 72k!' Looking closer, he saw the target worked on Wall Street. Maybe if he had made better choices, he pondered, he could be stealing legally like this guy . . . But he could not allow himself to indulge in fantasies like that – instead he just started calculating. Okay: two checking accs, two saving accs, one overdraft acc and one credit card . . . $2,000 from each. Total $12,000 from a single phish.

And everyday fifty of these little phishies swam into his account.

The spree in New York's Washington Mutual lasted just over a fortnight, netting him almost $300,000. Just as well, because his average weekly outgoings were in the region of $70,000. Every two or three months he would buy a new top-of-the-range Merc or BMW. First-class travel was axiomatic. He thought as much about purchasing a $10,000 Breitling watch as we might before buying a newspaper. He had a beautiful apartment on the Upper East Side, but only slept there two or three nights a week because he enjoyed the city's luxury hotels.

RedBrigade was earning more money than a Premiership footballer in England, but without the 50 per cent tax rate.

Nothing was out of his reach. He'd peel off the fifty-dollar bills and would see that look on the face of the cashier, meaning, 'Who the fuck is this guy?' He figured they thought he must be either a Trustafarian or a dope dealer. But in the Age of Plastic the super-rich were as likely to dress in T-shirt and jeans as in a Savile Row suit. Either way, the merchants always took the money – the jewellers, the car dealers, the wine sellers, the hoteliers – no questions asked. They could never be sure: perhaps this unshaven guy might own Google? And in any case, who cares how he made his money?

One thing kept bugging him. He had too much cash. One evening he came home with $77,000 in his pocket to add to the $300,000 already lying about the apartment. There was also $110,000 worth of money orders. RedBrigade had set up a global cash-out operation, so he would supply the card and account data to an East European middle man, who would organise the raids on ATMs before sending RedBrigade the cash. For that operation he had to start banking again himself. He was tired of trying to stay under the Reporting Guidelines – any transaction of more than $10,000 had to be registered with the Treasury under anti-money-laundering rules. Shit, he thought, who would have known how difficult it could be to get rid of money!

He was preparing another cash-out of $77,000. It would have been a simple stroll for a few blocks from his apartment, and then he thought, 'I've got so much money here, I can't be arsed.' He knew there was something very wrong with the whole picture. But the only thing that kept going through his mind was: 'CarderPlanet was one thing, but who would ever believe this Shadowcrew shit? Who would believe that I can walk into banks, day in, day out, and exit with fifty grand in my pocket? It's insane!'

When CarderPlanet finally closed down in 2004, it boasted not just the Russian- and English-language forums, but had added Korean, Chinese and even Arabic sections. 'CarderPlanet was a game-changer,' said E.J. Hilbert, a former FBI Special Investigator who spent several years on the investigation into the website, 'all the successors to Card-erPlanet took the site as their model. It is no exaggeration to say that it spread the practice of criminal hacking to all four corners of the globe.'

Websites modelled on CarderPlanet sprang up everywhere: *theftservices.com, darknet.com, thegrifters.net* and *scandinaviancarding.com*. There were many more, including one bound by the delightful acronym parodying American academic communities, IAACA (International Association for the Advancement of Criminal Activity).

But none succeeded like Shadowcrew during its two years of existence. And RedBrigade was one of the many carders on Shadowcrew who hit the jackpot. Law enforcement was just beginning to become aware of the extent of the business. Banks were effectively clueless, ordinary folk oblivious.

Hackers were streets ahead, and Mammon ruled everywhere – the hedge-fund managers, the oligarchs, the oil sheikhs, the Latin American mobile-phone moguls, the newly empowered black economic elite in South Africa, the old white economic elite in South Africa, Chinese manufacturers of global knick-knacks, techno gurus from Bangalore to Silicon Valley.

Hundreds of carders made vast fortunes during Shadowcrew, many of them sufficiently naive to piss it all away on the trappings of arriviste wealth. In those days there were no checks on your computer's IP address when you made purchases over the Web. There was no Address Verification System on the credit card: you could ship goods anywhere in the world (except Russia and other former Soviet countries), regardless of where the card was issued, and nobody would cross-check it at any stage.

This novel crime took root well beyond its Ukrainian- and Russian-language nursery. It began to globalise spontaneously. RedBrigade recalled how established Asian criminals would now communicate with college kids from Massachusetts who were talking to East Europeans, whose computers overflowed with credit-card 'dumps'. Behind some of the nicknames on Shadowcrew were criminal agglomerates like All Seeing Phantom, revered among his peers.

A good ten years older than most Shadowcrew members, RedBrigade saw no advantage in gaining recognition and respect by attempting to climb the hierarchy. He failed to see why ordinary members were in such awe of the moderators and administrators of the boards. Despite its success, Shadowcrew's managers had a puerile, almost brat-like aspect to their behaviour – hardly surprising as most were in their late teens or early twenties. He observed that CarderPlanet had been established and developed by real criminals, whereas many of the Shadowcrew team were dilettantes whose boundless hubris was fed by the unfathomable sums of money they were making.

The further RedBrigade kept away from these characters, the less likely he was to be spotted by law enforcement. All but a tiny minority of Shadowcrew members were unaware that the Secret Service had achieved deep penetration of the website.

In April 2003 Albert Gonzales, a young American of Cuban origin and one of the most senior Shadowcrew members, had been busted. He was known to the carders as CumbaJohnny. But they did not know that after his arrest he had turned informant, which was the critical breakthrough for the Secret Service. Gonzales ran a so-called Virtual Private Network (VPN) through which the website's leading actors communicated with one another. A properly maintained VPN renders detection by law enforcement very hard, if not impossible – unless of course the guy administering the administrators is also administering to the cops, as Gonzales was.

On 26th October 2004 the US Secret Service launched a series of raids across the United States, which led to the initial arrest and indictment of nineteen individuals for their role in *shadowcrew.com*. Several more were picked up later.

'Shadowcrew,' ran the indictment for criminal conspiracy, 'was an international organisation of approximately 4,000 members which promoted and facilitated a wide variety of criminal activities.' It was the biggest outing for the Secret Service's young posse of cybercops. The indictment presented in a New Jersey district court sounded dramatic. 'Administrators,' it continued, 'collectively controlled the direction of the organisation, handling day-to-day management decisions as well as long-term strategic planning for its continued viability ... The administrators had full access to the computer servers hosting the Shadowcrew website and, correspondingly, had ultimate responsibility for the physical administration, maintenance and security of these computer servers as well as for the content of the website.'

The media engaged with the Shadowcrew takedown in a rush of excitement, going so far as to suggest that this was the virtual equivalent of crushing the Corleone clan in Sicily. Coverage was helped because one of the indicted was a woman, Karin Andersson, aka Kafka, although the Secret Service had actually failed to uncover that the real criminal was her boyfriend, who was simply using her computer and IP address to commit crimes. Hardly a surprise, given that 96 per cent of hackers are male.

Doubtless the arrests were justified. But were the 'administrators' the guys making the money from Shadowcrew? No, they were not. It is true that among them were some so-called 'monetisers' (chief among them Gonzales who, notwithstanding his close ties to the Secret Service, later engineered an even more notorious bust – the hacking of T.J. Maxx's credit-card database).

But the cops faced a problem that would frequently recur: hackers are not typical criminals. True, their skills are exploited by real criminals to commit real crimes against real people. But the hackers are often oblivious to this aspect of their activity. They are Script's 'lone wolves', often uninterested in amassing a fortune and more concerned to elevate themselves as masters within their peer group. 'You have to understand,' JiLsi explained, looking back on the carding experience, 'that this was all a game. It was like playing Grand Theft Auto, except you are doing it for real. You pit yourself against living and breathing cops. And that makes the buzz so much bigger! It is about respect. It is about . . .' JiLsi paused for effect, *your reputation.*'

In one regard, however, the Shadowcrew bust of criminals operating on the Internet replicated the effect of a major takedown of a mafia organisation in the real world. It created a carding vacuum and triggered a monumental struggle for supremacy among the next generation of carders, who coalesced around two new websites that emerged the following year: CardersMarket and DarkMarket.

Part IV

14

THE ICEMAN COMETH

Santa Clara, California, October 1998

Max Vision was surprised when Chris and Mike, his two contacts from the FBI office in San Francisco, turned up at his front door in Santa Clara. He didn't recognise the third man, although later he learned that this was the FBI's computer-crime boss. But then this was not a social call. 'We're building a case on you, Max,' they said. 'You've really screwed up on this one.'

In a state of mild shock, Vision turned over his computer and everything else – he did not want to appear to be obstructing justice and, at the same time, he was not yet sure what the problem was.

His life was good – great, even. After putting a torrid adolescence behind him, he had moved from Iowa into a region where neither geeks nor unkempt long hair and ponytails were considered unusual or inelegant. Nor would they find it odd that he had changed his name to Vision from the more prosaic Butler. He had quickly become accustomed to the lotus-eating lifestyle of the West Coast and, to top it all, he was deeply in love with his intended bride, Kimi.

In his mid-twenties, Max Vision was a computer-security genius and one of the most respected and highly valued consultants in the Bay Area. He was also a civic-minded chap, who set up the website *whitehats.com*, which was dedicated to helping people and companies ensure themselves against malicious cyber attacks. Mr Vision would post the latest 'vulnerabilities' to which popular software was prone and explain how to patch them up.

Vulnerabilities were meat and drink to hackers, offering one of the main routes into third-party computers. They were digital holes in the armour of software and computer systems, which the manufacturer had failed to spot. Once a company like Microsoft or Adobe noticed that a hacker had penetrated Windows or a ubiquitous application like PDF Reader by using a particular vulnerability, it was then able to close it or 'patch it' by writing a specific security fix, as it is known. Next, it would alert its customers to download the fix and install it, thus blocking that route into the customer's computer. If the user failed to update the fix, the computer could still fall foul of a virus exploiting that particular vulnerability, should it come calling.

Super security hackers like Vision would often spot vulnerabilities before anybody else and so, in the spirit of good neighbourliness, he offered practical advice to users on how to protect themselves.

But his good deeds went further. He also gave his services free of charge to the FBI station in San Francisco, and the Feds were only too happy to accept the help.

No challenge on the Web was too great for Max Vision, no vulnerability too small for him to spot. But of course in order to seek out those vulnerabilities, he needed to probe computer systems all the time. He knew this put him at the centre of a profound dilemma that affected the computing industry with serious ramifications. In order to protect yourself from criminal or 'blackhat' hackers, it was sometimes necessary as a 'whitehat' hacker to ascertain how to break into systems – an act that might in itself have been illegal.

It is almost unavoidable for 'whitehats' to sniff around large public computer systems, just as 'blackhats' do. The difference is that the 'whitehats' will not exploit for personal gain any vulnerability they find. The 'blackhats' probably will.

Operating out of the little house he shared with Kimi, Vision found that whenever he came across a network anomaly or problem, he could not resist the urge to correct it. In 1998 he discovered a dangerous vulnerability on the networks serving a series of government agencies, including parts of the Pentagon. This was a hole in their defences through which all manner of mischievous worms could wriggle. Literally hundreds of thousands of government computers could be compromised by skilled hackers working anywhere in the world. Again demonstrating his patriotic commitment, Vision filled these holes with digital cement to ensure the security of his nation: nobody would be able to exploit this vulnerability ever again in those particular government departments.

Then came a turning point.

Both at the time and in retrospect it seemed insignificant. It was minuscule, an act so fleeting it was barely recorded by time: an electronic pulse almost impossible to conceptualise; one stroke of a key; one letter in pages upon pages of computer code, nothing but the Pavlovian twitch of a born hacker. For in all those government computers Max Vision left one tiny little hole open through which only he could crawl and, a little later, an eagle-eyed cyber investigator from the United States Air Force spotted that hole and traced it back to its architect.

And that is why his friends from the FBI came knocking on his door in Santa Clara, with the intimation that dark clouds were gathering. 'You've been causing all sorts of problems, Max,' they said. 'This is a national security issue – that's why the Air Force is here.'

Vision was upset and indignant. He had emailed the authorities in advance, telling them about his suspicions regarding the vulnerability and how he planned to scan them as a test.

How serious was this crime? His actions had not been motivated by financial or any other type of gain. On the contrary, he had performed a considerable favour to the federal agencies involved. Among other services, Vision had made safe the computer systems of military bases and nuclear research facilities, including the Brookhaven and Livermore National Labs. And given that the damage he had caused was minimal and that he had stolen nothing, how wise was it to prosecute one of America's most gifted computer operators for this offence?

The airman's discovery not only led to Max Vision's arrest on charges of releasing a malicious worm. The consequences were even more dire: that tiny hole drilled into the entry ports of computer networks grew and grew until it was transformed into an unholy abyss, the Taft Correctional Institution, a federal prison that lies in the desert north of LA. Vision was going to prison as a mature skilled hacker, not as a criminal. He had only encountered professional criminals when his contacts at the FBI were shooting the breeze with him. That was about to change, of course, as Max (and his hacking skills) was deposited in a low-security prison, many of whose inmates were incarcerated for fraud and other financial crimes.

Things looked bad for Max. But they were about to get worse. Not only had he received a two-year sentence in Taft, but a month after he arrived there, Kimi announced she was leaving him.

Abandoned by his wife for another man, forsaken by his erstwhile friends in the FBI, Max Vision tumbled down the abyss, at the bottom of which lay a deep depression. Here he landed next to a fellow inmate, one Jeffrey Normington, who extended a hand of friendship when nobody else would.

On his release from prison, Vision was unable to find regular work that paid more than the minimum wage. He applied for jobs and was offered senior positions in security companies abroad, but as he was on parole, he was not eligible for a passport. In Silicon Valley, nobody wanted to employ someone whose CV included an indelible conviction for computer crime.

His debts mounted as his despair deepened. Then one day friend Normington reappeared, promising a path out of the abyss and back into California's sunshine. The route was littered with goodies. Normington promised him a top-of-the-line Alienware laptop, a must-have but expensive accessory for hackers. That was just for starters. He said he'd find Vision an apartment and pay for it. Normington would arrange everything.

In exchange for a few favours.

Crime was not Vision's sole option. There were other avenues to explore. He could have gone to friends and family. But he was tired, he felt abandoned and Normington was convincing. Another turning point; another wrong turn.

Max Vision, all-round good guy, was discarded back into an abyss. In his place, Iceman emerged – all-round bad guy, albeit one whose alter ego, Vision, had form as a collaborator with the Feds.

15

CARDERSMARKET

Iceman watched from the sidelines as the US Secret Service outsmarted the brains behind Shadowcrew. He considered himself apart from most of this tawdry team, which had sought to mug unsuspecting individuals on the Net while allowing itself to be eaten from inside by informers, snitches and rippers.

Now that Shadowcrew was finished and a number of wannabes had sprung up to replace it, Iceman resolved to show the world how you beat the law. Above all, he wanted to show his mastery of cyberspace and its users.

For Iceman, the carding sites were anarchic emporia where money was barely relevant and freedom to act was everything. He believed sincerely that creating special market places like his own new site, CardersMarket, where people could exchange information, should not be regarded as a criminal act in itself, even if it might inspire some of the traders to commit crimes. His and similar sites were a signal that the Web, in contrast to other areas of life, should not feel constrained by heavy-handed state interference, and on the home page he addressed the police and administrators of the Internet quite directly:

MSG TO LAW ENFORCEMENT, HOSTING, & ISPS:

CardersMarket is a **legal** forum provided as a place where members are allowed to discuss topics of their choosing. Absolutely NO illegal content is permitted and any illegal content is removed immediately by staff. Discussion is not a crime. Operating a forum is not a crime. There are no credit-card numbers, bank accounts, pornography, warez or anything that could be deemed illegal in the United States nor in the international community. Any alleged business that transpires between our members is **not our business** and if it happens it happens **outside of our forum**. We do not condone or in any way participate in illegal acts here.

The deeper he involved himself in the carding world, the more tangled he wove his moral web. As Iceman, he never bought and sold credit cards. But Vision created other online persona who did trade in them. The ability to section off parts of the personality was a common trait among hackers. At times Vision even appeared to believe that his virtual characters were autonomous in thought and deed, and therefore morally distinct entities.

As Iceman, he sought to defeat both his criminal competitors and the police in order to emerge as the unchallenged master of the carding world. This required a dual-pronged strategy. First, he must identify and expose all snitches (Confidential Informants or CIs) and cops who were stalking the carding boards. Second, he must vanquish the competition – all the other carding boards vying for criminal traffic.

Long before the US Secret Service successfully engineered the closure of Shadowcrew, Iceman had identified that several of its key members were either informants for American and Canadian law enforcement or, perhaps, full-blown police officers. Those like Iceman who practised deception knew they must be equally skilled in perceiving the art in others. Experienced cyber thieves and cybercops alike knew that nothing encouraged disguise and dissemblance like the Internet. Iceman reasoned that spotting snitches was an essential part of the job.

When Iceman did uncover informants, he wrote famously vitriolic rants about them on the boards. Some members concluded that Iceman did protest too much. Was it possible that the master brain of CardersMarket was himself an informant? It certainly looked that way as he launched his master plan for annihilating the competition – a series of attacks on rival carding forums, aimed both at taking them out and absorbing their voluminous member databases into his own CardersMarket. Vision was quite open about his intentions: with his hallmark arrogance, he said he didn't believe that other criminal websites like *scandinaviacarding.com* or TalkCash 'had any right to exist'.

To underline his superiority, he first created a false digital trail, which made it appear as though the CardersMarket server was located in Iran, way out of reach of both law enforcement and other carders. In fact, the server was in California, but so great was Iceman's capacity for subterfuge that he did indeed convince everybody that the site was based in Iran. Naturally this added to the rumour mill: was Iceman an agent of Iranian intelligence, charged with sowing confusion among US law enforcement and raising funds for its covert operations?

Whoever he was, it was clear that he meant business. One after another, he successfully hacked the rival carding sites, hoovering up their databases, which included all the email addresses and passwords of the members, along with a record of all postings ever made. He then integrated all this information into CardersMarket before deleting the records on the original site.

His attacks were relentless – even the Russians were not spared his wrath. He had the temerity to hack *mazafaka.ru*, the iconic site that had replaced CarderPlanet in the affections of Russian hackers. But although his ego sometimes clouded his judgement, he knew perfectly well that destroying the Russian sites in the way he had the English ones would have been most unwise. The Russians included some of the most brilliant hackers in the world, and Iceman had no wish to provoke them. Furthermore, following the Shadowcrew takedown, the Russians had promptly left the carding party. That is to say, they departed – more or less en masse – from the English-speaking boards. The Babylonian exchange of criminals, informers, spies and police officers on the anglophone websites was becoming irritating and oppressive: it was getting in the way of business. The risk they ran was negligible, provided they kept away from countries where American law enforcement could act.

And so Russian hackers established a series of boards that were exclusively or predominantly Russian-speaking, including *mazafaka. ru*. US law enforcement found these much harder to infiltrate, while cooperation with the Russian police or the more influential KGB proved extremely difficult. The first line of defence of criminal hackers in Russia or Ukraine is always the ever-changing local slang. While some Western police officers could hold a conversation in Russian, it was much harder to keep up with the dynamic shifts in the language attached to a popular culture with which few in Washington or London could keep pace.

While the Russian sites rumbled along happily, by the summer of 2006 Iceman had killed off almost all English-language opponents. And when he noticed any of them attempting to resurrect themselves, he would launch a devastating Distributed Denial of Service (DDoS) attack.

DDoS attacks had emerged as the most common weapon in cyberspace. They were the work of so-called botnets, the cyber equivalent of the 1950s Hollywood classic, *Invasion of the Body Snatchers*. A virus 'captures' a computer, which then falls under the influence of a so-called Command and Control Server. The virus would infect thousands of computers in this way, which were referred to thereafter as zombies, enjoying the status of drones that carry out the bidding of the mighty C-and-C Server. To most intents and purposes, they continued to function as normal computers. An ordinary user would be unaware that his other machine was now a soldier in a vast Army of the Digital Dead. If an especially active zombie, the innocent victim might have noticed his or her computer running a little slowly, usually because it was being overworked to assist unseen in the distribution of billions of spam emails, either advertising penis enlargements and Vicodin or containing a new copy of the virus that could infect still more computers.

But often botnets are instructed instead to mount DDoS attacks whereby the zombies are all ordered to access a specific website at the same time. If a website or a server is subject to a DDoS, it simply collapses under the strain of having to accommodate so much computer traffic. The page freezes. If the attack is powerful enough, whole systems freeze.

His relentless use of DDoS attacks ensured that Iceman was widely loathed among the criminal hacking community for his arrogance. But his tactics also aroused the suspicion that he was working for the Feds, because so many of his victims were hackers and criminals.

However, nobody could argue with his figures and turnover, as CardersMarket now had several thousand members, all of them still active, buying and selling credit cards, bank accounts, viruses, identities and more. By August 2006 he was cock of the cyber walk.

There was only one thorn in his flesh. One criminal website wouldn't die. Every time he hit it, whether by clearing out its database and wiping all its files or by ordering his army of zombies to take it down from the Web, it just kept coming back like a weeble, those funny dolls that always spring back up when you knock them down.

The battle with DarkMarket had begun.

16

DARKMARKET

Cyberspace, 2005–8

As the souped-up car rolled down the western edge of the Alps, the sun bounced off the crisp Mediterranean, reinforcing the sense that this was going to be a stupendous weekend. The group of twenty-something Scandinavian lads led by Recka, the king of Sweden's carders, turned off the A8 and onto the Grande Corniche highway before snaking down through the mountains to Monaco.

One of the smallest and most densely populated countries in the world, the principality had been drowning in its own glamour for most of the last century. In 1956 it set a gold standard for post-war global celebrity hysteria when one of Hollywood's most alluring princesses, Grace Kelly, joined a real royal family by marrying Crown Prince Rainier, heir to the Monégasque throne.

Now, exactly fifty years after Monaco's marriage of the century, a group of DarkMarketeers armed with a trove of rare plastic booty were preparing a brief raid on this temple of decadence. Soon after passing the border from France to Monaco, the first casinos hove into sight. These cash factories have been underwriting the principality's budget since the 1860s. The locals call them 'Monaco's wallet' and they are the reason why the Monégasques pay no taxes. Why would they need to? A single room at the Monte Carlo Bay Hotel, for example, costs $800 a night, and if the guests can afford that, they can obviously throw silly money into the casino vaults. The result – a surfeit of lucre all round.

The indigenous population thus bathes gently in the huge pools of money which the super-rich fritter away on the blackjack and roulette tables. Guest residents often feel able to dispense with this cash so lightly because it's money that, under other circumstances, they would be paying in tax to those national exchequers where they or their businesses spend most of their time. As Monaco is a haven for tax evasion – and, according to the venerable Organisation for Economic Cooperation and Development, money laundering too – the authorities on this rocky outpost of fiscal freedom are used to not asking questions of visitors to their tiny land or the origins of their funds.

A perfect place, then, for a group of DarkMarketeers armed with twelve American Express Centurions, the fabled Black Amex cards, Olympian deities in the Age of Plastic who grant audiences by special invitation only to squillionaires from the West, Japan, Hong Kong and the Middle East. In America, the Centurion user has to pay a $5,000 joining fee and then subsequent annual fees of $2,500. But in exchange, Centurion Man receives free plane tickets, dedicated concierge services, personal shoppers and membership of elite clubs dotted discreetly around a world of which we inhabitants of Planet Drudgery have no notion.

And did we talk cash? Present your Centurion and swaddle yourself in the bucks, euros, sterling, Swiss francs or yen that the bank cashier will hand over with a hint of a smile that is reserved for someone of your value and status. A single Centurion could almost pay the ransom for a hostage captured by Somali pirates.

There is nothing unusual in a group of youngsters with too much money for their own good pitching up in Monte Carlo to spend, spend, spend with their Centurions – in this environment spoilt brats are the norm. They were determined to exploit their twelve magic tokens to the full. First a luxury hotel, then cocktails and a sumptuous meal before they hit the Casino. 'It was a crazy party,' one of them remembered dreamily, '2006 was the time when DarkMarket began to soar in the sky.' By the time they left two days later the young carders had taken out €400,000 on those Black Amex. Even they admit to being shocked at how easy it was. 'They didn't bat an eyelid. Nobody challenged us once, and you got the feeling that people did this sort of thing all the time.'

The Scandinavians were not alone in hitting the jackpot. Maksik, a notorious Ukrainian carder, was earning hundreds of thousands of dollars by reselling 'dumps and fulls', credit-card numbers with their PINs and the three digits on the back of the card. Cha0 in Turkey created a veritable factory of criminal activity, cashing out cloned credit cards, selling 'skimmers' around the world to other thieves so that they could steal card data on their own.

Darkmarket.com was founded in May 2005, but in the first few months of its existence it was a fairly lifeless affair. In the autumn of that year, however, it attracted some significant figures from other carding boards. The most energetic of all was JiLsi, the hacker from Sri Lanka, who had already founded one site, The Vouched, and had achieved moderator status on mazafaka's small but influential English-language section.

Before long, JiLsi had been appointed global moderator on Dark-Market, one rung below the kingpin status of administrator. He took it upon himself to elevate DarkMarket's profile. His aim was the same as Iceman's with CardersMarket – JiLsi wanted it to be recognised as the top criminal website in the English-speaking world. Working tirelessly from the Java Bean Internet café in north London, he succeeded in attracting hundreds of new members by May 2006. They were mainly English-speakers, although a number of Russians floated in and out as well.

Just as the site was becoming popular among carders the world over, its original founders decided to bring an end to DarkMarket because they feared its penetration by the security services. One of them even worried that it was becoming too successful. JiLsi and his friends wished to build on its growing reputation and simply reregistered the site as *darkmarket.ws* (the country domain for Western Samoa).

Now they could really get to work. Along with JiLsi, DarkMarket boasted the sponsorship of a renowned Russian hacker who went under the name of Shtirlitz, a veteran from CarderPlanet, who acted as a bridge between the Russian carding sites and DM.

There were others. Matrix001 had a look around DM. His reputation as a specialist in graphic design had been growing since he became a member of the International Association for the Advancement of Criminal Activity. He was unimpressed by what he saw – the message board was clunky and its security poor. He sent the administrator JiLsi a blunt message, pointing out that enemies like Iceman were hacking the website on a daily basis due to the inadequate software. Matrix offered to install a better system, which JiLsi welcomed, and Matrix began his ascent up the hierarchy.

More help was on the way. JiLsi was quick to promote a certain Master Splyntr to accept the post of moderator on the forum. Master Splyntr was the nickname of a notorious Polish spammer called Pavel Kaminski. In a typically adolescent reference, his nickname referred to the rat who trained the Teenage Mutant Ninja Turtles in the art of martial combat in the popular children's cartoon. In deference to his hero and his skills, Master Splyntr was also known among the spamming and hacking community as 'sensei'.

Master Splyntr's true identity had been revealed by the secretive British anti-spam organisation, *spamhaus.org*. The businessmen, techies, former spooks and God-knows-who-else comprising this team run an effective crusade to blacklist high-rollers of the spam, carding and child-pornography worlds. It scours the digital world for 'rogue' ISPs, those Internet Service Providers that turn a blind eye to the criminal activities of their customers. Kaminski, Spamhaus reported on its website, was one of the world's top five spammers, responsible for vast amounts of unwanted ads for penis enlargements, Vicodin and the rest.

Spamhaus's interest in Master Splyntr meant that he was a marked man, and five police forces from around the world launched investigations into his activities when he moved from spamming into the realm of carders. Kaminski was also linked to the wholesale distribution of malware, viruses and trojans. He was an established bad dude, and JiLsi was quietly thrilled at having enticed such a big fish into the waters of DarkMarket. He cultivated both Splyntr and Matrix001 assiduously. This was developing into quite a team and when Cha0, the Turkish criminal mastermind, joined the party, DarkMarket developed an undoubted aura of success.

To look at, there was nothing remarkable about DarkMarket. It functioned just like message boards that discuss the perils of parenting or the thrills of bee-keeping. It was harder to access because members had to be nominated and vetted, but this rarely proved a problem for those acquainted with the carding scene and with a determination to join. Actual business – buying and selling – was hardly ever conducted over the forum, for security reasons. Rather it was a place for vendors and buyers to meet; it was where manufacturers of skimming machines could find a market; it was an opportunity for holders of credit-card databases to recruit a team doing 'cash out' work (the critical job of going from ATM to ATM extracting cash from accounts). But the details of any deal were almost always hammered out in private messages held on encrypted icq networks. Once a deal was struck, it was back to the website to put in a request for the escrow service where administrators would ensure fair play.

The forum attracted ever more members, and business boomed. Key individuals acted as a bridge between Russian criminals and Western carders, but at the same time JiLsi noticed the geographical circle widening. Turkey was becoming an important cybercrime zone. The communities in Spain and Germany were growing very fast, while even those in France – whose carders felt, like most French people, more comfortable in a French-speaking environment even on the Web – brushed up on their English to enter the fray.

The Golden Age of DarkMarket was under way.

17

THE OFFICE

Renu Subramaniam's office was a terminal at the Java Bean Internet café. For much of the previous eighteen months Renu had been working on the Web against a background of grinding and screeching, as the modest Java Bean lay in the shadow of Wembley Stadium – and the stadium was undergoing a monumental reconstruction, which, by the middle of 2006, was already overdue and over budget.

In most respects, the café was like thousands of others dotted around the world. Its surroundings were not salubrious. Nestled between the Bowling Nail Bar and a rather dingy-looking chartered accountant's office, it housed several decrepit, bulky screens and sticky keyboards that were attached to unreliable computers inscribed with faux brand names, marking them as cheap knockoffs from East Asia. Heaven only knows what activities have gone on behind the rickety wooden partitions dividing the grimy consoles.

Bent over the screens, adolescents played online games for hours, often with unparalleled levels of concentration; backpackers composed amusing emails brimming with their impressions of newly discovered lands; curious teenagers and frustrated middle-aged men surfed weird porn sites; idealistic youths planned political protests, imagining that by dropping into these anonymous venues they had dodged Big Brother; drug dealers arranged drop-off points and methods of laundering money; and cyber criminals logged on to see the value of the latest haul.

Apart from its location in the shadow of the inchoate Wembley Stadium, there was one other peculiarity about the Java Bean. Usually the computers in Internet cafés are equipped with only limited protection from external attack. Viruses, trojans and other digital bacteria lie around these places, rather as their organic equivalents infest hospitals with lax cleaning regimes.

But Renu took his security seriously and persuaded the Java Bean's manager to install a special program on the café's systems called Deep Freeze. This restored the hard disks to an earlier configuration, which ensured that the network was no longer able to 'see' any malware it might have downloaded during the day, thus rendering the bad stuff ineffective and enhancing Renu's protection.

If the Java Bean was Renu's office space, then the filing cabinet that contained the secrets of DarkMarket consisted of a tiny memory stick. Renu usually kept this portable hard drive literally close to his heart. When he arrived at his office, he would plug the memory stick into one of the computer terminals and start working on DarkMarket.

Once logged in, Renu donned his pirate's mask to become JiLsi, one of eight administrators that ran DarkMarket during the site's three-year existence. Never more than four-strong at any one time, this team was one of the most influential units on the global carding scene. This most senior post did not bring them much in the way of extra revenue, but it was a privileged position that generated considerable respect among hackers and crackers. They also enjoyed access to great stores of information and held the key to virtual life or death – the power to exclude members for real or perceived transgressions.

There were two major drawbacks to attaining the exalted position of administrator. First, it was very hard work, regularly involving fifteen to seventeen hours of keyboard-hammering a day. There were no holidays for these people – they were expected to be on permanent call, every day of the year. Master Splyntr, for example, always carried a cellphone that alerted him when one of his fellow DarkMarketeers needed him and he would respond whenever it rang. JiLsi complained that he would log on at nine in the morning and would still be sat there at ten in the evening. Much of the work was drudgery: monitoring posts to check that the members were abiding by the forum's rules and that they were posting messages in the right section. Much of the time it was mere bureaucracy, mostly trivial and mind-numbing.

Second, the admin team was forever accessing the inner workings of the criminal websites. The digital trail it left behind on the Web was potentially much more visible than that identifying ordinary members, making them the primary target for cybercops.

This was paradoxical as it was 'ordinary' members who routinely made the most money from DarkMarket: the administrators would often assume the greatest risk for the least financial reward. Over a three-year period JiLsi and Matrix made a paltry amount of money, while Master Splyntr only charged for the upkeep of the servers, focusing elsewhere on his spamming empire.

Then there was the intriguing character Shtirlitz, who was there almost from the beginning. The nickname referred to the fictional Max Otto von Stirlitz. In the novels of Julian Semyonov, Stirlitz was a senior Nazi officer spying for Moscow during the Second World War. Characterised as the Soviet James Bond, Stirlitz became entrenched in Russian consciousness thanks to a series of popular films based on the books in the 1970s. Quiet, but with devastating good looks, Stirlitz remains a powerful patriotic symbol in post-communist Russia for his immense courage, intelligence and unswerving commitment to the motherland.

So we know Stirlitz the Soviet spy, but who was Shtirlitz the carder (who transliterated his name into English from Russian, hence the extra 'h')? Was he an agent for the KGB too? Or perhaps a double agent, working for the Feds or the Secret Service? Or was he a master carder? One member of CarderPlanet who had met him described him as being 'Aryan-looking and in his late twenties'. He regularly purchased counterfeit passports and at one point lived in Prague, the capital of the Czech Republic. On CarderPlanet he was described as 'a good guy and reliable', but later on other carders began to suspect that he may have emulated his fictional role model by morphing into one of America's most experienced law enforcement officials.

Whatever his true goals as one of DarkMarket's senior members, he was omnipresent but silent, logging relatively little activity. Likewise, a latecomer to the administration of the board, Lord Cyric appeared not to be involved in buying or selling at all. Each was too busy keeping everything afloat, while basking in their status as legends among the fraternity.

Equally, though, each harboured his own secrets, and some were not at all what they seemed.

Ironically, the one who took his personal security most seriously was in some respects the most transparent. This was Cha0. The Turkish criminal had come to the carding boards relatively late in the day. Unlike the rest, he was not a veteran of Shadowcrew or IAACA, but appeared out of nowhere in early 2006 as the owner of a board called *crimeenforcers.com*, an elegantly designed site that offered aspiring cyber criminals all manner of back-up services. It was especially notable for its animated tutorial lessons featuring a cartoon version of Cha0, walking the viewer through the finer points of carding.

Cha0 used DarkMarket to promote crimeenforcers (paid advertising was an important revenue stream for the boards) and his ubiquitous presence and relentless business transactions were soon translated into real influence. He joined DarkMarket in February 2006 and within seven months was appointed one of the bosses.

Unlike his colleagues, he was that rare breed, a geek with a brilliant criminal mind. His motivation for accepting the top role was simple – he could use it to advance his enterprise as a distributor of the accessories needed to perpetrate economic crime, such as 'skimmers' – machines that could read, store and transmit a victim's credit-card data.

But, as with the other leading figures on DarkMarket, Cha0's story eventually turned out to be more byzantine than that – appropriately enough, for a resident of Istanbul.

Leaving aside the anomaly of Cha0, the most successful thieves on Dark-Market did not help manage the site. They were men like Freddybb and Recka, the carders from Scunthorpe and Sweden, who just dropped in now and then to conduct business and then disappeared for days, weeks and even months. Law enforcement across the world has arrested a much higher proportion of geeks than it has hardened criminals in its cyber operations.

As they slaved away at their PCs, the four senior managers were collectively responsible for four main tasks. Protecting the website's servers and general maintenance were the responsibility of Master Splyntr and Matrix001. The quotidian threats to the site came not from law enforcement, but from DarkMarket's rivals and enemies elsewhere in criminal cyberspace, such as Iceman. Splyntr, Matrix and JiLsi would sigh whenever there was a dust-up between members. Splyntr became accustomed to a pattern, if a little weary of it. One carder would accuse another of some transgression, possibly baseless, possibly true. The accused would throw his toys out of the pram and before long the injured party had marshalled a botnet in order to launch a DDoS attack. Tens of thousands of computers under a single Command and Control machine would request access to DarkMarket and the site would go down. If it had been in the physical world, Splyntr muttered to himself, you'd just go beat the bastard up. But in cyberspace you have little choice except to close the site down, wait for the attacker to calm down or negotiate some sort of agreement.

As a consequence, the administrators had to monitor all the conflicts brewing between members and try to defuse them before they erupted. Your average cyber criminal has the manners of a chimpanzee and the tongue of a Sicilian fishwife. Anonymity breeds an intrinsic lack of trust across the Internet, and the criminal world is especially susceptible to this because of the potential threat from the police and from the perceived invulnerability conferred by the user's anonymity. So the insults on forums like DarkMarket escalate swiftly into open verbal warfare. Herein, incidentally, lay one of the trump cards held by police investigating cybercrime – in a community riven by a variety of suspicions, a skilled reader can manipulate disputes to his own advantage.

The admin team naturally decided the fate of members' status within the DM hierarchy. The four would go into a private conclave – a forum to which only they had access – to discuss whether, for example, a salesman of stolen credit cards had a sufficiently reliable record to be awarded the coveted title of Reviewed Vendor, which enabled him to sell cards without restriction through DarkMarket.

Naturally the administrators were also permanently scanning for the presence of cybercops, not to mention the 'scumbags and rippers' – those criminals who refused to adhere to the rules of the underworld.

Spotting 'rippers' was also a key part in the admin's third and most vital job – operating the escrow service to ensure fair play in the realm of the unfair. As with the original carding site, CarderPlanet, the successful management of escrow was a critical factor in transforming DarkMarket into the pre-eminent criminal website of its day. JiLsi ran the escrow, but the most important arbiter of the service was Cha0.

Finally, the administrators had to keep a sharp eye out for anyone using the site to distribute child pornography or to sell and buy drugs and weapons. This was not born of moral indignation, but of the belief that the police would be less energetic in their pursuit of the site if they restricted themselves to carding and identity crimes.

The first half of 2006 had been a mixed time for Renu. The bad luck had started in February. He had walked out of the Java Bean café following a hard day's work and headed for a night on the Martell and crack-pipe. The next morning he woke to find his invaluable memory stick was not in its usual place, nestling close to his chest. He had left the damn thing in the café!

He was seized by panic. When he walked into the Java Bean he went straight to the manager to enquire whether anyone had handed it in. The manager shook his head. 'You've just lost me a quarter of a million pounds!' screamed Renu, temporarily forgetting that he alone was responsible for the catastrophe. He was less worried about his own limited funds than about the money and data that he was holding in escrow.

Over the next few weeks JiLsi mounted a damage-control operation. He had to reassure DarkMarket members who had placed their trust in him that their security had not been compromised. Meanwhile, in the real world, Renu struggled to meet the payments on the mortgages he had taken out on dingy properties across north London. DarkMarket was prospering, but JiLsi was not enriching himself. On the contrary, he was sinking into debt and approached some 'friends' for a loan. Being a fugitive in cyberspace was no preparation for coping with this more traditional 'underworld'.

Even after the loss of the memory stick, Renu continued to devote himself selflessly to DarkMarket and its progress. But the stress of running the site was overwhelming him. Above all, he realised that DarkMarket and CardersMarket were now engaged in a fight to the death. The website was vulnerable, but JiLsi was even more vulnerable still, and sometimes he felt extremely weary of the whole affair.

Iceman upped his attacks, raining down DDoS assaults and throwing at DarkMarket any other digital weapon that he could lay his hands on. Carders around the world lined up behind one or other of the sites, arguing that the opponent should give way and allow one megasite to dominate. This indeed was Iceman's central argument: competition in this instance did not increase efficiency; it only led to acrimony.

By September 2006 the relentless attacks were driving Renu to despair. His dependency on crack cocaine was also becoming marked at this time, a dangerous development both for his own security – not to mention his health – and for the security of DarkMarket itself.

He decided to discuss the attacks on DarkMarket with Master Splyntr, who was at this time a moderator, two rungs below JiLsi, the key administrator. For a long time Master Splyntr had been arguing that JiLsi should allow him, Kaminski, to take over the servers. Kaminski argued that he had a much better security arrangement in place and, if he were to take over, it would relieve the pressure on JiLsi.

Master Splyntr was JiLsi's reserve choice. He had asked Cha0 first but the Turk had dismissed the offer, doubtless not enthused by the thankless work involved in maintaining servers. Nobody else would commit and so JiLsi felt he had no choice but to invite Master Splyntr.

Kaminski received the call at about 11.30 in the evening in early October 2006. 'My servers are ready, JiLsi,' he said. JiLsi hesitated no longer, happy at last to relinquish responsibility for his vulnerable servers, 'Okay. Let's move!'

Perhaps anticipating their irritation, JiLsi didn't consult his fellow administrators when handing over control of the server to Splyntr, although in the event none of them seemed to object. They were quickly convinced of its wisdom – Splyntr proved a more efficient manager of the service than JiLsi.

Kaminski was as good as his word: his servers were effective and secure. Not only that, but when anyone tried to discover where the DarkMarket servers were really located (whether fellow hackers, law-enforcement, military or intelligence services), they could not track them beyond an anonymous server in Singapore.

Master Splyntr was appointed administrator. Traffic through the site began to grow again. Every time Iceman hacked DarkMarket and destroyed its database, Master Splyntr would have it back up and running within twenty-four hours. And although Iceman was unques-tionably the most gifted technician in the game, his arrogance had alienated hundreds of carders. DarkMarket grew ever stronger and nothing, it seemed, could stop its rise to the top. But Iceman still had one last throw of the dice.

18

SUSPICIOUS MINDS

Iceman's outer calm belied his absolute fury. He had lost track of time. It might have been three in the morning; it might have been three in the afternoon. But when engaged in a major hack that can take hours and hours, it was easy to become disoriented. For the most obsessive hackers, time and place evaporate. When the fury descended on Iceman, there was no real world – only the bidding of Nemesis, the goddess of retribution, mattered.

She now appeared in several forms. The first was El Mariachi, an embittered carder whose website, The Grifters, Iceman had destroyed. El Mariachi was shouting from the digital hills that he had incontrovertible proof of Iceman's real identity as an FBI collaborator. His accusation was echoed by Lord Cyric, El Mariachi's lapdog, constantly yapping and growling across the carding boards. Like many others, Iceman detested Lord Cyric.

Vitriolic accusations were hurled from one carding site to the next. It was the equivalent of a war between several mafia clans except that nobody really knew who belonged to which family, who was an informer and who was a Fed. It was chaos.

But when Iceman discovered what he then believed to be the truth, he sat almost dumbfounded in his comfortable apartment in the centre of San Francisco, paid for by Jeffrey Normington and another partner, in exchange for a regular stream of stolen credit-card numbers. From here amidst the stale pizza crusts and Coke cans, Iceman would administer CardersMarket and obsessively hack other carding sites. In October he had succeeded in hacking the very heart of DarkMarket's servers.

He started examining all the administrators' traffic and then spotted some IP addresses that looked odd. Anyone can look up IP addresses and see where they are located – which company or individual is associated with them, and the name of their parent Internet Service Provider. One was registered to a company called Pembrooke Associates. Iceman looked high and low on the Web for information about the company, but there was nothing except on a website listing businesses. Here was the company name and a phone number. He then performed a reverse search on the phone number and found its associated address: 2000 Technology Drive, Pittsburgh, PA.

When he read the address, it was enough to make even Iceman shiver. He had come across it only a couple of weeks earlier, after one of his colleagues on CardersMarket had found a template document on a website, which included the acronym NCFTA and that same address in Pittsburgh. When Iceman looked up this organisation, he discovered it was the National Cyber Forensic Training Alliance, a quasi-governmental body that assists a variety of US law-enforcement agencies in their work on a broad range of cyber-security issues.

Deep in his virtual existence, Iceman suddenly felt the chill touch of the real world. He had always suspected that law enforcement was lurking around every corner, but this was unambiguous – he was convinced that it could not be a mistake. Having believed for many months that he was untouchable and the man controlling the carding community, Max Vision was suddenly worried.

After lengthy consultations, three of Iceman's colleagues at Carders-Market – silo, c0rrupted0ne and dystopia – decided to contact Matrix001 from DarkMarket to share their suspicions about the IP address and the FBI, and to plan a way forward. Matrix001 was the one administrator whom nobody believed was attached to law enforcement in any way, so they sent him the evidence about the NCFTA and Technology Drive in Pittsburgh, with a stark message sent over icq:

> *dystopia:* we've known it for a long time, but we finally
>   have proof
> *dystopia:* matrix, DM is a sting site
> *dystopia:* 100%

cOrrupted0: we worked hard to try and make peace and if we go public Law Enforcement is going to come after us HARD but if we dont say anything we are responsible for all those who get fucked over

siloadmin: happy days to you, you're an admin of a sting site!
siloadmin: Pembrooke Associates 2000 Technology Dr Pittsburgh PA 15219. something fa jmiliar 2000 Technology Dr?

Matrix smelt a rat. He trusted no one as a rule, but he was especially suspicious of cOrrupted0ne and silo. CardersMarket had for a long time acted with unbridled aggression towards DarkMarket, hoping to destroy it by any means available. He examined the document and, despite not having English as a mother tongue, immediately spotted that it was riddled with errors:

matrix001: the word document is a fake
matrix001: didnt anyone of you guys notice the typos in it?
matrix001: oh and there is no company or any other name on the top line
matrix001: saying ncfta
matrix001: just the address
matrix001: oh and just to mention one typo: it's spelled available not avaliable
matrix001: you guys want me to continue?

Siloadmin's response was defensive, as if he was annoyed with himself for not noticing the typos:

siloadmin: listen matrix
siloadmin: I know the shit looks fake, typos etc
siloadmin: but thats what was pulled
siloadmin: I didnt make this shit up

matrix001: no company in the whole world would ever
   have such a document
matrix001: its totally ridiculous

This could quite easily have been a set-up and the exchange convinced Matrix of exactly that. Accusing rival boards of being a sting operation organised by law enforcement was a common practice designed to scare off members so that they would join the competition. If members were to desert DarkMarket, Matrix was convinced Iceman and CardersMarket would recruit them immediately and that might threaten DarkMarket's very existence.

Furthermore, silo, dystopia and c0rrupted0ne appeared very keen – perhaps too keen – for Matrix to open another file, a compressed zip file, known as an rar. Zip files were some of the most notorious carriers of trojan infections, and he was certain this one was designed by the CardersMarket crew to suck all DarkMarket's secrets from his computer. He began to wonder whether Iceman and his cohorts were now on stage two of an audacious plan, designed by the FBI, to wipe out DarkMarket.

It was by now about a quarter-past nine on a freezing November morning in central Germany, but Matrix knew he had to act swiftly. He immediately contacted his fellow DM administrators and warned them that Iceman and his cohorts were about to denounce DM:

matrix001: I did not download the file and open it,
   therefore i said my rar is not working
matrix001: I bet it was a trojan
matrix001: and if you check the info they passed it's quite
   bogus . . .
matrix001: But take a read yourself . . .

19

DONNIE BRASCO

Pittsburgh, October 2006

Special Agent Keith J. Mularski of the FBI's Cyber Division was distraught, and it wasn't just because the Steelers were having a mediocre season after the previous February's sensational victory in the Super Bowl. As a season ticket holder at Heinz Field, the Steelers' home stadium, Mularski had always acknowledged that football was not a matter of life and death – it was more important than that. But for once his problems were even more serious than football.

For months and months he had been working as a cyber Donnie Brasco, immersing himself in the Web's ever-expanding pool of criminality. True, his life was never in danger the way that Agent Joe Pistone's had been when he assumed the identity of Brasco in the lairs of New York's toughest mafia families. But it had taken Mularski a hell of a lot of work securing his bosses' agreement for the unprecedented operation to go undercover in cyberspace. It was expensive to mount and contained the great danger of being denounced as entrapment. So FBI chiefs were scrutinising his every move for signs of a slip-up. What had just happened was no slip-up, though. It was a head-on collision.

The timing was, atrocious. He had come a long way without his cover being blown. He was on the verge of enlisting the help of several foreign law-enforcement agencies to assist in his long-term strategy of executing a spectacular series of busts around the world. He had created and then nurtured a character, chosen a name and back story, and this figment had become real for many global cyber thieves in a remarkably short space of time. Mularski was a close confidant to several of his targets.

Now, because of the carelessness of a colleague who had left a file with a trace of the National Cyber Forensics Training Alliance letterhead on a computer, he was threatened with exposure and the collapse of an immensely intricate operation.

This was also the FBI's first major foray into cybercrime. Until now the US Postal Inspection Service, but above all the US Secret Service, had dominated cyber investigations. By 2004 it was clear that cyber-crime was one of the fastest growing sectors of organised criminal activity worldwide. More and more organisations, institutions and individuals were being hacked into. Credit cards were the biggest problem, because of the sheer volume being misused or stolen. But large companies were now victims of industrial espionage in which their commercial secrets were being stolen and sold on to competitors by some of the very hackers who were involved in credit-card fraud. Cisco Systems had allowed a Chinese competitor to steal and copy the plans for one of its most advanced servers – so not even supposedly computer-savvy corporations were immune.

The haphazard approach to network security, both in government and in private industry, was beginning to spook the White House, Congress and the Pentagon. Most government agencies and ministries were either unaware of their vulnerability or so overwhelmed by the number of attacks launched against them that they buried their heads in the sand, in the hope that the problem might just disappear.

However, that was not an option for the Pentagon. It was swamped trying to manage the fallout from Titan Rain, a series of sustained attacks on the Defense Department's computer systems, originating in China and designed to gouge out all the classified secrets sitting in unwisely exposed files.

The big banks were still reeling from the so-called pvv (pin verifica-tion value) vulnerability that had cost Citibank and the Bank of America tens of millions in stolen cash during the Shadowcrew period, and although they had solved that problem, hundreds of other banks were still spewing out cash from their ATMs to carders.

In a word: chaos.

The implications were not hard to fathom. Before long, large amounts of taxpayers' dollars would be diverted into the related problems of cybercrime, cyber industrial espionage and cyber warfare. No self-respecting law-enforcement agency would want to forgo a slice. From the FBI's vantage point, the US Secret Service stood to gorge itself on three-quarters of a rich budgetary cake. First mover among the cybercops, and still basking in the glory of the Shadowcrew take-down, the US Secret Service was naturally eager to assert its primacy in this embryonic field.

The FBI, the largest and most powerful law-enforcement agency in America, had other thoughts. Its Director, Robert Mueller, was keen to move into cyber both to get the funding but also because he was instrumental in trying to refashion the FBI to become less of a police force and more of a domestic intelligence agency. Mularksi's plan was not merely about busting criminals, it was about gathering information as well. This change of direction at the very top helped overcome the objections of some senior officials and Mularski, who had backed his request to mount the bold undercover operation with a dazzling pres-entation, got his authorisation. So when the Iceman fingered him, it was not just Operation DarkMarket that was teetering on the brink of failure. If this went south, those future tax dollars went with it and the apparent ability of the FBI to manage cyber operations. A heavy burden weighed on Mularski's shoulders.

His initial reaction was despair. The game was up, he thought, and his hard-working team would have to prepare a humiliating explanation for the hierarchy, some of whom would be muttering, 'We told you so!' But one of the reasons the FBI had selected Mularski for its agent-training programme in the first place was because he was quick-witted in tight spots. And it was only minutes before he decided he would not give up without a fight.

The fortunes of Mularski's family had closely followed those of twentieth-century Pittsburgh. His great-great-grandfather had secured a passage from Hamburg in 1892, arriving in Baltimore with just a dollar in his pocket. Keith may have been an all-American boy, but the ethnic identity of many of the city's European communities remained strong – Polish, in Mularski's case.

Interspersed among the modest wooden houses, Art Deco cinemas and dance halls of Pittsburgh's now-picturesque South Side are the churches and community centres of the many Slavic communities – Czech, Polish, Serbian, Slovak, Ukrainian and more – who gravitated towards this strategically placed city in western Pennsylvania. Andrij and Julia Warhola, a couple of Rusyns from rural north-eastern Slovakia, emigrated to Pittsburgh in the early twentieth century before dropping the final 'a' of their surname and giving birth to one of the most influential figures in twentieth-century art.

Mighty steel bridges and inscriptions to the Norfolk and Western Railway are some of the reminders of Pittsburgh's central contribution to America's global economic dominance of the twentieth century. Steel from these factories was moulded into battleships, planes, cars and industrial plant that spread across the world. Decades have passed since the black clouds that spewed from the steel-producing hydra last cloaked the city in darkness, distributing poisonous particles that once conferred the highest incidence of pulmonary disease in the United States.

The smog no longer hangs over the city, and Pittsburgh is now regarded as one of the most desirable places to live in the entire United States. The sun shines brightly and, after fifteen years of poverty and decline, the city quietly refashioned itself during the 1990s as an East Coast centre of the high-tech industry.

Mularski was one of those who fled the city in the 1980s after graduating in history from Duquesne University. At the time, there was nothing left. His father could have been the reincarnation of Willy Loman. One of the first to suffer the downturn in the stumbling giant's fortunes, Mularski senior was laid off from his sales job in the 1970s and had been unable to find another post. The family lived precariously off the earnings of Keith's mother, an executive assistant.

Pittsburgh's population had shrunk by one-third in young Keith's lifetime. He had no intention of watching it waste away any further, so he moved with his new wife to Washington DC. Taken on by a large furniture retailer that operated countrywide, Mularski demonstrated real skills in management and sales. At first glance, the work of a sales manager appeared to have little in common with cybercrime, but the techniques he learned with the company provided firm foundations for his work as a cybercop with the FBI.

'Social engineering' – the art of persuading somebody to do something that is objectively not in their interest – lies at the heart of cybercrime. How, the crook ponders, can I persuade my target to give up their password? To open an email with a trojan hidden within its code? Even to turn a computer on?

There are some obvious options available to the cyber thief. The two tried-and-tested methods are free music downloads and pornography. The sexual drive is one of the most powerful of all – it has to be, because in evolutionary terms finding a mate has often proved a hazardous business. We are prepared to take huge risks to satisfy our sexual desires, and computer-virus manufacturers were swift to grasp this. The promise of a pair of breasts is often all that is needed to tempt an unsuspecting user to press on a hyperlink that will download a destructive piece of malware onto his machine. If he's lucky, he'll actually be redirected to the picture, although that's scant compensation for handing over all the secrets on his desktop to a faceless controller far away. Not by chance was one of the most successful viruses spread via email with the subject line 'I Love You'.

While sales managers tend not to spread viruses, they are, like cyber thieves, accomplished engineers of the human soul. Their job is to convince potential customers to invest in items that are either unwanted or unnecessary. 'To sell something you have to someone who wants it – that's not business,' the mobster king, Meyer Lansky once remarked. 'But to sell something you don't have to someone else who doesn't want it – that is business.' At the very least, sales managers can persuade customers to buy more expensive items. So when the recently minted Agent Keith Mularski was accepted into the infant Cyber Division of the FBI, he brought with him a prized asset – the ability to cajole, josh, empathise, exhort, inveigle and entice. For a cop, he was a very convincing criminal.

By the year 2000 Pittsburgh had been transformed. It had always benefited from huge philanthropic bequests. Stamped everywhere around town are the marks of Carnegie, Heinz and Mellon, collosi of America's industrial surge on either side of the turn of the twentieth century. Part of the city's reinvention after the collapse of manufacturing lay in its investment in computer science and technology at the Carnegie Mellon University (CMU), rated as one of the world's top twenty higher-education establishments.

Founded by the towering Scottish-born industrialist, Andrew Carnegie, the university began as a technical school and merged with the Mellon Institute of Industrial Research in 1967. During the bleak years of the 1980s and early 1990s, the CMU studied the demise of Pittsburgh and researched ways of resuscitating it. The university was also well known for its work in the area of computer security. Outside of the Massachusetts Institute of Technology and Silicon Valley, Pittsburgh arose as a rare outpost of intense geekdom in the United States, with a specialist bent towards security issues.

The expertise of the CMU explains much about the new Pittsburgh, including the emergence in 1997 of the National Cyber Forensics Training Alliance, a not-for-profit organisation with support from the banks and various corporations, aimed at bringing together professionals from academia, the private sector, law enforcement and intelligence to act in the face of growing network insecurity. And that is why Keith Mularski returned home soon after the millennium to work in the unassuming glass-fronted offices on 2000 Technology Drive.

As he stared out of one of those windows on the fourth floor, he was aware how he was almost single-handedly responsible for this entire FBI operation. He was working with a great team, but it was he who had persuaded his bosses, in the teeth of deep scepticism, to give him the go-ahead. It wasn't only the reputation of the Feds and their budgetary concerns on the line – it was his job, for God's sake.

Then he remembered what he was really good at: sales. Or, better still, social engineering.

When the news flashed around the criminal bulletin boards that DarkMarket belonged to the Feds, he calmed down, reminding himself that self-pity helped no one. He needed to launch a counter-attack immediately. He approached Grendel, perhaps the most mysterious DarkMarketeer of all. In real life, Grendel worked for an entirely legitimate high-end security company in Germany, but he also offered his services against payment to major cyber criminals. DarkMarket depended on his Virtual Private Network (VPN), which was an almost complete guarantee of anonymity – but beyond that, Grendel had also constructed four 'shells', software that can render users effectively invisible.

Grendel was able to produce the previous verifiable logins from the shells, none of which mentioned Pembrooke Associates anywhere. Mularski proudly boasted to all members of both CardersMarket and DarkMarket that this was his VPN service, and the only person to have come up with the Pembrooke Associates login was . . . Iceman. Using his sales techniques, the Nemesis Mularski was flipping the searchlight away from himself and shining it right into Iceman's eyes.

The typos on the headed notepaper that Matrix001 had spotted were the cherry on the cake. Iceman had a history of flinging wild accusations at anyone who irritated him and, during his tenure as the master of CardersMarket, almost everyone had irritated him at one point or another. He had few friends out there. Equally, the idea that Iceman was up to his old tricks as a confidential informer for the Feds took root once again – a thesis that Mularski fanned energetically.

Far from destroying DarkMarket, Iceman had achieved the opposite. It emerged stronger than ever and was now recognised by almost everyone as the primary English-language criminal carding site in the world. Mularksi's quick thinking had averted a real disaster.

20

A CUNNING PLAN

JiLsi was as pleased as punch. CardersMarket and Iceman were still on their feet, but reeling from the counter-punches that followed the revelations about DarkMarket as a sting site. A majority of carders now believed (wrongly) that CardersMarket was the sting site and Dark-Market kosher. In consequence, DarkMarket started growing again, towards its eventual membership of 2,000.

Of course there were still rumours that maybe all was not what it seemed among the administrators of DarkMarket, but by this stage there were as many pack animals among the carders as there were 'lone wolves' from the pioneering days of cybercrime. The pack had turned on Iceman and was running with DarkMarket.

By December 2006 the DarkMarketeers were doing a sterling job. JiLsi was proud of his achievements – at last he was a respected family member, recognised for his selfless and efficient work. He had built up a great team: Matrix, Master Splyntr and Cha0 were first-class administrators, and all members had confidence in their escrow service. Shtirlitz and Lord Cyric provided back up and cred-ibility. They were quick to spot rippers and scammers, summarily dealing with these bottom feeders whenever they emerged from the cyber sewers. Ever more deals were being struck between members, and the revenues began their ascent towards the golden days of Shadowcrew and CarderPlanet.

It had been more than two years since the Shadowcrew bust and a sense of complacency had also set in. The 'lone wolves', who now comprised a minority on the boards, never let their guard down. They took care not to incriminate themselves. Recka, the fraud king from

Sweden, scrupulously avoided the trade in American credit or debit cards, as this would place him squarely in the sites of US law enforcement; the Swedes and other Europeans he could handle, but he was careful not to poke the Americans in the eye.

But many of the carders, especially the younger ones, were lax in their security, eschewing the use of encryption in their icq chats and failing to maintain proper VPN and tunnelling systems to mask their IP addresses. In Pittsburgh, however, Mularksi was steadily building a database with a program of his own design, which was able to cross-reference the activities of individual carders – he was reading their messages, logging their icq and IP addresses and, where possible, linking these to E-Gold accounts.

Unbeknownst to the users of this digital currency facility, government agencies had enjoyed full access to the records of E-Gold, the carders' favourite method of transferring money among themselves, since February 2006. This followed the arrest of its founder, Douglas Jackson, in Florida on suspicion that the service was being used for money-laundering. Few (if any) of the cyber criminals, though, had put two and two together with respect to E-Gold. Russians eschewed such Western-based companies, registered in Belize, preferring WebMoney instead, based in Moscow beyond the reach of Western law enforcement.

Armed with this growing body of evidence, Mularski made contact with the police in a number of European countries as autumn turned to winter in 2006. He talked to the Serious Organised Crime Agency (SOCA) in the United Kingdom, to the Federal Police in Germany and, later on, to the regional force in Baden-Württemberg.

He also approached the OCLCTIC in Paris, the recently formed and prosaically named Central Office in the Struggle Against Information and Communication Technology-related Crime. The reception he received here was a touch chilly. The French police are generally keen to cooperate with the United States, especially in the areas of terrorism and cybercrime, but traditional suspicion of America and its intentions in Europe still runs deep in French society. Any government that appears to be cosying up to the US is in danger of losing electoral brownie points, and so it cautions its organs to be circumspect in their dealings with Washington agencies.

The boss of OCLCTIC, Christian Aghroum, thought it ridiculous that every time he and his officers sought the assistance of a company like Microsoft, they ran the risk of an outcry, containing predictable accusations of the police being in the pocket of giant American corporations. The fact was, Aghroum knew, that you couldn't really start combating cybercrime unless you had a degree of cooperation with companies like Microsoft. Articulate, and a shrewd analyst of the political minefield that surrounds international policing, Aghroum was resigned to the fact that neither politicians nor the public in France had any idea about cybercrime and what you need in order to defeat it. Most French people seemed to harbour the illusion that you can combat and contain transnational crime from within your own borders, especially if the criminal in question could not speak French.

But Mularski was in for an even greater shock than the well-known issue of Gallic anti-Americanism. OCLCTIC, he was told, had already been working for several months with the US Secret Service on a case related to . . . DarkMarket. A parallel investigation was under way and he had known nothing about it. Moreover, the US Secret Service showed no inclination to share information about their investigation. A few months earlier the boss of the Secret Service's Criminal Investigation Division had testified to Congress that due to its close cooperation with 'other federal, state and local enforcement . . . we are are able to provide a comprehensive network of intelligence-sharing, resource-sharing and technical expertise'. He forgot to tell that to the team investigating DarkMarket, because they refused even to share with the FBI who they were targeting. Matters were about to get complicated for cybercops and cyber thieves alike.

Most DarkMarketeers were not focusing on law enforcement at the time (except the ones collaborating with Mularski). Rather, they wanted to assert the site's supremacy by finishing off Iceman. JiLsi took it upon himself to administer the fatal blow. If he succeeded, it would be his finest hour and his reputation would be considerably enhanced. He had also had enough of Iceman's repeated incursions, which created endless extra work for him; and the bilious rhetoric, Iceman's trademark, was also getting to him.

JiLsi's plan was simple. He created an anonymous email account, which he used to send messages to Iceman's Internet Service Provider. He warned the ISP that CardersMarket, which it hosted, was a criminal site and its owners were involved in major credit-card fraud. When Iceman discovered the account from which the denunciatory emails were being sent, he used JiLsi's password, MSR206 (the name of the legendary credit-card cloning machine used by all good carders), and – hey presto! – it worked. Iceman discovered JiLsi was bad-mouthing him to his own ISP. This was unforgivable. JiLsi had indeed crossed a line that no (dis)honest carder should ever breach, regardless of how bad relations became: he had ratted on a member of the fraternity. Worse than that, he had been caught doing it.

Iceman disseminated the news far and wide. Before long it came to the attention of Cha0.

In the aftermath of the Iceman accusations, everyone was still feeling a little jittery. Were the Feds on the case? But more than this, if they were, 'Who the fuck was working with them?', as one of the DM administrators put it. Iceman, Splyntr, c0rrupted0ne or Silo from CardersMarket; Shtirlitz, the enigmatic 'Russian'; or perhaps Dark-Market's new moderator, Lord Cyric? Or someone else?

The two people whom nobody had hitherto accused of working for the police were Matrix001 and JiLsi. They had occasionally accused the latter of incompetence (and not without reason). But police work? Never. Iceman had long known JiLsi's password from his hacking forays. But now everyone appeared to know it. There was some suspicion that a third party had infiltrated a trojan onto JiLsi's beloved memory stick and that they were now monitoring every keystroke he made, thus becoming privy to DarkMarket's deepest secrets. Or maybe JiLsi was not who he said he was . . . maybe he was somehow connected with the mystery company from 2000 Technology Drive – Pembrooke Associates?

A few days before Christmas 2006, JiLsi logged onto DarkMarket as usual to check out the traffic. He wasn't on for long before heading out again to attend to his real-life affairs. That afternoon he was back. 'Username: JiLsi,' he typed. 'Password: MSR206.' In a blink, the machine returned 'Incorrect Username or Password'. Automatically JiLsi tried again, assuming he had made a typo. The result was the same. He tried again and again.

There was no room for doubt: JiLsi, spiritual owner and chief administrator of DarkMarket, had been excluded from his own site. Panicked, he tried to log onto www.mazafaka.ru. No dice. The Vouched – another of his sites – no entry.

It wasn't long before cold turkey kicked in. JiLsi had never known such a painful downward spiral. His entire life had been snatched away from him – or at least the only thing that really meant anything to him. He was angry, hurt and upset. Who had done this, and why? His response was to lose himself in the anaesthetic qualities of Martell chased by a pipe of crack. The pain receded for an evening and a night, but he awoke to a misery more intense than the previous day.

JiLsi finally managed to establish icq contact with Cha0. The chat left him reeling. 'We know you have been working for Scotland Yard and the High-Tech Crime Unit,' Cha0 told him. 'Your decision to rat on Iceman was the ultimate proof. We know that you are working with law enforcement. You have been excluded from all sites.'

JiLsi was speechless. Everything he had worked for had disappeared in an instant, and now he was the fall guy. What next? Where to? Despair and drift, JiLsi, despair and drift.

Part V

THE DRON LEGACY

Calgary, Alberta, 2006

From his early days advertising on Shadowcrew, Dron had always received the warmest reviews for his work. 'I received Dron's skimmer yesterday afternoon,' one satisfied customer posted on DarkMarket. 'Spent the evening testing it and am very, very impressed. Dron has got a first-rate product here, one that's well worth your time and money.'

Dron had been as good as his word. 'Shipping was fast. The packaging was discreet,' the poster continued. But it wasn't the efficient dispatch of goods that made Dron so popular, it was the aftercare service he provided that ensured clients came back for more. 'Now, customer service, for me, that's really where Dron comes through. He sent updates to his buyers on a regular basis and when I emailed with my concerns or questions, I invariably had a reply within twenty-four hours. Pretty damn impressive.'

Thanks in large part to the Internet, the culture of consumer rights and expectations has finally filtered through into the criminal world. If a criminal was shafted by a vendor on the Internet, it would be difficult to track the offender down and deploy the traditional method of expressing one's unhappiness at shoddy service – physical violence. Instead, criminals selling illegal wares over the Web have to compete by offering the best service.

In another age, Dron would have risen swiftly to the top. He may have left school at fifteen, but he combined this entrepreneurial flair with a creative streak. It was after his father had taught him how to play the stock market on the Internet that he came across the criminal bulletin boards and, as a twenty-four-year-old, signed up to Shadowcrew, DarkMarket's most successful predecessor, in the spring of 2004.

But his greatest skill lay in an innate engineering ability. From scratch, he taught himself how to design and build skimmers that fitted the two most popular ATMs around the world. These were complicated and intricate devices and worth every penny of the $5,000 he charged for each one (discounts offered on bulk sales, naturally). Not only would he respond to queries from customers, but he dispatched each product with an instruction manual, the appropriate software and a free USB cable.

His library also revealed how seriously he took his job. Alongside *Document Fraud and Other Crimes of Deception* stood *Holograms and Holography* and *Secrets of a Back Alley ID Man*. But perhaps his most important volume was *Methods of Disguise*. When dropping into one of his home town's many Internet cafés in order to manage his sales and marketing over the Web, Dron would generally wear a black baseball cap and black jacket. But for his forays into the post office, or when he was cashing out a credit card as payment for one of his skimmers, he would prefer a red cap and blue windcheater.

The United States Secret Service had first spotted Dron as a significant presence on Shadowcrew. Of course, the administrator on Shadowcrew, Cumbajohnny, was an informant for the Secret Service. But Dron did not belong to Cumbajohnny's Virtual Private Network, the chief means by which the Secret Service monitored members' activity. He was not in the United States, nor was he an easy target. Hence he was not a priority. But the Secret Service did not forget Dron. Instead, they started to build a relationship with him.

Although a youngster compared to the US Postal Inspection Service, the Secret Service has the longest history in fighting cybercrime. The US SS was formed in 1865, not to provide armed protection for the President – that was one of Congress's central responses to the assassination of President McKinley in 1901. The original and abiding purpose of the agency was to detect, investigate and then seek the prosecution of anybody found manufacturing or dealing in counterfeit currency. Soon after it was established, Congress also charged the agency with investigating financial fraud.

In the wake of the Second World War, the Bretton Woods agreements established the United States as the undisputed leader of Western economies and the dollar as the chosen reserve currency in the capitalist world. Although the Soviet Union and China rejected the dollar's supremacy, both communist superpowers were nonetheless eager to accumulate as many greenbacks as possible. In a world where most governments kept a tight rein on foreign-exchange flows across their borders, the ubiquity of the dollar as a form of payment greatly increased the attraction of issuing counterfeit US currency.

The result was an internationalisation of the Secret Service's operations, as crooks and governments around the world sought either to enrich themselves or to undermine American power by printing their own dollar bills. Wherever you are reading this, you can be fairly confident in the knowledge that there is a Secret Service operative in a nearby location. But while the agency has a long arm, there are nooks and crannies that not even it can reach – in the 1990s, for example, the *superdollar* spread around the world. The US government believes that these batches of fabulously accurate but nonetheless fake $100 bills emanated from printing presses in North Korea – one of the few areas that are off-limits to the Men in Black.

Taking a bullet for the Prez and chasing dodgy dollars are tough enough jobs, but in 1984 Congress requested a further expansion of Secret Service activity to include the investigation of credit- and debit-card fraud, counterfeit documents and computer fraud.

Over the next two decades the organisation that is, by some way, the most secretive American law-enforcement agency developed a specialisation in cybercrime, leading to an operational capability second to none. But the Secret Service employs only 6,500 people. The FBI, by contrast, is almost 30,000 strong. More recently, the US SS has been absorbed into the Department for Homeland Security, which has wounded its pride. There is no love lost between the two agencies. Whether this is due to the Secret Service's inferiority complex or the FBI's superiority complex is hard to tell – it's probably a bit of both. Either way, they have a history of niggling disputes, which impact on major operational issues.

After the Shadowcrew takedown, the Secret Service decided to nurture a relationship with Dron, who had joined DarkMarket in late 2005, where his reputation as a seller of skimming machines grew so rapidly that he soon established his own website, *www.atmskimmers. com*. For many months the Buffalo office of the Secret Service toiled to establish Dron's whereabouts. The vendor was using the Israeli email service Safemail, because he knew that the company blocked the sender's IP address, which meant that the recipient could not track him down. The Secret Service finally got its break in January 2006 when Safemail agreed to release Dron's IP addresses after the US SS's request had forced its way through Israel's dilatory criminal-justice system. Dron, it turned out, was using a variety of computers located throughout the Calgary area in Canada's oil-boom province, Alberta.

The next eighteen months were to prove an exacting period for Detective Spencer Frizzell of the Calgary Police Service. The Secret Service offices in Buffalo and Vancouver would provide him with one IP address, which they received from Safemail each time the undercover agent exchanged an email with Dron. These addresses always belonged to some Internet café or other. By the time he had actually located the place, the bird had of course flown. Until he started on this case, Detective Frizzell had no idea that there were so many Internet cafés in Calgary or how popular they were. He felt increasingly as if he were looking for a needle in a haystack.

For months, Dron's use of Internet cafés appeared to be random. One day he would pop up here, the next day three miles away. Sometimes he disappeared from Calgary altogether, raising the fear that he was gone for good. But he always returned and, after several months, Frizzell had a major breakthrough. Pinning flags on a map, he spotted that all of Dron's Internet cafés were close to the stops on Calgary's Light Rail Transit, on the line that runs from Somerset to Crowfoot. He also noted two or three shops that Dron seemed to favour.

That meant he had enough information to apply for a surveillance team. He came up against the usual objections that cybercops the world over encounter. Who are the victims in Calgary? What is your evidence of turnover due to criminal activity?

Frizzell received his authorisation, but only for a limited period and with very few human resources. Generally, when he received a tip-off from the Secret Service that Dron was online, he would grab anyone he could from the office and head out for somewhere along the Light Rail Transit.

The Calgary detective performed a heroic job for more than a year, slowly narrowing down the suspects until he was convinced he had the man. What he didn't know was that he was at just one of the sharp ends of a larger Secret Service operation that included not only Dron, but also a number of targets in Europe. The US SS had contacted SOCA in London and the OCLCTIC in Paris. 'That's the way we operate,' said the Secret Service spokesman, Edwin Donovan. 'We really push out our collaborative effort, working with police all over the world. We go to the agency that's working these type of crimes and say that we have this target – and of course sharing information is a key in these cases.'

So the Secret Service was sharing information with the police in Britain, Canada and France. But one group of agents they still weren't sharing it with was their colleagues at the FBI. The evident rancour between the two US agencies sowed confusion among the Europeans – in the end, the French worked with the US SS, the Germans with the FBI and the British politely balanced the two. This resulted in a moment of profound irony, as the only people in the world who knew that the FBI and Secret Service were targeting the same person, JiLsi, belonged to a foreign police force, the Serious Organised Crime Agency in London. It got worse – officers from SOCA realised that the competing American forces were actually investigating each other's undercover agents as suspected criminals. Eventually a senior British civil servant gently informed a higher authority in Washington that perhaps the FBI and the Secret Service should put aside their differences, at least for the duration of the investigation.

22

DUDE YOU FUCKED UP

Baden-Württemberg, 2007

It was a pleasant evening in early May, although it didn't feel much like springtime to Matrix001. The external world receded as his mouth dried and his eyes ran over the email one more time.

> Your landline is tapped.
> Cops in UK, Germany, France are onto you . . . Hide evidence.
> Warn others . . . Cops know matrix-001 is detlef hartmann
> from eislingen . . .
> You only got a few weeks before cops hit in uk and france . . .
> Warn all carders you can get hold of.

What did this mean? Who did it come from? He looked at the sender's address again: *auto432221@hushmail.com*. That was probably randomly generated. And it was impossible to identify anything about the author, except that his English appeared to be fluent.

Matrix decided he should consult his fellow DarkMarket administrators and a couple of other confidants. What, he asked, did they all make of this? Their replies were oddly bland, in some cases almost indifferent, mere warnings for him to keep an eye out.

In Pittsburgh, Keith Mularski felt anything but indifferent. The email extracts that he and the others had received from Matrix meant only one thing: the operation was being leaked. And if it was being leaked to Matrix, who else was being tipped off? The timing could hardly be worse, as for several months the FBI had been planning the first wave of DarkMarket arrests. It was bad enough having to deal with an uncooperative Secret Service. The German police from the federal state of Baden-Württemberg (LKA) had heard that their French colleagues were preparing a DarkMarket related bust, but the French police had snubbed them, saying that their presence at a planning meeting in Paris with Britain's SOCA and the Secret Service would be unnecessary.

The anonymous hushmail sent to Matrix001 triggered an anxiety among the investigating police forces that would linger for many months. They needed to know whether the leak was a result of carelessness or an inside job, or indeed whether a hacker had penetrated one of the investigating teams' computer networks. Every time something went wrong, the suspicion that there was a traitor among the ranks bubbled up to the surface. Morale could not help but suffer.

Mularski's attempts to coordinate the first arrests were proving difficult. The fear for any cybercop is that, if one fraudster is taken in without the others, news will spread like wildfire across the boards that something bad is going on and targets will simply disappear. Hence the Secret Service's obsessive secrecy . . .

Wait a minute, thought Mularski, that's probably where the leak came from – the Secret Service! He carefully considered the possible culprits: a) the Secret Service; b) someone from inside his own operation, which he doubted because the FBI's security had been ratcheted up since Iceman had spotted the Fed involvement; c) SOCA knew about Matrix, but the British were always the most tight-lipped of the lot; and d), of course, the Germans – he simply didn't have enough experience to judge the Germans, although had he detected a slightly abrasive relationship between the regional force in Stuttgart and the Federal Police Agency a couple of hours' drive to the north in Wiesbaden, both of which had been privy to the DarkMarket story? He couldn't be sure.

For the moment, speculation had to go onto the back burner. Mularski's immediate concern was to get in touch with Frank Eissmann of the regional police in Stuttgart and discuss the Matrix investigation before the young German did a runner. Stuttgart decided it was time for the case to go on steroids and Eissmann brought forward Matrix's planned arrest date. This in turn created problems for the police in London, Calgary and Paris, who had finally agreed at the London

meeting in early April to pounce on their suspects on the same day
– 12th June. SOCA was still feeling a touch awkward because the Secret
Service had been watching JiLsi since the days of Shadowcrew. The
Feds and the SS both wanted to bust him.

But Matrix did not do a runner. Indeed, his chats and emails that
the German police were intercepting indicated that he was not phased
at all by the hushmail. Perhaps the decision to speed up the Matrix
case had been premature?

Exactly one week after the first email, he received a second, on 10th
May. This time it was from *auto496064@hushmail.com*, and auto496064
was a tad upset:

> Dude you fucked up.
> Our network gave you german carders a fair warning and what
> do you go and do? Talk to the fucking FBI!
> You are so damn dumb you deserve to go to jail.
> However we intercepted communications between the FBI and a
> german guy calling himself 'iceman'. They've got an undercover
> cop baiting you, waiting for you to buy/sell some stuff. We ain't
> got the name yet. But you might be able to help us blow his
> cover.
> And do yourself a fucking favour. Until we know who the under-
> cover cop is, don't buy from any of those guys.
> Because you were so damn clever, to tell the FBI we are on to
> them, they may hit earlier! Delete any info on your homecom-
> puter, even if it is fucking encrypted, and use *only* internet
> shops.

Matrix went into denial and ignored it. He put it down to another
game being played, similar to those he remembered from the Iceman
affair. But the cops went berserk. This time the surveillance that had
been placed on *Detlef Hartmann's* computer connection picked up the
email when he opened it. Frank Eissmann (who was confusingly understood to be 'iceman' by the mysterious auto496064) could not believe
that somebody appeared to be monitoring all DarkMarket communications. The fear spread among officers that the entire DarkMarket investigation had been hacked, and that the bad guys knew everything about
the case that the police did.

Mularski, too, was shocked. He did spot one important anomaly, though – the writer of the anonymous email may have had totally fluent English, but he wasn't American because he spelled favour with a 'u'. So who was he?

23

MATRIX SQUARED

29th May 2007. People were starting their Tuesday in Eislingen. One of Germany's countless anonymous communities where a broken traffic light or a stray cow may be the biggest news story for many months, Eislingen has a routine that is rarely disrupted. Life in Germany gets going an hour or two earlier than it does in Britain or America. By six-thirty in the morning there is already a steady stream of people on their way to work, dropping in at the local Tchibo café. Here they exchange what little gossip there is over coffee, topped unappealingly with condensed milk, but compensated for by creamy cakes or a smoked-ham *weggle* (a bread roll in Swabia's all-but-incomprehensible dialect).

Yet today was destined to be a special day in Eislingen, for the twenty-first century was about to arrive. Halfway down H. Street, Detlef Hartmann hauled himself out of bed, dimly aware that he had something important on his mind. With the mist still clearing from his brain, he checked his hushmail account for any encrypted messages and scanned his website to see if it required any maintenance. He found nothing untoward.

Then he remembered. His parents were returning from their holiday over the border in Austria. Action stations. He and his brother had just a day to clear up. Desiccated spaghetti stuck like industrial cement to the plates; ashtrays supporting small mountains of cigarette butts lay higgledy-piggledy among the beer cans, bottles and indeterminate items of clothing – a typical monument built by teenage boys when left to their own devices. Detlef decided to take a quick bath before clearing up and was just drying himself when the doorbell rang. He shouted down to his brother to open it.

Detlef's irritation at being disturbed just after nine-thirty in the morning increased a notch when his brother shouted something about a delivery for which he had to sign. Striding downstairs, Detlef prepared to remonstrate with the postman for having got the wrong address. 'Come on,' said his brother impatiently, shivering a little in the draught as Detlef made his way down the hall.

'That vehicle is illegally parked,' thought Detlef with his characteristic eye for precision when he saw a black van on the street outside. Standing in front of it was a postwoman. She was dressed in a uniform that Detlef could only describe as ceremonial. Her tie had a small, tightly drawn knot, while on her head she wore a stiff peaked cap. She looked very earnest.

The postwoman almost bowed as she presented Detlef with an A4 envelope in one hand and a pen in the other. As he reached out for the pen, she stepped back theatrically. 'What the hell is going on . . .?' But before Detlef could finish the thought, four men had jumped on him and he was lying on the ground with his arms behind his back. 'You're under arrest,' one of them screamed, while from nowhere several other officers streamed into the house. Detlef just lay there, dressed only in pyjama bottoms. It was raining and it was cold, about ten degrees Celsius. A boot clamped his neck to the icy ground, while the cable binding his hands dug into his skin. Repeatedly he mumbled, 'What on earth is going on here?' while feeling as if he had stumbled onto the set of a second-rate movie.

Ten minutes later he sat opposite Officer Frank Eissmann from Baden-Württemberg's LKA. The officer was staring gloomily at the detritus in the kitchen, the epicentre of teenage chaos. 'God, this place is a bloody mess,' the detective observed.

By way of explanation, Detlef said that his parents were on holiday. 'I can see that,' Eissmann muttered to himself.

Then for a few minutes the policeman and his charge fell silent. The only noise came from Detlef's chattering teeth. The front door had been left open and, following his short sojourn in the rain, his body temperature was falling. An urgent shout came from upstairs: 'The computers are still running!'

Finally it dawned on Detlef what was happening. Despite the cold and confusion, he thought quickly and asked the officer if he could put some clothes on. It was not entirely disingenuous – he was freezing cold. Eissmann hesitated. Okay, he agreed, warning that it was strictly irregular, but he would allow the lad to get dressed.

As he walked upstairs, only one idea was going through Detlef's brain. 'Turn off the computer! Turn it off! Shut it down! Shut it down!' he thought. Detlef knew the police did not have his password, so if he could manage to disable the computer, there would be no evidence. He reasoned that as long as they didn't have his password, they had nothing.

In the bedroom Eissmann's colleague stood in front of the computer with his hands primed like a goalkeeper to protect the machine from any interference. As Detlef struggled to put on a T-shirt, he stumbled and grabbed hold of the cable leading to the plug, pulling it out of the wall socket. The humming stopped. 'Shit, shit!' screamed the officer, 'the computer's down.' Eissmann charged into the room. 'Right, that's it. You've had it – that's the last thing you'll be doing for a long time.' He dragged Detlef back downstairs into the kitchen. Eissmann thrust a piece of paper in front of him with a lot of officialese written on it, but the only thing Detlef remembers is the hand-written scrawl: '. . . *suspected of forming an organised criminal syndicate*'.

Despite his fury, Detective Eissmann did allow Detlef a brief exchange with his brother. Detlef told him not to worry and that everything was going to be okay. His brother said nothing, but looked at him as if he was completely bonkers. Finally, before pushing him out of the house, Eissmann asked Detlef whether he wanted to take anything with him. 'Can you recommend the sort of thing I'll need?' Detlef replied, a touch perplexed. 'This sort of thing has never happened to me before.'

As he stared out of the car window en route to the police station, his mind drifted back to the two anonymous emails he had received a couple of weeks earlier. What had he been thinking? Why hadn't he reacted to them? Try as he might, though, Detlef was not really sure what he could have done. He was not a hardened criminal with safe-houses and a mafia network at his disposal. He was just a young and rather naive student. He barely knew what a criminal conspiracy was, let alone that he might be part of one.

Detlef was still pondering all this when the police car pulled up in front of a large white building at the end of the aptly named Asperger Street in the Stammheim district of Baden-Württemberg's capital, Stutt-gart. Had he glanced up to one of the windows on the top floor, he would have spotted the cell where Ulrike Meinhof, the charismatic leader of Germany's left-wing terror group of the 1970s, the Red Army Faction, had hanged herself in 1976.

Since then, Stammheim prison had been redesignated a male-only jail. But Detlef was taken there by a female officer. As soon as the inmates saw a woman, they went wild, screaming obscenities from their cells about what they would like to do with her.

With every step, Detlef's fear about his new circumstances grew. How did a respectable middle-class boy find himself in this situation? He had finished high school with excellent grades and was preparing to go to college. His parents adored him and were grateful for all his help with his three younger siblings. Now the harmless boy from Eislingen was in Stammheim, the most notorious detention facility in all Germany. After stripping and searching him, the warders gave him oversized prison clothes, but no shoes. His new pyjamas looked so big they reminded him of wading trousers. Food arrived, but he had not yet fully understood that he was there to stay. He was in shock. Slowly he realised that this was the final stage of the little journey he had begun five years earlier. It was just one day after his twentieth birthday.

24

THE FRENCH
CONNECTION

Marseilles, June 2007

Because they had effectively stopped talking to each other, the two US agencies launched their separate DarkMarket raids in parallel. With the Secret Service in attendance, Detective Spencer Frizzell had arrested Dron in Calgary four days before the FBI-backed Matrix operation in southern Germany.

For weeks Frizzell had been narrowing down the 'usual suspects', visiting the countless Internet cafés from which Dron had been working. Finally he singled out the ordinary-looking twenty-six-year-old who switched between his three 'casual' uniforms as he went about his business. The target lived in a decent apartment in downtown Calgary, conveniently positioned for the Light Rail Transit, naturally.

But neither Frizzell nor the Secret Service agent was quite prepared for what greeted them. The suspect, Nicholas Joehle, had about 100 skimming machines in production. Had he sold them all, it would have netted him $500,000, along with hundreds of blank plastic cards ready for cloning and holograms ready to be counterfeited. Of course the mere possession of these machines was not a crime in itself, but Frizzell was able to ascertain that Joehle had earned some $100,000 in skimmer sales during the period under investigation, a little under twelve months.

It is one thing for law enforcement to arrest a suspect of criminal activity over the Web. It is quite another mounting the evidence for charges to be brought. The virtual and transnational nature of the crime makes it extremely tough to convince a prosecutor to take the case on, and difficult to prove in court. Outside the United States, convictions in this embryonic area of the law tend to bring shorter sentences than conventional crime, which means that police forces are compelled to invest a lot of resources for some fairly unspectacular results. But the issue with somebody like Dron is that the more successful he became, the more his output would drain local and global economies. The potential losses from as skilled an operator as Dron were enormous. Nonetheless, there are tens of thousands of active cyber criminals out in the ether, and only a tiny fraction of them are ever likely to get caught.

Although he was taciturn and uneducated, Joehle was clearly talented. His combination of entrepreneurial and engineering skills would probably see him bounce back, once he had gone through a court case and imprisonment. He had already passed his know-how onto other members of DarkMarket, one of whom was building a vast factory of skimmers halfway around the world. But ultimately that was the responsibility neither of Dron nor of Detective Frizzell – the speed with which skills are communicated over the darkside of the Web is another compelling reason for national police forces to improve their communication with counterparts abroad.

Once Dron and Matrix were taken out, the police would need to move fast against their next targets before the DarkMarketeers noticed the sudden, and largely inexplicable, disappearance from the Internet of their regular contacts. The Secret Service was in better shape here, because Cha0, in his capacity as DarkMarket administrator, had already excluded Dron from the board.

While Dron was still posting on the board, Cha0 had exploited his authority to extract the secrets of the young engineer's trade. As soon as he and his team (for Cha0 had several accomplices) had got the knack, he shut down Dron's membership, just as he had done with JiLsi in December 2006. Dron would no longer be able to advertise on DarkMarket, and because most of the other boards had been liquidated in the battle royal between DM and CardersMarket, the young Canadian's marketing strategy had been severely hampered. With Dron out of the way, Cha0 meanwhile was busy attempting to establish his own near-monopoly in the sale of skimmer machines.

Because Dron had been banned from DarkMarket, his three French partners – Theeeel near Paris, and Lord Kaisersose and Kalouche in Marseilles – would not have noticed that Spencer Frizzell had taken him out of circulation. Nonetheless the Secret Service did not know when Matrix, the most prolific DarkMarket administrator, would be taken down by the German police backed by the Feds. And his surprise removal from the board would probably freak remaining DM members.

In Sweden, Recka knew straight away that law enforcement was on the march. He had been exchanging friendly messages with Matrix on a daily basis, and he didn't buy the curious post that Matrix popped up with in early June 2007. My mother, Matrix explained, has had a serious accident and so I will be absent for a while. Any experienced cyber thief would immediately have concluded that the police had taken over his nickname (they had) and that this was just a feint.

Lord Kaisersose, Theeeel and company were different, of course – they were French. France was developing a peculiar contribution to cybercrime. French criminals were as doggedly francophone as the rest of their compatriots. France's language policeman, the Académie française, had observed with unease the exponential growth of English as a global lingua franca during the 1990s. But it was pleased to note that in the digital world most French hackers and geeks were committed to battle against English, the primary source of linguistic impurities.

This meant two things: cybercrime in France was initially genuinely national – nothing like as cross-border as elsewhere in the world. The country had pre-empted the Internet with the roll-out in 1982 of its very effective information technology called Minitel, which transmitted text onto a video screen along conventional phone lines. As a consequence, the French were much further advanced in their understanding of information technology than most of the rest of the world. The Minitel system, through which customers could look up phone numbers, check their bank accounts, send flowers or talk dirty using the *messageries roses*, was notably more secure against hackers than the Internet, which partly explains why the Web is only now eclipsing Minitel in France. So the French were less vulnerable to early viral infections on the Internet. Furthermore, relatively few French hackers spent time on boards like CarderPlanet, Shadowcrew and DarkMarket.

Second, the advance of spam emails in France has been slow. The returns are far less tempting than those generated by English, Spanish and, latterly, Chinese mass spam mailouts. The market is simply too small. And until recently the eighty or so officers at OCLCTIC did not bother to monitor cyber threats originating in other countries (in contrast to the French military and intelligence communities, which have a highly advanced cyber capability). Operation Lord Kaisersose (the Marseilles crew) and Operation Hard Drive (Dron and Theeeel) went some way towards helping OCLCTIC agents spell out to their political masters why the French police had to engage more effectively with international law enforcement. Perhaps most astonishingly, when OCLCTIC made their arrests – complete with dozens of armed officers charging their way into addresses in Marseilles and outside Paris – there was no coverage at all in the French press: not a single item.

When arresting Theeeel, the police were mildly shocked to find that he was just eighteen years old – the youngest DarkMarketeer to be arrested anywhere in the world. He had become involved in carding to assist the funding of his university studies. If some young women find that they can only make their way through college financially by occasionally selling their bodies, it is quite predictable that young geeks must be tempted to top up their income, too. And as Theeeel discovered, once the money starts rolling in, it's hard to kick the habit.

At first, French officers believed that Lord Kaisersose belonged to one of the many gangs of petty criminals that populate Marseilles, France's very own Odessa: another engrossing port with an inimitable culture (and in Marseilles's case a fabulous cuisine as well). From their surveillance, the cops had learned that one of Kaisersose's accomplices, Dustin, owned a restaurant an hour outside the city and had form for minor fraud offences.

But when OCLCTIC officers, along with local Marseilles cops, raided the apartment of the suspect, Hakim B, in central Marseilles, they realised that Lord Kaisersose was in a higher league. Apart from the large variety of computer kit, the flat was furnished in a tasteful and elegant manner. Hakim was no street thug. He was a gifted hacker whose brother, Ali B., happened to work for DHL. There are few businesses more valuable to cyber criminals than the international courier trade. With Ali an insider at DHL, Hakim had ample means of shifting goods and cash in and out of Marseilles without anybody noticing. And that was important – because Hakim was one of the biggest resellers of dumps from the Ukrainian carding king, Maksik.

Over a two-year-period Maksik had sold Hakim the details of 28,000 credit cards, which had a 'cash out' value of around $10 million. Using his team – Ali, Dustin and one or two others – Hakim would send the cards to ATMs throughout southern France. He was careful never to use any French cards, only American ones. Had the US Secret Service not approached OCLCTIC in this case, Lord Kaisersose would have remained elusive to this day – and very much richer.

25

THE INVISIBLE MAN

Renukanth thought he could start a new life. His exclusion from DarkMarket had triggered a depression that lasted for three weeks. The site that he had nurtured from nothing was the only thing that mattered to him and it had been snatched away. As the winter of 2006 gave way to spring 2007 and his initial shock receded, a strange sense of liberation slowly overcame him. He found he was able to give up smoking crack and drinking. The fog in his brain started to lift and he returned to the gym, in an effort to lose some of the weight that had developed during his days as DarkMarket's obsessive administrator. JiLsi was small, and it was a short journey from being stick thin to bulbous fat.

After a few weeks he sent a request to the DarkMarket administrators to allow him back onto the site. This they did, although they rejected his request to return as administrator. Instead, they conferred a unique – if meaningless – honorific title, Respected Member.

He could no longer wield the power of life and death over the website's members, but he continued to assist its smooth functioning. One member had worked a credit card scam at a Texaco garage in Portsmouth on England's south coast. Somebody had installed a mini-camera in the ceiling above the point-of-sale machine at the checkout. Not only were the cards being skimmed, but their owners were being filmed inputting their PINs. Unfortunately for JiLsi, he agreed to act as Escrow Officer purely as a favour to the other member. But worse than this, he asked another member, Sockaddr, to cash out the cards in the United States. Sockaddr was the primary undercover Secret Service agent on DarkMarket.

But JiLsi's activity on the board became less frequent – his carding days were coming to an end. Although he had yet to work out what to do next, he was pretty sure that it was time to go straight. He had to extract himself from the mess he was in.

Renu's sixth sense was also telling him that something strange was happening. He would watch, listen and smell for the faintest rustle, like a deer alert for danger. He thought he had noticed a couple of animals stalking him. From the corner of his eye he became convinced he could see a pack of lions around the Java Bean café. He would also scan the heavens for circling vultures.

Was this paranoia, or were his two parallel lives as Renu and JiLsi in danger of colliding? Whatever the truth, it was best to plan for all conceivable outcomes. He could no longer blithely dismiss the obvious signs: a car parked near the café for too long; strangers dropping into the shop who just didn't fit – wrong demographic, wrong clothes. After a couple of weeks Renu started varying his route to and from the Java Bean. Sure enough, he had company. These were the lions.

The vultures were members of a less-organised but equally threatening team who had issued warnings regarding certain financial obligations that Renu had assumed after the disastrous episode with the memory stick more than a year earlier. They now wanted their pound of flesh. Might either group be willing to negotiate? Or would he have to flee them both?

Mick Jameson had taken over as lead officer for the JiLsi case a couple of months earlier, in March. For more than half a year his employer, the Serious Organised Crime Agency (SOCA), had been tracking JiLsi following a tip-off from Keith Mularski. Both the US Secret Service and the FBI had been targeting JiLsi for a long time, thanks to his hyperactive posting on virtually every criminal website out there (almost to the point where, if JiLsi wasn't on your site, you weren't really kosher). His distinctive chirpy avatar, the pirate with an eye-patch and tricorne, was irrepressible.

SOCA was the only police agency that was privy to both the FBI and the Secret Service DarkMarket operations and, to a degree, Britain's anti-organised-crime force acted as a passive peace-maker, at least ensuring that the arrest date for Lord Kaisersose and Theeeel in France should be the same one as that for Matrix in Germany and JiLsi in England.

A surveillance team had been focusing their cameras and listening devices on the Java Bean since February. Officers had been tailing Renu. They had clocked him meeting a few people, often speaking in Tamil. They had seen him hand over cash and memory sticks to others, who would pull up in cars before shooting off again. They even stumbled across a second DarkMarket user who also frequented the Java Bean. But it was Renu they wanted. They had taken pictures of his screen with a telephoto lens. One of Jameson's colleagues had infiltrated DarkMarket as an ordinary member and so they were able to monitor a lot of JiLsi's postings. In addition, Mularski was feeding them invaluable intelligence. But they did not yet have definitive proof that Renukanth Subramaniam was JiLsi. For that they would need to arrest him.

The various police forces had resolved to move against him in the second week of June. Some measure of agreement had finally been reached between the Secret Service and the FBI – 12th June was D-Day. That plan was then wrecked by the anonymous emails sent to Matrix001. If JiLsi's arrest was botched, then there was a good chance that word would get out through DarkMarket in a matter of minutes, and many years of painstaking preparation would have been in vain.

And then Jameson's worst fears were realised – a couple of days after Matrix's arrest, JiLsi went AWOL. One morning JiLsi had been walking not to the Java Bean, but to the nearby Wembley Park station, heading for the centre of London. As he passed IKEA on the North Circular, London's traffic-clogged inner ring road, he noticed a peculiar-looking man. Or was it a woman? He couldn't decide. Androgynous was perhaps the best description. He continued on his way to Wembley Park. Just as he was walking towards the underpass by the Tube station, he noticed a long-haired man on the bridge above who was watching him and talking on his phone.

After hopping on the Jubilee Line into town, JiLsi changed onto the Piccadilly at Green Park before finally getting out at Leicester Square, but, as so many people do at that station, he used the wrong exit and had to double-back towards the square itself.

His heart froze: Mr Androgyny was right there. And going across Leicester Square, packed with tourists and street artists, Renu almost bumped into Mr Long Hair. There was no doubt about it now – he was under serious surveillance.

He dived into a Chinese restaurant and wolfed down some lunch as he considered his options. He emerged into the sunlight before slipping down St Martin's Street, the lane that narrows into a passageway alongside the National Gallery before arriving at Trafalgar Square.

Milling around Nelson's Column, visitors were admiring the extraordinary twelve-foot-high statue that occupied the Fourth Plinth, where exhibits are rotated every eighteen months or so. *Alison Lapper Pregnant* depicted the eponymous British artist naked and with child. Ms Lapper had been born without arms, and the decision to mount the statue caused a great deal of fuss at the time. It drew in the crowds and, as Renu made his way through a tidal wave of tourists, his minders were buffeted behind him. He jumped on the first available bus and made his way upstairs. As it turned left into St Martin's Lane, he looked down from the upper deck and caught a glimpse of both Mr Androgyny and Mr Long Hair, looking desperately around in search of their vanished quarry.

Renu disappeared. But he wasn't the only one – JiLsi had made his last-ever posting on the Internet.

A couple of weeks later Renukanth was heading towards one of several properties, which, if he didn't own, he had certainly taken out a mortgage on. He had almost reached the house, which lay slap bang under the landing path for Heathrow Airport, when his phone rang. It was his mate who lived there, warning Renu to stay away. The police had just raided the house and were brandishing a warrant for his arrest.

SOCA's lead officer in the JiLsi investigation, Mick Jameson, had already visited Renu's main address in Coniston Gardens, and a few others as well. Apart from his work as JiLsi on DarkMarket, the Sri Lankan was also a serial mortgage fraudster. He had repeatedly lied about his professional and financial circumstances in an effort to secure funds from lenders on a variety of properties in north, west and south London. Britain was not subject to the same sub-prime frenzy that had seized the financial industry in the US. Nonetheless, the notorious system of self-certification, whereby your word was considered sufficient proof as to your income, combined with the practice of lending up to five times an applicant's salary (in more sober times, this figure was never more than three) meant that mortgage fraud was relatively easy in the UK. So competitive was the market that turning a blind eye had become best practice in the banking industry.

When the phone call came, though, Renu was more concerned to negotiate the deep waters into which he had swum than to consider the fine print of his various scams. He decided on the spot to go underground. For three weeks he slept rough, avoiding any of the addresses that he assumed were now under some form of surveillance. When he received the tip-off about the police raid he had about £500 with him.

Life had been frenetic and risky before, but Renu had always enjoyed his slightly spook-like existence: never staying long at a single address, surreptitiously passing memory sticks to shady-looking contacts and, of course, being lauded as a master of the carding sites, without anyone knowing who he was. At first, he thought dossing down in cardboard boxes under the arches with a group of alcoholics would contribute to that mystique. But as the money ran out and his lifestyle deteriorated to the point where it was almost hand-to-mouth, Renukanth Subramaniam – unfit, unkempt and unwell – decided that running and hiding were a dead end.

On 3rd July 2007 he walked into Wembley Park police station and gave himself up. The easy part of Operation DarkMarket was complete.

Interlude

THE LAND OF I KNOW
NOT WHAT AND I KNOW
NOT WHERE

Tallinn, Estonia

Four days before the official voting day of its general election in the spring of 2007, the tiny Baltic country of Estonia, with a population of just 1.25 million, offered its citizens a world first: the opportunity to cast their ballots in a parliamentary election without getting up from their PC. If the experiment worked, the ultimate aim would be to instigate a full 'virtual election' four years later in 2011.

Much was at stake if Estonia were to make this significant leap towards a digital future – not only did the systems have to work, but they had to be secure from outside attack as well. A year earlier Estonia had officially inaugurated its Computer Emergency Response Team (CERT), whose main job was to react to any breaches (whether accidental or malicious) in the Internet domain that bears the country's suffix: .ee. That involves constantly monitoring the flow of Internet traffic in, around and out of the country for any abnormal patterns.

The man responsible for the entire country's computer security is the quietly spoken Hillar Aarelaid, sporting the look of someone who has only recently got out of bed, and that unwillingly. He may appear distracted, but Aarelaid has a single-mindedness that saw him rise through the ranks of Estonia's police force, where he started as a simple traffic cop in the sticks. 'But I loved computers, so first I got a transfer here to Tallinn and eventually I was appointed Chief Information Officer for law enforcement throughout the country.' Just as well – he definitely looks like a geek. He definitely does not look like a cop (except, at a pinch, an undercover narcotics officer from the 1980s), so perhaps it was for sartorial reasons as much as anything else that he left to run CERT in 2006.

On the day of the virtual election in 2007, CERT and Hillar's former colleagues in law enforcement were on high alert. 'And sure enough,' he explained, 'we spotted somebody had launched a botscan on the electoral system.' Somebody, it seems, had sent out an automatic probe, which was instructed to search for any ports on the electoral servers that might have been left open by mistake. 'This was not very serious, as botscans are pretty easy to detect,' Hillar continued, 'but nonetheless it was a genuine security threat.'

He then puffed himself up – as much as somebody as laid-back as Hillar can – to announce proudly that 'Fifteen minutes after we first spotted the botscan a policeman was knocking on the door at an address in Rapla, fifty kilometres south of Tallinn, enquiring of the inhabitant, "Why are you running a botscan against the electoral computers?"'

In the world of cyber security, fifteen minutes from the detection of mischief to an officer arriving at the location of the mischief-making computer is more than impressive – it's brilliant. 'It was lucky for us that we had done such a good job,' Hillar said, 'because when the first big attack came at the end of April, we were well prepared.'

That 'big attack', two months after the election, marked another cyber 'first' for Estonia as it was subject to a sustained assault on its networks, which eventually forced it to close down its Internet links with the outside world. Some argue that this was the first-ever incidence of cyber warfare.

I had sought out Hillar a month after my visit to Google in Silicon Valley. My eastward journey led me to Tallinn, the picturesque capital of the most northerly Baltic state. The wall of the old town protects a rich mix of Scandinavian, Germanic and Slavic architectural styles. These reflect how the past imperial aspirations of Estonia's neighbours to the north, the east and the west finally gave way to Estonia's primary indigenous culture just over twenty years ago, after the collapse of communism (although Russians still make up just under a quarter of the population).

Sitting cheek by jowl with the Orthodox, Lutheran and Catholic churches are faux-bucolic restaurants for the tourists and, after a hearty meal, snappy nightclubs to round the evening off with some dancing. Estonia hosts fewer stag nights for drunken young Englishmen than neighbouring Latvia, but it, too, has a sleazy side. Amongst the clubs is the evocative Depeche Mode Baar, which only plays records by the eponymous 1980s band from Essex and is decked out as a shrine to the cultural legacy of Britain in the early days of Margaret Thatcher.

Tallinn's strange but welcoming atmosphere was heightened because I arrived only a week before midsummer's eve and the dawning of the fabled White Nights. Dark does not descend until just after midnight, and the light starts returning an hour and a half later. In a week's time it would be light for twenty-four hours of the day.

This jumbled crossroads of imperial ambition, peculiar modern cultural icons and the dreamy nature of light form an ideal backdrop for the annual gathering of the Cooperative Cyber Defence Centre of Excellence (CCDOE), the NATO-backed complex that researches all aspects of cyber warfare. The characters at this conference live in a contemporary Wonderland where convention is oft disregarded – pony-tails and wire-rimmed glasses earnestly exchange information with starched military uniforms about 'SQL injection vulnerabilities'. Besuited civil servants are deep in conversation with young men in jeans and T-shirts detailing the iniquities of 'man-in-the-middle attacks'.

To grasp even the very basics of cyber security in its rich variety, one must be prepared to learn countless new idioms that are being constantly added to or amended. Otherwise you can listen to a conversation that in basic vocabulary and syntax structure is unmistakably English, but is nonetheless completely meaningless to those unschooled in the arcane language. It is, of course, embarrassing continually having to ask people fluent in the tongue why a 'buffer overload' can have alarming consequences for the security of your network, but geeks are not a patronising clan and are generally happy to oblige.

Estonia may be small, but it is the most wired country in Europe and one of the leading digital powers in the world, from where – among other inventions – came Skype. Free wireless can be found in most places, as connectivity is considered a basic right, not a privilege. You won't find hotels gouging your wallet for Internet access here.

However, I was talking to Hillar Aarelaid not about Estonia's go-ahead approach, but about its fabled position in the now fast-growing history of international digital strife.

In early 2007 the Estonian government announced its intention to move the memorial to the fallen of the Red Army during the Great

Patriotic War (as the Russians call the Second World War) from its position in the heart of Tallinn to the city's main cemetery, which is frankly not far from the centre. Russia and its leadership perceived this to be an intolerable insult, even as proof of a resurgence of fascistic Estonian nationalism (all 750,000 of them) and a snub to those soldiers of the Red Army who had sacrificed their lives in liberating Estonia from the Nazi yoke.

The dispute over the bronze soldier escalated. The Russian media, both inside Estonia and across the border in Russia, stoked the genuine worries of Estonia's Russian minority and before long matters had reached breaking point. On the afternoon of 27th April hundreds of young ethnic Russians, citizens of Estonia, gathered in the centre of Tallinn. The protest against the removal of the memorial remained peaceful and good-humoured until one group attempted to break through a police cordon protecting the statue. Violent clashes erupted and spread quickly – by the evening the old town, a UNESCO heritage site, was ablaze as cars were set on fire, shop windows were smashed and their contents looted.

As the disturbances threatened to spread, Moscow issued warnings citing Estonian police brutality, and the country that had gained its independence from the Soviet Union less than two decades earlier, was gripped by uncertainty and fear. It was highly unlikely that Russia would offer Estonia 'fraternal assistance', to use the Soviet euphemism for sending in tanks. After all, Estonia was by now a member of NATO and it seemed inconceivable that Russia would want to trigger NATO's defence guarantee – all for one and one for all – because of a bloody statue!

Thankfully for all of us, the Kremlin indeed showed no inclination to render any fraternal assistance, but as Tallinn's centre crackled and fizzed with rioters and flag-burners, hackers were opening up a new front in this peculiar conflict.

That evening the websites of Estonia's President and several government ministries started receiving inordinate amounts of spam email, while the Prime Minister's photo on his party's website was defaced. Russian-language chat rooms began to exhort hackers to launch attacks on Estonian sites and were distributing the software to do so. According to sources quoted in a US Embassy telegram to Washington (c/o WikiLeaks), the initial attacks were technically unsophisticated and 'seemed more like a cyber riot than a cyber war'.

Over the weekend, however, the attacks escalated from spam showers to DDoS attacks. Hackers had created dozens of those pesky botnets, suborning infected zombie computers around the world and forcing them to request Estonian websites. These were mighty assaults – the presidential website, 'which normally has a two-million megabits-per-second capacity, was flooded with nearly 200 million Mbps of traffic', according to the US Embassy cable. This was still manageable, but on 3rd May 'the cyber attacks expanded beyond Government of Estonia sites and servers to private sites'.

At about ten o'clock that evening Jaan Priisalu received a call at his home on the outskirts of Tallinn. 'They told me that the channels were all going down at work,' he remembered. As the Chief of IT Security at Estonia's biggest bank, Hansabank, Priisalu went into overdrive. 'I then got an SMS, which informed me that our Internet banking service had gone down.'

It was action stations all round: tens of thousands of computers were swamping Hansabank's systems with requests for information. Priisalu immediately started to delve into the frenetic electronic activity and soon discovered that Hansabank was under attack from a botnet comprising some 80,000 computers. Following the attacks back to their origin, Priisalu found they were coming from a server in Malaysia. Not that this amounted to evidence of anything at all, for beyond Malaysia the attackers had successfully masked their real origin. But he realised immediately that he was dealing with a very serious attack. 'It was massive,' he said. A botnet of 80,000 computers is a big monster that can completely paralyse a company's entire system within a matter of minutes.

Thanks to Priisalu's precautionary measures, Hansabank was well prepared with powerful servers. These were alternative websites that could mirror content (thus making it more difficult for DDoS attacks to succeed). However, even though Hansabank's site remained online, the US Embassy's key Estonian source reported that it cost the company 'at least 10 million euros ($13.4 million)'.

The next targets were the Estonian media, including the daily paper with the most frequently visited news website. 'Imagine, if you can, the psychological effect,' said one observer, 'when an Estonian tries to pay his bills but can't, or tries to get the news online but can't.' The government was on high alert, deeply worried that the escalating attacks represented 'a frightening threat to key economic and societal infrastructure'.

By this time Hillar Aarelaid and his team had fully mobilised. Estonia's CERT responded by expanding the country's broadband 'pipeline' into the country with the assistance of its friends abroad, notably in Finland and Sweden. 'We had been expecting that something like this might happen and we had been on alert,' Hillar remembered. 'This was where the Russians made a mistake. If you want to succeed with an attack like this, you need to know your enemy really well and you need to be close to your enemy,' he said, explaining that the Russians had failed to anticipate the high level of Estonia's preparedness. 'Had they thought it through,' he continued, 'they would have known that our systems were on high alert because of the recent elections.'

Thanks to the coordination of the government, the police, the banks and CERT, the impact of the attacks on ordinary citizens was kept within reasonable boundaries. Hansabank maintained its online banking, but the other two largest banks were unable to. Instead people simply switched to using their branches. Mobile phones were interrupted and, once the government ordered the shutdown of Estonia's links to the outside world, communication with the country was tricky for a few days. Contrary to initial reports, traffic lights in Tallinn did not stop working, but there was some interruption to the work of the government and the media.

The attacks continued at varying degrees of intensity for two weeks, culminating in a massive assault on 9th May, the date of the Red Army's victory over the Nazis in Europe. At this point, exhausted by the relentless flood of DDoS attacks, the Estonian government decided to cut off the country's Internet system from the rest of the world. The DDoS attacks declined to a dribble, eventually coming to an end on 19th May.

The implications of the Estonian events were grave. In political terms it was perfectly clear that the attacks came from Russia, but predictably the government in Moscow denied all responsibility for them. And it is perfectly possible that there was no official involvement. Researchers were unable to track down the precise origin of the attacks. Assuming that they did come from Russia, however, the government must have known about them because of their omniscient monitoring system, SORM-2. Having said that, there was so much extraordinary Internet activity going on in Russia at the time that maybe even the fabled SORM-2 was having a hard time keeping up with everything. Who can say? Because one thing that the attack on Estonia made quite clear was that you can make a very shrewd guess as to who has instigated events like these, but you cannot ever be certain.

Like all governments, the Russian government was evolving its own unique attitude towards the Internet, its function and the relationship between the state and the end user. Moscow recognised as early as the 1990s that the political and security importance of the Internet was such that it deserved the full attention of one of the country's most enduring and successful institutions: the secret police. In short, the FSB (intimate successor to the KGB) developed the ability to monitor every packet of data zinging in, out and around the country. This system goes under the appropriately sinister acronym of SORM-2, the Система Оперативно-Розыскных Мероприятий, or the System for Operative-Investigative Activities.

SORM-2 is truly frightening. Should you request information over the Web from your computer in Vladivostock or Krasnodar, then when it reaches your Internet Service Provider, a duplicate package dutifully trots off to FSB central in Moscow, to be read, mulled over, laughed at and (who knows?) used in evidence against you, at the FSB's pleasure. At the very least, it will be stored.

Not only does SORM-2 require that Russian ISPs feed *all* Internet activity through to the FSB's headquarters, but it adds insult to injury by compelling the ISPs to purchase the required equipment (at a cost of more than $10,000) and to fund the running costs of the service. These costs are of course passed on to consumers, who thus end up paying quite directly for a mighty tool of oppression of which they are the principal victims.

The Russian state has the capacity to know who is doing what, when, to whom and, probably, why over the Web. Of course, a sneaky Russian computer-user might concoct a plan to circumvent the all-seeing SORM-2 by encrypting their data and Internet browsing. But remember – encryption is illegal in Russia and one file with a digital lock on it would be enough to buy you a one-way ticket to Siberia.

That does not imply that the Internet regimes of Western governments represent a model of free speech. On the contrary, as our dependency on the Internet increases, so the desire, ability and will of governments to control it strengthen. Despite habitual protests by civil servants and politicians that no such process is under way, the tortured and slow death of Internet privacy in the West, especially in the United Kingdom and the United States, is a sad – albeit visible – reality and is probably inevitable.

The response to 9/11, in the name of combating terrorism, severely curtailed our freedom from state interference on the Web. The main tool in the US was the Total Information Awareness (TIA) programme, although even the Bush administration, with its congenital tin ear, eventually realised that the name had so many Orwellian associations that it should be renamed the Terrorism Information Awareness programme.

The TIA afforded DARPA, the Pentagon's research and detection wing, considerable access to data gleaned from private communications. Although the programme was eventually closed down, many of its powers were retained by government and distributed among different agencies in the United States.

Elsewhere, in a landmark case, the Supreme Court consented to the FBI deploying key-logger trojans onto the computers of suspects, although under court supervision. This enabled the FBI to log everything that the suspect would do on his computer, just as the cyber criminal does when he infects a third-party computer with a key logger. At the turn of the millennium the European Parliament confirmed the existence of Echelon, the United States's global spy programme that is allegedly capable of homing in on digital communications anywhere in the world.

In a directive issued under the UK's presidency of the European Union, Internet Service Providers in Europe were obliged to start storing all computer traffic (this applies to mobile phones as well) for between six months and two years – data that a variety of governmental agencies can access under national legislation. If these moves towards digital surveillance continue, Western governments (usually in the name of anti-terrorism strategies and law enforcement) will be in an ever better position to monitor the movements and habits of their citizens.

Researchers at the London School of Economics best described our chosen path. In June 2009 they asked the reader to imagine:

the government having a deaf security agent following every single person everywhere they go. The agent cannot hear the content of any interactions, but can otherwise observe every minute detail of someone's life: the time they wake up, how they drive to work, who they talk to and for how long, and how their business is doing, their health, the people they meet in the street, their social activities, their political affiliations, the papers and specific articles they read, and their reaction to those, the food in their shopping basket, and whether they eat healthily, how well their marriage is going, the extra-marital affairs, their dates and intimate relations. Since most of these interactions are today mediated at some level by telecommunications services, or are facilitated by mobile devices, all of this information will now reside with our internet service providers, ready and waiting for government access.

At least in the West, we stand a fighting chance of resisting some of the more draconian powers that various branches of government are seeking to acquire over civil Internet activity.

Given the strength of the civil-liberties community in the West and the KGB's comprehensive surveillance of the Internet, one might assume that Russia would represent an implacably hostile environment for cyber criminals. Yet the Russian Federation has become one of the great centres of global cybercrime. The strike rate of the police is lamentable, while the number of those convicted barely reaches double figures. The reason, while unspoken, is widely understood. Russian cyber criminals are free to clone as many credit cards, hack as many bank accounts and distribute as much spam as they wish, provided the targets of these attacks are located in Western Europe and the United States. A Russian hacker who started ripping off Russians would be bundled into the back of an unmarked vehicle before you could say KGB.

In exchange, of course, should the Russian state require the services of a hacker for launching a crippling cyber attack on a perceived enemy, then it is probably best for the hacker to cooperate.

2007 was the heyday of a loose organisation of companies based in St Petersburg known as the Russian Business Network, or RBN. This mysterious acronym offered to host websites for individuals and companies – it was known as the king of bulletproof hosters. Companies that offer this service are essentially letting their customers know that they are not interested in the content or function of a website and, in exchange for much higher fees, will resist any legal or digital attempts to bring down the sites.

Not all bulletproof hosting is intended as a way of circumventing the law, but criminals and pirates frequently avail themselves of such services. They are virtually indispensable for individuals and groups involved in the distribution of child pornography, for example, and the RBN was known to include such clients on its books, as several security companies' research departments have identified.

These hosts have also proved invaluable for people distributing spam email, as these operations require huge, secure capacity in order to spew forth their billions of dubious adverts and viruses. Nigerian 419 scams, counterfeit medicines, the now-fabled penis enlargers and many other products (real or imaginary) are dumped on the world from bulletproof hosts. Many spam messages conceal viruses or links to infected websites, which, if activated, may turn a computer into a single footsoldier in a botnet army.

As the Russian Business Network was booming in 2006 and 2007, Spamhaus, the secretive anti-spam operation in Cardiff, listed it as controlling 2,048 Internet addresses. It described the RBN as 'among the world's worst spammers' and home to vast 'child pornography, malware, phishing and cybercrime-hosting networks'.

The RBN's primary significance lies in the profitability of such bulletproof hosting organisations, which are able to charge $600 or more a month. For legitimate websites, the cost would be one-tenth of this.

But its secondary role is, in many respects, the more interesting one. The attacks on Estonia began with millions of spam emails swooping down on the computer networks of the Estonian government. Subsequently François Paget, who works for the US computer-security giant McAfee, analysed the content of the spam to discover that they were identical to the standard RBN mailouts. Furthermore, Andy Auld, the head of cyber intelligence at Britain's Serious Organised Crime Agency, reported that in their brief field-observation of the RBN in St Petersburg, British police were able to establish that the RBN could operate in part because it bribed local law enforcement and the judiciary.

It is possible that the RBN instigated the attacks on Estonia but highly unlikely. More probably it was either paid to launch them or the authorities leaned on them to participate in this act of patriotism. This connection between a complex of St Petersburg-based Internet Service Providers that specialised in criminal activity and the cyber attack on Estonia highlights one of the greatest conundrums at the heart of computer crime and computer security.

There are three main 'threats' on the Internet, each manifesting themselves in a variety of guises. First, there is cybercrime. In its most basic form, cybercrime consists of 'carding', the theft and cloning of credit-card data for financial gain. Beyond carding, there are all manner of other scams. One of the most lucrative, for example, is called 'scareware', which was perfected by a Ukrainian-based company called Innovative Marketing. IM employed dozens of young people in Kiev, the Ukrainian capital, most of whom believed they were involved in a start-up company that was selling legitimate security products. Except they weren't.

The company was sending out rogue adware, which, once installed on an individual's computer, would trigger a pop-up on the browser warning the user that their machine had been compromised by a virus. The only way, the advert explained, to rid their computer of the electronic critters now crawling all over their hard disk and RAM was to click on a link and purchase 'Malware Destroyer 2009', to name but one of their countless products.

Once you had downloaded Malware Destroyer (for €40), IM would instruct you to remove your existing anti-virus system, such as Norton, and install their product. Once installed, however, it did precisely nothing – it was an empty piece of software, although now of course you were open to infection by any passing virus and you had paid for that dubious privilege.

A researcher for McAfee in Hamburg, Dirk Kolberg, began to monitor this operation. He followed the scareware back to its source in East Asia and found that the administrator of IM's servers had left some ports wide open, so Kolberg was at liberty to wander into the server and peruse it at will. What he uncovered was quite breathtaking. Innovative Marketing was making so much money that it had established three call centres – one for English speakers, one for German and one for

French – to assist baffled customers who were trying to install their non-functioning products. Kolberg worked out from trawling through the receipts he also found on the server that the scareware scam had generated tens of millions of dollars in revenue for the management, in one of the most theatrical examples of Internet crime.

Beyond scareware, there are pump-and-dump schemes, which involve hackers moving into financial sites and digitally inflating share prices, before selling their holdings and then allowing the stock to collapse. There are also payroll schemes, whereby criminals hack into a corporation's computer and add phantom employees to the personnel database. However, the hackers give these employees real salaries, which are dispatched monthly to so-called 'money mules'. For a small consideration, these are instructed to pass on the money to a bank far away from where the crime is actually committed.

Just as the Web offers boundless possibilities to the creative mind in the licit world, so criminals can let their fantasies run free on the Internet.

The second major area of malfeasance on the Web is cyber industrial espionage. According to the annual threat report published by the American telecommunications giant, Verizon, this accounts for roughly 34 per cent of criminal activity on the Web and is almost certainly the most lucrative. Communications technology has made the theft of industrial secrets much easier than in the past. Until computers became widespread, stealing material involved physically breaking into a company or, if it were an inside job, finding ways of actually removing and distributing the data being sought.

No such difficulties now: industrial thieves can hack into a corporate system and then sniff around for blueprints, marketing strategies, payrolls or whatever else they are seeking, before downloading it. When Max Vision was not yet the fabled Iceman, he worked across the West Coast as a penetration tester – companies would pay him to attempt a digital break-in. Speaking to me in the orange jumpsuit that is his prison uniform, Vision said, 'In those years, there was only one company which I failed to break into, and that was a major American pharmaceutical company.' This is understandable – the value of pharmaceutical companies resides in their research, and the loss of formulae for new treatments can result in the loss of hundreds of millions of dollars and the collapse of share prices.

Vision was absolutely livid that he was unable to crack this one system. 'Of course, I then launched a phishing attack on them and I was inside within five minutes, but it's just not the same.' What he means by that is that he sent infected emails to company email addresses, and it was but a matter of minutes before one of its many thousands of employees had fallen for the trap. So even if you have an unbreachable digital fortress, you have only overcome one of several major security challenges.

Similarly, these days it is much easier to perpetrate an inside job in a company because of the ease with which data can be collected and stored. We know that Bradley Manning, the man accused of having removed the US diplomatic cables that were subsequently published on WikiLeaks' website, managed to download all the material onto a CD marked as a Lady Gaga album.

We also know that Stuxnet – to date the world's most sophisticated virus – must have been planted on its apparent target in Iran's nuclear facilities by somebody (wittingly or otherwise) infecting the computer systems with a memory stick or CD. Iran's nuclear operating systems are not connected to the Internet. But they are still networks, and their infection by Stuxnet proved that they were within reach of a professional intelligence agency.

Stuxnet represented a significant escalation in the third major threat: cyber warfare. This piece of malware was so complicated that researchers estimated it must have taken in the region of several man-years to develop, which means that a dedicated team of coding engineers must have been working on it for an extended period. Organised crime does not operate in this fashion. The only entity capable of developing Stuxnet was a nation state with a lot of resources to devote to the design and manufacture of both defensive and offensive cyber weapons. Nonetheless, whoever designed Stuxnet borrowed huge amounts of computer code and techniques from the many tens of thousands of blackhat or greyhat hackers out in cyberspace. Criminal hackers are a great driver of creativity in all areas of the Web's darkside. Military, private-sector, police and intelligence agencies are always quick to adopt the tools that crackers and hackers are developing.

When Stuxnet was successfully infiltrated into the control system of several nuclear facilities in Iran, the authorities admitted that it led to a major breakdown in the operation of a highly sensitive station. It could have resulted in an explosion. Its existence proves that the doomsday scenarios proposed by the so-called cyber warriors are no longer only theoretically possible. Serious though it was at the time, the attack on Estonia was the equivalent of a playful pre-match kick-about, compared to what Stuxnet heralds.

The cyber warriors are also referred to as cyber securocrats – these are the prophets who warn that the sky is about to fall on our heads. Among the most articulate of this breed is Richard Clarke, who describes the following scenario in his book *Cyber War*:

> By the time you get to the Situation Room, the Director of the Defense Information Systems Agency is waiting on the secure phone for you.
>
> FEMA, the Federal Emergency Management Agency, has reported large refinery fires and explosions in Philadelphia and Houston, as well as lethal clouds of chlorine gas being released from several chemical plants in New Jersey and Delaware.
>
> The National Air Traffic Control Center in Herndon, Virginia, has experienced a total collapse of its systems . . .

Most securocrats continue by arguing that the only way we can prevent a digital Pearl Harbor or Cybergeddon is to put money into their think-tanks and companies in order to step up research into the threat.

In fact, this is already happening. The Estonian events accelerated the move towards the militarisation of cyberspace. NATO first agreed to create the majestically titled Cooperative Cyber Defence Centre of Excellence in Tallinn in 2005. Despite an enthusiastic reception for the idea of a cyber-war operational institute, member states proved reluctant to put any money on the table (with the understandable exception of the host country, Estonia). The project wasn't mothballed, but it struggled to advance much beyond the stage of some attractively designed headed notepaper.

'As soon as the attack happened, however,' noted Peeter Lorents, an eminent Estonian mathematician and one of the Centre's co-founders, 'the atmosphere changed and we started getting real support from both Brussels and Washington. Indeed, my first reaction on hearing about the attack was to call France and order two cases of Cristal Champagne to be delivered to Mr Putin. By launching this attack, the Russians had surely secured the future of our centre.'

Alarm bells were certainly ringing in Washington. A number of events immediately preceded or followed on from the Estonian incident, and together these convinced the incoming Obama administration in 2009 that cyber defence needed to be strengthened at all costs. In particular, a few months after Estonia, it dawned on America's huge global surveillance operation, the National Security Agency (NSA), just how serious the loss in April 2001 of an EP-3E Aries reconnaissance plane to the Chinese Air Force really was. Although the pilot had succeeded in destroying the software before it went down, the hardware was intact and, as soon as it fell into Chinese hands, they began to reverse-engineer the state-of-the-art technology that would enable them to monitor and decode encrypted communications. Soon after Obama's election to the White House the Chinese started testing their new toy, and their new capability at intercepting communications was observed by the NSA. The Chinese, it seems, wanted to indicate to Washington that it had successfully cracked the technology.

The United States government did not stop at putting its weight behind the cyber-defence centre in Tallinn, which, since 2008, has been conducting major research, including complex cyber military exercises. Computing networks had become so critical a part, both of the Defense Department's infrastructure and of its offensive and defensive operational capability, that Robert Gates, the Secretary of Defense, made the momentous decision to create a new military domain – cyberspace.

This fifth military domain – a sibling to land, sea, air and space – is the first-ever man-made sphere of military operations, and the rules surrounding combat in it are almost entirely opaque. Along with the domain, the Pentagon has set up USCYBERCOMMAND to monitor hostile activity in cyberspace and, if necessary, plan to deploy offensive weapons like Stuxnet. For the moment, the US is the acknowledged leader in the cyber offensive capability.

'Cyber offensive capability' should not be mistaken for an ability to deploy conventional weapons that are enhanced by computer systems. The best examples from this latter arsenal are the drones (which the US has regularly deployed in Afghanistan and Pakistan) that can undertake surveillance and fighting missions while being piloted by a computer operator in Nevada.

Cyber weapons are the hacking tools that enable a cyber soldier to penetrate the computer systems of an enemy's CNI (Critical National Infrastructure), such as their energy and water grids. Once in control of the system, the military doctrine goes, the cyber commander can order their shutdown (or, as we know from Stuxnet, trigger a very damaging explosion) so that within a matter of days the affected society will be reduced to Stone Age technology.

That, at least, is the idea. For the moment, the United States is the acknowledged front-runner as developer of offensive cyber weapons. But the Chinese, the French and the Israelis are snapping at their heels, with the Indians and British not far behind.

The militarisation of cyberspace was foreseeable. Where this is leading us is, by contrast, understood by nobody. Writing in *The New Yorker*, the ever-perceptive Seymour Hersh teased out the implications of the Chinese having nicked the secrets from the reconnaissance plane's hard drive:

> The EP-3E debacle fuelled a long-standing debate within the military and in the Obama Administration. Many military leaders view the Chinese penetration as a warning about present and future vulnerabilities – about the possibility that China, or some other nation, could use its expanding cyber skills to attack America's civilian infrastructure and military complex. On the other side are those who argue for a civilian response to the threat, focussed on a wider use of encryption. They fear that an over-reliance on the military will have adverse consequence for privacy and civil liberties.

The urge for the military to establish itself as the chief arbiter of cyber security appears widespread. In October 2010 President Obama charged the National Security Agency, which is part of the Pentagon, with assisting the Department of Homeland Security and the private sector in domestic cyber security. In China the People's Liberation Army is the primary institution governing foreign and domestic cyber security, while in the Middle East the Israeli Defence Force is the inspiration for the extraordinary research into computer warfare, which allows Israel to punch high above its weight in this field.

But what, one may legitimately ask, has any of this to do with cyber-crime?

The threats in cyberspace are real and dangerous. Ideally, a demo-cratic state would ensure that this critical technology should benefit, not ruin, the lives of its citizens. Equally, the state should resist the temptation to infringe our rights and privacy. Allowing the military to assume a lead role in defence of civilian networks is most unwise. Yet given that cyber weapons have the potential to cripple a country's Critical National Infrastructure (and ruin people's lives in the process), there must be provision for the military to intervene in extreme situ-ations. Those circumstances should be both exceptional and verifiable.

Separate agencies should be responsible for policing the three sepa-rate threats – cybercrime, cyber industrial espionage and cyber warfare. Recognised police agencies like the FBI or the US Secret Service should assume responsibility for cybercrime. Corporations and companies should either develop their own network security system or pay a company specialising in cyber security to do it. Civilian government should establish its own network defence, while the military should protect its systems.

On the surface that seems straightforward enough. But in the real world the edges are already blurred, encouraged by the interconnectivity of the Web. Then there is the hitherto insoluble two-part conundrum at the heart of the cyber security: what does a cyber attack look like?

To answer this, a cyber defender requires two vital pieces of know-ledge. From where does this attack originate? And what is the attacker's motive? Faced with a skilled cyber aggressor, not even the best defender can answer these questions. One may only calculate and – acting on a supposition – this can lead to wrong decisions, misunderstandings and, eventually, conflict.

Let us assume that our police agency, the corporate sector and the military dutifully stick to their task of protecting the state against their designated perils. There are still two actors who are ever present across the spectrum of threats: the spook and the hacker. The former seeks to crack the conundrum (although not necessarily to share the resulting knowledge); the latter is actually responsible for formulating the conun-drum precisely in such a way as to render it insoluble.

The intelligence agency sniffs around the Web like a black cat against a dark background, never making a sound and socialising only when its team seeks to dissemble, recruit or confuse. This phantom-like behaviour is part of the spook's DNA, but it is also explained by the intelligence service's fascination with, and even admiration for, its primary opponent in cyber: the hacker.

Until recently, network defenders were confident that when an attack was under way there was a hacker masterminding it. This has changed in the last five years with the emergence of 'off-the-shelf' malware. Many criminal hackers now make their money not by compromising credit cards, bank accounts or similar cunning scams, but simply by selling trojans, viruses and worms that they have developed. They are user-friendly programs that do not require specialist knowledge to deploy them. The most common form is the botnet. Hackers will hire out botnets to be used in DDoS attacks for purposes such as extortion or revenge for a day or two, or maybe for a week or a month. Naturally, hackers selling a botnet or virus have the technical ability to control the length of hire because they can simply programme in its obsolescence, about which their clients – presumably petty jobbing criminals – can do nothing.

Yet the emergence of a secondary market on the Net for 'off-the-shelf' malware will not alter the fundamental truth that behind any cyber attack – whether it is criminal, corporate espionage or warfare – lies a gifted hacker. Mounting cyber attacks that are genuinely damaging, rather than merely inconvenient, invariably requires highly specialised and technical skills. This means that even if a hacker is working on behalf of a boss (be it a *capo*, a CEO or a Commander), he will still need to know a great deal about the intended target *if* he is to design the right product. Whichever team of hackers designed Stuxnet, for example, had to know not just about the Iranian nuclear facilities that were the presumed targets; they also needed to understand the Siemens PLC network that ran it and the very specific compressor designed by Vachon, a Finnish company (although manufactured in China), as well as the Taiwanese company whose RealTek digital certificate was spoofed to fool the Iranian system's anti-virus program. Anyone smart enough to work on Stuxnet would have been smart enough to work out its intended victim.

In this respect, hackers are the key to cyber security as they hold the solution to the conundrum. Find the hackers and you will have made serious strides towards uncovering the truth.

The overwhelming percentage of funds that governments are now channelling into cyber security are devoted to 'digital solutions' – they are fighting the power of gadgets with gadgets. The money going into understanding hackers, their culture, their minds, their intentions and their vulnerabilities is negligible. But how do you find a hacker? And, on the Internet, how do you know if your new-found friend is a hacker, a police spy, an intelligence agent, an Air Force investigator, a prankster, a terrorist or an alien?

Everything revolves around trust. And building trust means being patient and nurturing relationships. Yet time is at a premium in the world of cyber security. Nowhere did the difficulties relating to trust and time become clearer to me than when DarkMarket's locus shifted away from its origins in Britain, Germany and the United States towards a country whose economic and geo-strategic importance is growing at a rate of knots – Turkey.

BOOK TWO

Part I

26

BILAL IN PITTSBURGH

Pittsburgh, Pennsylvania, February 2008

One crisp winter morning in 2008, Inspector Bilal Şen of the Turkish Police stared out of his office window at Pittsburgh's Hot Metal Bridge. Straddling the Monongahela River a tad east from where it joins the Allegheny to form the majestic Ohio, the bridge used to transport molten metal from the great Eliza furnace on the north side to the rolling mills on the south.

But today he had no time to reflect on Pittsburgh's snow-clad post-industrial aesthetic. He had just read something disturbing on the DarkMarket boards. According to apparently reliable information coming out of Istanbul, Cha0, the cyber criminal under investigation by Inspector Şen, was 'one of the big boys, rich and powerful'. For a Turk, the phrase was easy to decode: the target had friends in high places, a Turkish copper's worst nightmare.

Inspector Şen had been working at the National Cyber Forensics Training Alliance for almost three months. On his first day he had been waiting in reception to be greeted by the organisation's boss when by chance Agent Keith J. Mularski strolled in, bright and charming as always. He introduced himself and, on learning that Bilal was from Turkey, immediately started telling him everything he knew about Cha0, DarkMarket's notorious administrator and master criminal. Mularski and Şen were a splendid match.

When he entered the office area on the fourth floor of 2000 Technology Drive, the Turkish policeman was struck by the appearance of the place, which looked more like an insurance company than the frenetic high-tech environment familiar from TV programmes like *CSI New York*. One room that was tucked away was littered with the tools of computer forensics, machines that offer up the innermost secrets of any digital device. But this tech examination room was barely visible and was sealed to prevent the intrusion of any trojan or other malware from contaminating objects under investigation (as with their organic counterparts, computer viruses are sometimes airborne). That aside, the offices were quiet, orderly and unremarkable.

On that first morning, Keith showed Bilal the whiteboard in his office with the name 'Cha0' atop the pyramid of criminals connected to DarkMarket. Inside, the Turkish policeman felt a twinge of shame. With the support of colleagues in Britain and Germany, the Feds had taken down two of DarkMarket's most energetic administrators, JiLsi and Matrix, six months earlier. Arrests had already been made in Britain, Germany, Canada and France, and further arrests in the United States were being prepared. So the officer from Ankara felt it a stain on his national pride as well as on his personal reputation that his fellow Turk was now among the most-wanted cyber criminals in the world.

Turkish police, and particularly its organised-crime department, had come a long way in the previous decade, and Bilal was determined to prove that even with many fewer resources available to him than to his counterparts in Western Europe and America, the young Cyber Crime Unit based in the Turkish capital, Ankara, was capable of playing in the big league.

Police officers from around the world were always dropping in and out of the FBI offices. They came to learn from their American counterparts, but also to build networks of mutual assistance. Cooperation between police forces from different countries usually groaned under the weight of intolerable bureaucratic procedures, and personal friendship among cops was the quickest way to bypass that.

Bilal had come on a three-month attachment. As a Turk, he was a novel, if potentially very useful contact for the Feds. In 2003 he had been one of the two co-founders of the tiny Cyber Crime Unit in Turkey's Anti-Smuggling and Organised Crime Division. And compared to the perpetrators, the inspector had no resources.

For his part, Bilal Şen wanted to learn from the FBI. Not that he was inexperienced. He had joined the police as a fifteen-year-old in 1989, signing up for the gruelling eight-year officer training course

– the longest in the world. This was odd, as with his small stature and thoughtful manner, Inspector Şen resembled a Turkish Hercule Poirot more than the traditional image of a tough Balkan cop moulded by rural bandits, urban narco syndicates and a brutalised criminal-justice system.

Police college had proved a taxing regime. However, what pained Bilal most were not the spartan quarters and unforgiving assault courses, but the complete absence of computers. From a young age he had taken any opportunity to sneak into the local games arcade in his home town of Eskişehir that sits midway between Istanbul and Ankara in northern Anatolia. He was only about six years old when he came across the game River Raid. Every minute of his spare time was spent flying a two-dimensional fighter plane up a river, firing on tiny helicopters, ships, tanks and dirigibles while trying to refuel at the same time. Gripped by that mysterious fusion of repetition and occasional reward that keeps so many children, adolescents and young adults glued to their computer screens, Bilal had an obsession with games that mirrored that of many proto-hackers at the same age. Equally, he was gripped by the same determination to win.

Perhaps that stubbornness helped the raw recruit through his first posting at a village police station in the middle of Anatolian nowhere. Although this was by now the mid-1990s, the only machine here was an ancient manual typewriter. Taking down witness statements was considered below his dignity as an officer, but Bilal was so determined to improve his typing that he spent many an hour banging on those keys. When he wasn't doing that, this remarkable autodidact was teaching himself Mandarin.

When he applied to join Ankara's elite Organised Crime Unit, the chief there asked Bilal why he was learning Chinese. 'With China opening its doors to the outside world,' he answered, 'we are soon going to need Mandarin-speakers in the Department for Organised Crime.' That reply swung it for him and he landed the job.

Once in the Turkish capital, the young detective signed up for a Masters at Ankara University, again off his own bat and in his spare time. He selected a topic unknown and unstudied in Turkey – 'The Opportunities and Risks of E-Government' – in which he considered the relationship between privacy, civil rights and cybercrime.

Bilal Şen began to monitor the proliferation of Internet crime in his country, one of the few Turkish policeman with the capacity to do so – the only other organs of state already aware of the strategic importance of cyber security were the military and civilian intelligence agencies, but they, of course, never advertised their capabilities or motives.

Together with a colleague, Bilal set himself the Herculean task of persuading the unwieldy Interior Ministry to divert some of its precious funds to the establishment of a Cyber Crime Unit. It took three years of pleading, cajoling and politicking. Fortunately, he had a collaborator who had mastered the Ottoman art of striking the right tone with the appropriate bureaucrats in the Interior Ministry.

As with all the cybercrime units springing up in police forces around the world, Turkey's new department was able to exploit the fact that virtually nobody else in the ministry understood the dark side of computers. Once given the go-ahead, the two men found themselves oddly free from outside interference, as nobody else had a clue what they were doing and they were hardly a burden on the Exchequer.

While the Inspector's own government was scarcely aware of his work, his counterparts way across the Atlantic had soon taken note of his achievements. In the summer of 2007 as police in Germany and Britain arrested the DarkMarket administrators, Matrix001 and JiLsi, Turkey's cybercrime team had put one of the most notorious cyber criminals, Maksik, behind bars. A major player on DarkMarket (he had supplied amongst others the French hacker, Lord Kaisersose in Marseilles with 'dumps'), Maksym Yastremsky from the north-eastern Ukrainian city of Kharkov had assumed he would be safe in Turkey – not only did no cyber criminal ever get arrested there, but relations between Ukraine and Turkey had never been more cordial, especially in the underworld.

The Ukrainians also adored the country for its gorgeous coast – Antalya's beautiful beaches had become a de rigueur destination for cyber thieves from both nations.

The US Secret Service had been tracking Maksik for two years. They had successfully stolen the secrets of his laptop in 2006 and then set up meetings between him and an undercover Secret Service agent in Thailand, Dubai and Turkey. In the past, cooperating with the Turkish police had proven awkward, if not downright impossible. But in arresting Maksik while he was languishing in Antalya's blistering sunshine, Turkish police had sent out a signal that on cybercrime, they were keen to cooperate and they had the know-how to do it.

Although the JiLsis and Matrixes of this world were no longer treading the DarkMarket boards, the rest of the crew were still active – indeed, DarkMarket was again experiencing a surge of criminal activity. Ironically, the key to that revival lay in the arrest of another cyber criminal: Iceman.

In September 2007 US law-enforcement officers had finally tracked down Max Vision at his hideaway apartment in downtown San Francisco. CardersMarket had crumbled with Iceman's demise and so, while mazafaka controlled the Russian carding scene, DarkMarket was now the unchallenged champion of English-speaking cyber criminals. Directly or indirectly the site was still generating hundreds of thousands of pounds of illegal profits every month and it remained as popular as ever among carders and hackers.

There were now three key players on DarkMarket: Cha0, Master Splyntr and Shtirlitz. The mysterious Lord Cyric would soon join them. Cyric's presence on the carding scene was generating enmity and adoration in equal measure among carders. Those who loathed him believed him to be the FBI plant, Mularski, although there was also a suspicion that Master Splyntr and Shtirlitz were actually working for, or with, US law enforcement. The one thing that everyone agreed upon, whether cop or hacker, was that the most serious criminal remaining on the board was Cha0.

In contrast to their bulging dossiers on his fellow DarkMarketeers, Mularski and Şen knew just two salient facts about Cha0 himself: he lived in Istanbul; and he had a thriving business selling so-called 'skimmers,' that essential tool of the fraudster in the Age of Plastic. But the detectives had no real name for Cha0; no physical address; no IP address and no known associates. Either Cha0 didn't exist (not impossible) or he never made mistakes.

If it was the latter, then Cha0 would appear to have perfected a system of disguising his digital tracks so that the forensic sleuths found it impossible to home in on his location. Part of that masking system was provided by Grendel, who helped out DarkMarket (against payment) in his spare time. This was ironic as Grendel was also providing the shell system that disguised the location of Mularski's servers. Grendel had originally been invited to provide these services to DarkMarket by

JiLsi – in real life he worked for an IT security company in Germany. It was ironic, but somehow very DarkMarket, that he ended up offering security to criminals and cops alike on the website.

Despite intense efforts, Bilal Şen had failed to match Cha0's style (or MO, as the police describe it) with any known criminals in Turkey itself. The two fundamental aspects of the Internet's darkside seemed to coincide in his personality: he was a geek with mesmeric technical skills, but he was also a gifted criminal who attended to every last detail and left nothing to chance. It was also possible that Cha0 was the collective name of a well-organised syndicate, although linguistic analysis strongly suggested that only one person was actually formulating his posts and messages on the Internet.

So when Bilal got the message from Istanbul that Cha0 was 'one of the big boys', he was not only worried, but he knew that from now on he would have to tread carefully even in a country that was modernising as fast as Turkey.

After the millennium Turkey had become an increasingly attractive venue for hackers, crackers and cyber criminals. In the late 1990s much cyber criminal activity had clustered in certain regions of the so-called BRIC countries. An economist from Goldman Sachs had conferred this acronym on Brazil, Russia, India and China as the leading countries of the emerging markets, the second tier of global power after the G8 (though, politically, Russia straddles the two).

The BRICs shared important social and economic characteristics. Their economies were moving and opening after several decades of stagnation. They had large populations whose combined efforts registered huge growth rates, while a resurgence in exuberant and sometimes aggressive nationalism accompanied the transition to the status of dynamic global actor. Their education systems offered excellent basic skills. But, combined with extreme inequalities of wealth, this spawned a new class of young men, poor and unemployed, but – in contrast to earlier generations – with great material aspirations as they absorbed the consumer messages that are an intrinsic part of globalisation. To meet these aspirations, a minority started beavering away in Internet cafés, safe from detection by law enforcement or indeed anyone else, where they found myriad online opportunities to educate themselves in the art of hacking.

Turkey qualified as an honorary BRIC, with an economy that, when compared to Russia's, for example, looked much more dynamic. The country's population, at around eighty million, and its growth rates were increasing even faster than those of the acknowledged BRICs. Everyone recognised its strategic importance, nestling against the Black Sea and Mediterranean Sea while bordering Bulgaria, Greece, Iran, Iraq, Syria, Armenia: there is barely a neighbour that hasn't experienced a major upheaval or war in the past two decades. The unpredictable has been ever present in Turkish politics but, as the millennium turned, Turkey's burgeoning economic power and sophistication emphasised its pivotal role in several vital geo-strategic regions – the Middle East, Central Asia, the Black Sea and the Balkans.

The country had been slow to develop its Internet infrastructure in the 1990s, but in recent years it had begun to catch up rapidly. Istanbul, Turkey's economic engine, hosted an explosion of successful start-ups along with the design, media and service companies that benefited from them.

On the downside, the size of the country, its improving infrastructure and the broadening education of the youthful middle class represented an opportunity for cybercrime. Until Bilal Şen's unit was properly up and running in 2005, there was little to prevent crackers and hackers from operating on the Web from inside Turkey without fear of detection. The Cyber Crime Unit was beginning to make a difference, but it was an uphill struggle. If Inspector Şen were able to track down Cha0, it would be an important feather in the unit's cap.

But just before the Inspector was due to return to Turkey from Pittsburgh in mid-March 2008, he received another alert that further complicated his investigation into Cha0. This time his Istanbul contacts provided details of a baffling interview given to a well-known news organisation, Haber 7, by a Turkish hacker named Kier, who confessed that he was a fugitive from the law.

Haber 7's reputation was based in part on the spiritual backing it received from a huge domestic Islamist movement, called The Gülen Community, which promoted the philosophy of its leader, Fethullah Gülen, who was living in exile in the United States. As a Community news organisation, Haber 7 was broadly sympathetic to the governing AK Party, which was pro-Islamic but democratic.

The young hacker, Kier, had approached the news organisation to claim that not only did he know Cha0, but, he hinted, the person or

people behind DarkMarket's most successful mystery avatar were planning to expand his/their criminal empire. The article included a photograph of the hacker talking in an Istanbul café. The photograph was
taken from the back, but some of the hacker's profile was visible.

Bilal did not yet know that the hacker was a young man named Mert
Ortaç. This odd character was thought to be an accomplice of another
cyber criminal called Cryptos, who had been arrested in January 2008
for allegedly hacking into the Akbank, one of Turkey's biggest financial
institutions. In many respects, the Akbank case was a bigger deal than
DarkMarket because the team had actually hacked into the bank's main
system, by means of a vulnerability in its operating system. But neither
the Istanbul police nor the Anti-Organised Crime Division had the
faintest idea where Ortaç had been hiding. And suddenly he popped
up talking to a journalist.

Despite being under surveillance both by the Istanbul police and by a
posse of intelligence agents, Ortaç told the paper that he had given them
all the slip in December 2007 and gone underground. He had surfaced
only once to convey his strange and fragmented tale to the newspaper.

The Istanbul police were red-faced about his cameo appearance. The
implications of his interview – the ease with which he had evaded
capture – were troubling. To compound the police's misery, the hacker
warned them that the arrests in the Akbank case would have no impact
on the security of Turkish banks because an altogether more formidable
criminal was now in the process of skinning them for all the money
he could – and that his name was Cha0. (Bilal Şen, of course, had
heard of Cha0, but this was the first time he had been talked about in
public – and by a mystery man.)

Ortaç had alleged that Cha0 was being protected by government
officials. The interview at least confirmed for Şen that Cha0 existed.
Nonetheless, when he read it, the Inspector felt himself looking into
the abyss. Who could possibly be protecting Cha0, and why?

27

THE SUBLIME PORTAL

Looking up from his notes, Inspector Şen felt his unease gradually mutate into fear. Now, it emerged that Cha0 himself had sent a message to the news channel Haber 7 in response to Ortaç's interview. It was an extraordinary outburst, seasoned with strong pinches of megalomania and iron conviction. 'I am the ultimate Law Enforcer on Dark-Market,' he thundered. 'I prevent the work of cops and rippers. I create the rules and everyone will obey.'

The Inspector's contacts soon indicated that Cha0 might well be beyond the law. Şen spoke to his oldest friend in the Istanbul police. It was frightening stuff: both men were worried that Cha0 might have a mole inside the police, who would obviously be informing his boss of the investigation's progress. If they were unable to trust their team, their backup and, most importantly, their superiors, then how could they possibly take the case any further?

In the first interview Mert Ortaç had spoken a great deal about the secret police and other forces at work in the DarkMarket case. In some countries, this might smack of conspiracy paranoia, but in Turkey it would be unwise to discount it. Mert had implied that the entire Dark-Market operation could touch people at the very peak of economic, military or political power.

The country's complicated political structure had assumed a new shape since the AK Party became the dominant force there in the elections of 2002. Given that more than 90 per cent of Turks were Muslim, the fact that an avowedly Islamic party had won a landslide victory was not in itself surprising. The AK Party insisted that its religious faith was subordinate to its commitment to democracy, much as many moderate conservative parties in Europe refer to themselves as *Christian* Democrats.

But Turkey boasted another ideological tradition of immense power – Kemalism. Named after modern Turkey's founder, Kemal Atatürk, its guiding principle proposed the complete separation of Church and state. The ubiquitous presence of Atatürk's image in shops, homes, offices, barracks, hospitals and prisons reflected a deep reverence for his legacy of secularism among Turks (as well as a fear of arrest for non-compliance).

Kemalism, however, comes in a variety of flavours. Its two most fervent supporters come from the secular middle-class elite: intellectuals, professionals and civil servants on the one hand, and the so-called Deep State on the other. Both view the AK Party, and each other, with suspicion.

The Deep State is an appropriately sinister name for the military-industrial complex that acted as the ultimate arbiter of Turkish politics in the post-war period. As one of only two NATO members to share a border with the Soviet Union (the other was Norway), the country played a key role in the Cold War, and its allies, led by the US, were happy to turn a blind eye to the egregious abuses inflicted by the military on its own population.

During its repeated interference in political life, Turkey's security establishment sank its teeth deep into the country's economy as well, until it was sometimes hard to distinguish between the predator and the prey. It protected this enmeshed and lucrative involvement by appealing to Kemalism: if it considered its business interests were threatened by the fragile democratic order, the military would intervene, claiming the need to protect the Atatürk heritage. By tradition, the armed forces let nothing or anybody stand in their way. To paraphrase an old Turkish saying, 'Shake hands with the Deep State and it'll rip your arm off.'

But for the last fifteen years or so successive Turkish governments have instigated a series of reforms, partly in a bid to meet the membership criteria of the European Union. Notwithstanding fears that it has a hidden extremist Islamist agenda, the new rulers from the AK Party have pushed through some of the most liberal changes in Turkish society, such as the abolition of the death penalty. In another attempt to consolidate the primacy of the rule of law, the AK Party has been weaning the country's regular police forces away from the military.

This process has led to some remarkable and very positive changes. Parts of the civil service began to understand that their primary job was not to feather their own nests, but to provide services to ordinary people; and that an efficient Turkish state enhances its international influence and standing.

But the slow birth of a new Turkey has not been a painless process, nor has the outcome ever been predictable. It has been accompanied by a titanic political struggle in which shifting alliances between opaque forces can prove deadly for anybody who, wittingly or unwittingly, comes between them.

The main theatre of war between these forces was opened officially in 2007 with the launch of the so-called Ergenekon investigation. Ergenekon, which refers to an epic legend of ancient Turkic lore, was more recently the name of an alleged Deep State conspiracy, which saw leading military, intelligence and political figures collaborate with organised crime, journalists, lawyers and other professionals. Their supposed aim was to restrict the influence of democratically elected governments, in particular the AK Party. But according to prosecutors and pro-government media, the plot went further – the Ergenekon members were planning a military coup in 2009 to restore the power of the Deep State over the elected government.

Since 2007 police have made hundreds of arrests of senior military and intelligence figures in what are called the Ergenekon 'waves'. But along with these, they have picked up dozens of journalists and lawyers whom they accuse of working with Ergenekon for pecuniary or ideological advantage. The small but articulate class of liberal intellectuals and the larger middle class have warned that the democratic government is resorting to the sort of intimidation usually associated with the Deep State. In a sign of the times, the Ergenekon indictment relies heavily on digital evidence – mobile-phone taps, instant messaging and computer files, demonstrating the growing cyber abilities of the domestic intelligence services.

Bilal Şen had no role to play in any of this, except that his diligence, commitment and youthful energy appeared to align him with the new Turkey rather than the old. Yet, like most Turks, he was keenly aware of the sensitive political context within which he and everyone else worked. The last thing any Turkish cop wanted was to become an innocent pawn crushed in a struggle between the Deep State and the democratically constituted government. Almost all Turks avoided public discussion of Ergenekon if they could. But all knew that the Ergenekon investigation hovered in the background of many major criminal cases, whether or not it contained overt political implications.

Bilal would have to take care, but he was not about to give up the chase.

While in Pittsburgh, he and Mularski developed a firm friendship and the FBI agent shared all the intelligence he could on Cha0. Between the two of them, they began to build on their sparse dossier. Mularski was able to call on his vast archive as one of DarkMarket's key players, and Şen was able to read the Turkish runes. The Inspector wanted to assess Cha0's personality to see if it matched any known cyber criminals back home: a lot of documents were scanned, then sent back and forth between Ankara, Istanbul and Pittsburgh.

If things weren't baffling enough already, they took an even stranger turn soon after Inspector Şen returned home to Ankara. A weird image was circulating on the Web.

Bilal could barely contain his anger and frustration. Agent Mularski had sent him a photograph, which had appeared on Haber 7's website and then the San Francisco-based *Wired* magazine. Sitting on a chair in his underpants was the mystery man, Kier, being compelled, it appeared, to hold up a piece of paper on which was written:

1   I AM KIER. MY REAL NAME IS MERT ORTAÇ

2   I AM PARTNER OF THE MEDIA

3   I AM RAT. I AM PIG.

4   I AM REPORTER

5   I AM FUCKED BY Cha0

Half of Istanbul's police force was looking in vain for Kier – or Mert Ortaç, to give him his real name – but Cha0 had succeeded not only in tracking him down, but in kidnapping and humiliating him as well. It was perfectly possible that the man's life was in danger. What in God's name was going on?

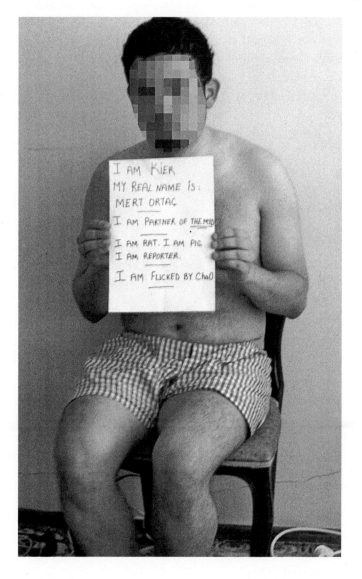

For Bilal Şen, it was axiomatic that to take at face value anything related to the Web was unwise. As an experienced surfer of criminal boards and a student of people's Internet behaviour, he knew that people lied, cheated, exaggerated, deceived and conspired as a matter of course. But the history of DarkMarket in Europe, and especially in Turkey, went beyond this quotidian dissimulation to evolve into a surreal tale of skulduggery, espionage and betrayal. And one with no apparent end.

Part II

28

CIAO, CHA0

From his research on DarkMarket with Keith Mularski, Inspector Şen knew that Cha0 had his own website: *CrimeEnforcers.com* (a play on the phrase Law Enforcers, which the criminal fraternity long ago reduced to the acronym LE as it cropped up so frequently in online discussions).

On the CrimeEnforcers home page, Cha0 explained its aims and services:

> *We are private organisation for your special developing requests. We are focused at Electronic and Computer Engineering. If you need special hardwares (especially hi-tech) nor software that can not be done or even discuss in your Country because of any reason such as laws etc. then u are at the very right place.*
>
> *We are offering absolutely anonymous & offshore developing for your projects. We dont care what you want to do with hardwares and softwares you requested to be done by us.*
>
> *Needless to say, your privacy is very important for us and we dont share with anyone else because of any reason. We don't need your Name, Adress etc. We only need your email. You will have a certificate and account for secure login to our private forum for tracking your development, you even may ask question to engineers who engineering your project.*
>
> *If you reach this Web Site then you already know us. We are not cheap developers and we cant make partnership with you. If you wish to your dreams to come true then u have to have*

enough money to invest for your dreams. You even have to pay
for request for quote from us for your project.

Once you adapted to his slightly mangled Globish, Cha0's business plan became clear. He was offering logistical services and backup for anyone interested in exploring a career in cybercrime. Rather than commit the crimes himself, he was making it easier for less-skilled computer users to engage in the practice. Computer crime was beginning to ape business models from the real world.

On other pages of *CrimeEnforcers.com* you could review Cha0's wares. His signature product was the skimmer, and it was not long before Cha0's mail-order service for skimming devices flourished into a significant business.

CrimeEnforcers also offered mobile credit-card readers – portable point-of-sale (POS) devices of the sort you find in most restaurants. In early 2007 police officers in several parts of England uncovered a ring of petrol-station attendants who had bought a job lot of these devices, which, it is thought, originated either from the Canadian DarkMarketeer, Dron, or from Cha0's factory. When the customer handed over a credit card, the attendant would swipe it deftly under the counter through the illegal reader to register its details, before swiping it again through the legitimate machine.

For those taking their first uncertain steps in the field of cyber criminality, CrimeEnforcers was replete with helpful tips that made the process so much easier. For absolute beginners, CrimeEnforcers posted helpful videos in which an animated Cha0, blessed with an electronic voice that still betrayed the distinctive timbre and lilt of the real man, offered tips and guides on how to choose the best ATMs when planning to execute a crime.

He taught his audience, for example, that installing skimmers on ATMs where there was a high concentration of illegal immigrants was a bad idea (not much ATM traffic, a lot of prying eyes and too much criminal competition). Instead, he suggested placing them near night-clubs, 'where rich children will often use their parents' credit cards'.

As a reliable supplier to criminal industries, Cha0 saw his name spread rapidly across the Internet, so it became extremely important to him to consolidate his reputation and escape detection.

Axiomatic was the general use of Globish, a second language of bastardised English, which had become the lingua franca of the Web, acting as a cipher that enabled Brazilians to communicate with Koreans and Bulgarians with Indonesians; soon the spelling and usage of even native English-speakers started to develop in many peculiar directions on the Internet. One could hazard a guess at the origin of a message-poster, but it was usually impossible to identify with any accuracy his or her nationality.

The same did not apply to Russian or Chinese. Posters on Russian-language criminal websites littered their comments with local slang, which some linguists may have been able to follow, but only the most gifted would be able to replicate without being spotted as a non-native speaker. FBI agents would give nothing away on an English-language board, but on a Russian board they would have a struggle getting past the first login. Although US law-enforcement and intelligence officers have used native Russian and Chinese speakers on occasions, they have certainly never possessed anything approaching the financial and linguistic resources to take control of a Russian site in the way they partially appropriated DarkMarket.

On English-language sites, however, one was much less certain of an interlocutor's true identity. The agency of the Web enabled, and even encouraged, people to change their personalities. This was by no means restricted to the criminal world. Dating sites were already home to some of the most sustained and intense mendacity in history. In chat rooms, people liked to impart a sense of their own talent and importance, which rarely corresponded to the mundane reality of their lives. The Web fostered this because people were unable to check up on their virtual partners' behavioural traits. Everyone was discovering that on the Web they could lie without fear of exposure or opprobrium.

Criminals were not only subject to the same laws on duplicity, but were especially good practitioners. DarkMarket provided ample proof. In chatlogs the fiendish Devilman, for example, would project an image of a young fast-living ladeez' man (although he reserved his most persistent affection for cheap 'dumps'). But when detectives knocked on the door of 62 Lime Tree Grove, Doncaster, the two-up, two-down semi where Devilman's real-life alter ego, John McHugh, resided, they were greeted by a man in his early sixties whose first response on being informed of his arrest was, 'Would you mind if I go and put my dentures in first?' In court, when it came to sentencing, he included among his mitigating circumstances the fact that he had already had one hip replaced and was waiting on a second, so his mobility was severely restricted.

But serious cyber criminals had to generate trust to do business: their reputation was crucial. In DarkMarket, you could only achieve the title of Vendor by proving to the administrators and to the satisfaction of the buyers that you could provide the market with stolen credit cards that genuinely worked. These transactions were overseen by five administrators (three after JiLsi was thrown off the site and Matrix arrested) – Master Splyntr, Shtirlitz and Cha0 (and later Lord Cyric played a role, too).

Cha0 joined DarkMarket in February 2006, but his considerable abilities ensured a rapid rise up the hierarchy. Once he had consolidated his position as a prince of DarkMarket, he was able to focus on his real business strategy. He wanted to become the premier vendor of skimming machines and illegal readers worldwide. There was a significant demand for these devices and, if he could create a monopoly, then he would move into the next phase of his plan for maximising his revenue with minimal effort.

Our man from Istanbul was also in charge of DarkMarket's crucial Escrow Service, perhaps the pivotal position in the entire operation. Acting as an honest broker, he would ensure that neither a buyer nor seller of credit cards and other illegal data could rip each other off. In that sense, DarkMarket was a mafia operation in the original meaning of the phrase. It acted as the policeman or arbitrator of a criminal market, just as the men of honour started by policing the agricultural markets of Sicily in the second half of the nineteenth century, before moving into the trade in illegal weapons and building permits.

Cha0's reputation as a scrupulously honest escrow broker was built on his success as a wholesaler of skimming machines. Everybody trusted him. He, by contrast, trusted no one. He never gave away his IP address; he never sent a message that might implicate him in wrongdoing without encrypting it; and nobody could locate him digitally.

Accepting that Cha0 had created a black hole in cyberspace where he was safe and invisible from the cops, Bilal Şen decided he would have to rely on more traditional policing methods to track down his suspect – the 'plod' factor has proved surprisingly important in the work of cybercops.

29

SOFTLY SOFTLY

Istanbul, Turkey, 2008

Still anxious that Cha0 might enjoy protection from above, Bilal Şen nonetheless persevered with his investigation. He promised to maintain close contact with Agent Mularski in Pittsburgh once he had returned to Istanbul. They had discussed the possibility of requesting the use of Cha0's Escrow Service on DarkMarket to see if they could smoke him out that way, but quickly concluded that this was too laborious and unlikely to yield results.

The other thing they knew about him, of course, was that he traded in skimmers. Digitally he was impossible to track down. But if Cha0 was selling these skimmers, Bilal reasoned, there were two weak points to his operation – their manufacture and their dispatch.

Skimming ATMs was becoming such a popular sport in Turkey that ever more police officers were now schooled in how to spot them, once they had been put in place. Many of the devices were shoddily built and installed by amateurs. But flicking through the arrest and confiscation reports, the Inspector had observed that in some areas their design and style were not only improving, but it appeared that they were being manufactured in large numbers. Somewhere there must be a factory. Intelligence alerted Şen to the possible presence of skimmer factories in Romania and Bulgaria, so he sent out assistance requests to their respective police forces. The other possibility was that Cha0's operation was masquerading as a legitimate business and ordering them from licensed manufacturers of card readers inside Turkey.

Once he had acquired the skimmers, Cha0 would somehow have to distribute them. Mularski and Şen had uncovered some evidence suggesting that his products were going as far abroad as the United States, New Zealand and South America, and that some were bulk purchases. In that event, he was unlikely to be using personal couriers. Given the numbers he was beginning to shift, this was probably prohibitively complicated. Bilal pondered the reasons for the increase in productivity, but drew a blank.

He was unaware that one year earlier, in the late spring of 2007, Cha0 had fallen out with Dron, the Canadian skimmer specialist whom the Secret Service and Detective Spencer Frizzell of the Calgary Police were preparing to arrest. Cha0 claimed that Dron was 'a difficult character' who irritated his customers and had therefore sullied the good reputation of DarkMarket. The many positive messages about Dron's service suggested that Cha0's motivation may have been different – certainly other carders on the board maintained that Cha0 had deliberately targeted Dron for his own reasons.

About a month before the young Canadian skimming expert and salesman was picked up by Detective Frizzell, Cha0, using his position as administrator, announced that Dron would be excluded from Dark-Market and would not be allowed back. Cha0 could now activate his plan to dominate the skimming market and move into action.

DarkMarket had provided a vital platform for Dron's wares – a large number of his devices were sold to carders who had spotted his paid adverts on the board. DarkMarket was also used as the primary advertising vehicle for *CrimeEnforcers.com*, through which Cha0 was selling his own skimmers. Cha0 also offered packaged solutions to wannabe cyber criminals, including training, manuals and all the equipment needed for a start-up operation.

But once he had removed Dron from the equation, he changed his business model: interested parties were no longer at liberty to purchase his skimmers; they had to hire them instead. Cha0 would send them out, but with a little added modification.

After Dron's expulsion, Cha0 was in a position to jack up the unit price of the skimmers – from now on they would cost $7,000 to hire, up from $5,000 to buy. For this, clients would receive a PIN pad along with the skimmer. They would install the skimmer on the mouth of an ATM and lay the PIN pad over the existing one. When bank customers inserted their cards and typed in their PINs, these were both recorded on the fake pad and the skimmer. The two fraudulent devices would then be detached and Cha0's client would download the information onto a computer using a USB lead.

With Dron's skimmers, the client would then be able to use that information to obtain funds fraudulently. But with Cha0's skimmers, the data downloaded onto the computer was encrypted. The only person who possessed the key to decrypt this information was . . . Cha0. So the youthful criminal who had so painstakingly placed the skimmer and PIN pad onto the ATM could not simply go out and clone credit cards himself – he would have to send the information back to Istanbul. Cha0 would then organise the cash-out. Once he had the money, he would then send a cut to the client who had actually done the hard work. He was effectively renting out his skimmers – a much more profitable strategy than Dron's outright selling.

This was a daring business model within the world of cyber criminality. If it succeeded, Cha0 stood to make untold sums, creaming off a huge percentage of illegal skimmer transactions around the world. All he had to do was maintain his supply of skimmers and ship them forward, without being detected. Not beyond the wit of man. Obviously there might come a time when a competitor might seek to undercut his strategy, or indeed return to the old-style simple sale of skimmers. But until then, by controlling the most influential board in the English-speaking world, Cha0 could enjoy the high life. And enjoy it he did.

By 2008 Istanbul was well on the way to becoming the city with the highest growth rate in the world. The population had been rising almost uncontrollably for fifteen years and it was now home to about fifteen million people, an estimated two million of whom were unregistered migrants, not just foreigners, but Turks and Kurds from Anatolia who were streaming into the city that straddled the mighty Bosphorus, the grand body of water separating Europe and Asia.

In contrast to many cities in East Asia, notably in China, Istanbul has not achieved this phenomenal and invigorating growth at the expense of its glittering legacy. History inhabits almost every building. Everywhere reveals the rich traditions of more than a millennium of Byzantine history and 600 years of Ottoman grandeur – two of the most magical, violent, successful and awe-inspiring imperial constructs of all time. Contrary to popular imagination, for much of its history the Ottoman Empire was renowned for the tolerance that its rulers displayed towards the three 'Peoples of the Book', Jews, Christians and Muslims. Its reputation for violence originated in the bloody massacres of its distant past, only to re-emerge during its slow demise in the nineteenth and early twentieth centuries.

In the Turkish republic that arose from the ashes of Empire after the First World War, Istanbul had experienced some depressing times: first, when its status as the country's capital was lost to Ankara, an Anatolian upstart to the east; and later, during the Cold War, when a merciless military sought to suppress the city's independent spirit. Its infrastructure began to crumble and people actually started moving away, its population stagnating at about two million. But since the early 1990s Istanbul had been making swift strides towards regaining its place at the top table of the world's most dynamic and intriguing cities.

Crowded, noisy and exuberant, with economic activity flying back and forth between its European and Asian sectors, Istanbul could sometimes feel suffocating, as tens of thousands of rickety cars and trucks plied their way across its two continental bridges. On the European side, the traffic shuffled at a snail's pace around Taksim Square or along Dolmabahçe, the former imperial gardens, which looked across at Asia. Even when the weather was cool, the dust kicked into the back of the throat. But in the last decade, the city has been brimming with possibilities – artistic, commercial and political – and there can be few greater pleasures in life, at the end of a hard day's work, than taking a ferry from Europe while staring at the Bosphorus and heading for a scrumptious meal in Kadıköy on the Asian side.

For all the fears that the ruling AK Party might represent a fifth column of Islamic fundamentalism, since it came to power Istanbul's youthful middle class has seized economic opportunity with both hands and begun to create successful manufacturing, design, high-tech and service companies that compete with the best from Europe, America and Asia.

Of course, policing the city is a complete nightmare, especially since few inhabitants have any trust in a force that for many decades was a key symbol of the repressive state apparatus.

New crimes engendered a new breed of cop, and Bilal was not associated with any of the old traditions of the Deep State, nor had he antagonised any especially powerful people, so he was welcomed in

Istanbul when he arrived from Turkey's capital, Ankara, aiming to discover the distribution network for Cha0's skimming operation.

This being Istanbul, however, Inspector Şen was looking for a needle in a haystack. Legal, semi-legal and illegal export/import had for centuries been a trademark of the city's economy – shifting goods out and bringing them in. Since the 1960s vast quantities of white goods had found their way to Istanbul through the Balkans from Germany, where some two million Turks had migrated since the 1960s as *Gastarbeiter*. But the volume of this trade had gone through the roof since the collapse of the Soviet Union: new markets had opened up in Russia, Ukraine, the Caucasus and in several Central Asian republics with their Turkic languages.

But Bilal had to start somewhere and so he chose the three biggest shipping firms in the city. First, he and his assistants spent half a day training the staff of the courier companies in the art of spotting a skimmer. They are most often registered as spare parts for vehicles or as machine tools. The staff were given skimmers to handle, to get used to their weight and shape.

Unproductive days went by and Inspector Şen decided he should return to headquarters in Ankara. Weeks passed and he began to experience a familiar despondency. But then, just over a month later, some good news came through from Istanbul – a man had entered one of the shipping companies with a package bound for Finland. It turned out to be a skimming device. The receptionist was calling from the back office with the news that the package had also included a PIN pad.

'Bingo!' thought Bilal, telling the receptionist to let the sender go: they had already captured his image on CCTV. After many months the Inspector had at last hit upon a lead. Unsurprisingly the man had used a fake ID, but then Bilal got a second break. The suspect had also given the courier company three phone numbers – and one of them was a real. They checked the name to identify the legal owner of the phone: it didn't seem to belong to a criminal. But they monitored the mobile number, and the man with the package was using it – the phone was active.

'This might be the guy who will lead us to Cha0,' thought Bilal.

But he was faced with a dilemma. It was at about this time that the news organisation, Haber 7, published the photograph of the humiliated hacker, Mert Ortaç, and pressure was ramping up both on the Istanbul police, who were tasked with finding Ortaç, and on Bilal, whose primary target was Cha0. Bilal had to speed things up, but he knew he must not allow impatience to jeopardise the operation.

By abducting Ortaç, Cha0 had betrayed anxiety and vulnerability for the first time. But why had Ortaç's revelations in Haber 7 so unsettled him?

Cha0 knew that Ortaç was Turkish. Cha0 also seemed to believe that Ortaç was a police informant. Furthermore, he had worked out that Ortaç was on the run and in a state of fear. If the police had picked him up before Cha0 did, there was a real risk he might start blabbing.

But who on earth was Mert Ortaç and how had he become involved in this extraordinary criminal affair? It had all begun the previous spring when, unbeknownst to Ortaç, Matrix and JiLsi were about to be arrested, marking the end of Phase I in Operation DarkMarket and the beginning of Phase II.

Part III

ORIENTATION

Within a year DarkMarket had taken me a long way from the head-quarters of Google to a restaurant in Cihangir, the chic district just below Taksim Square in European Istanbul. Opposite me danced the effervescent smile of Mert Ortaç. After spending several hours in his company, I concluded that the adjective 'mischievous' had never fitted anything on this earth as snugly as it did Mert.

During one lazy dinner in Kadıköy, my friend, Şebnem, and I had our iPhones lying on the table. Suddenly, they alerted us to the simul-taneous arrival of text messages. My message had been sent from Şebnem's phone. Şebnem's from mine. Both read, 'Greetings from Mert!' As we read the texts, Mert's bubbling laughter burst from across the table, along with an explanation that he had successfully hacked the international roaming system. As a result, he continued, he was in a position to send a message from any mobile phone in the world to any other – in the wrong hands (like Mert's), such a skill could turn life into an endless series of Shakespearean plots based on misunder-standings, both tragic and comic.

I had been corresponding with Mert while he was in jail, from where he had sent me snippets of a tale that outdid all other DarkMarket legends in its sheer invention. Whereas I was conscious, when talking to most other characters involved in DarkMarket, that they were holding things back, Mert was overflowing with information, anecdotes and mind-boggling stories.

It is critical that hackers, cyber criminals and cybercops maintain a full grip on their compartmentalised lives – they must know the bound-aries between the real and virtual, and they must be able to disengage as they move from one life to the other. Mert had utterly failed to identify in his own mind when he was speaking the truth and when not.

Life would have been incomparably easier if Mert had been an unashamed fantasist who simply talked nonsense. Tracking down the hackers, members and cops associated with DarkMarket was among the most enervating experiences in my journalistic career. But nothing was quite so exasperating as the attempt to establish the veracity of Mert's story. Actually, that is not quite accurate: much of his tale turned out to be true and verifiable in essence, but embellished at times with such frills and twirls that it was transformed into something quite different. Bizarrely, when Mert told straight untruths, they often related to the most mundane matters that were the easiest to check. He told me boldly, for example, that he was born on 10th April 1982. In fact, he was born on the same day four years later.

In the following chapters I tell Mert's story largely as he told it to me. But there are two key moments when his narrative simply doesn't add up, where I am unable to confirm his claims; indeed, in the first instance, one of the main characters flatly denies Mert's version of events. When we arrive at those moments, I will alert the reader.

The ultimate test of Mert's credibility lay in his answer to the question that has vexed many aficionados of the cyber underground since the inception of DarkMarket. Who was Lord Cyric?

30

THE DREAM WORLD OF MERT ORTAÇ

Istanbul, Turkey, May 2007

Mert Ortaç drew in his breath as he was shown into the drawing room of the opulent guesthouse. The room reminded him of the Sultan Suite at the Çirağan Palace, the late nineteenth-century masterpiece built at the behest of his imperial highness, Sultan Abdülaziz, and acquired more recently by the Kempiński hotel chain. Swirls of gold leaf adorned the sofas and chairs, while the wallpaper, with its Arabic patterns, glittered as it caught the sun.

In fact, the Çirağan Palace stood only 800 yards away from the guesthouse, which was itself sealed off in a heavily guarded compound. Agents stalked the environs and scowled at anybody with the temerity to try to park there. Set at the very edge of Beşiktaş district, the mansion stared imperiously from atop a hill in Europe, across the Bosphorus Straits to Asia. Most surprising was that the drawing room, into which they had shown Mert, boasted no portrait of Kemal Atatürk, modern Turkey's revered founder. Portraits of Kemal are de rigueur throughout Turkey, and not just in private and public offices: they will often be found in every room of a building. Not in this room, though, despite this being the guesthouse at the Istanbul regional headquarters of the Milli İstihbarat Teşkilati (MİT), Turkey's National Intelligence Agency.

In most anxiety-inducing situations, Mert would react either by giggling gently behind his infectiously mischievous smile or he would cut and run. On this occasion, neither was appropriate. Mert was transfixed by the elegant waiters as they served tea and coffee. Above

all, the image of their immaculate white gloves as they placed the
refreshments on the table in front of him stayed in his mind. He felt
a surreal sense of well-being and controlled excitement. But this did
not last long.

Accompanying him was a colleague from the Senior Sciences Technology Institute, but Mert did not know the three others who greeted
him. Once the waiters had silently withdrawn, these men turned their
attention to Mert. 'We wish to ask you a few questions,' one of them
began. Then they placed a digital recorder on the table in front of him.

Before long he was sweating under the pressure of the interrogation.
But this was not the third degree. Instead, for six and a half hours
Mert was required to solve a set of fiendishly difficult mathematical
problems. Under normal circumstances he would not even have
attempted answering them without a computer. His three hosts asked
him to use a methodology popular in coding that involved dividing the
number fifty-two into odd numbers. It was highly advanced maths and
he only had a pen and paper to assist him.

The young computer programmer had already failed the selection
exam that would have made him eligible as a probationary member of
the Intelligence Agency. He passed his foreign-language test (English)
and his maths, but failed his Turkish-language exam abysmally. Nonetheless the Agency was still fascinated by his computer skills. His
programming ability was genuinely remarkable and he had an extraordinary record, so they took him on as a freelance collaborator.

Back in 2003 Mert was the subject of a criminal investigation for
fraud. He was only seventeen at the time, but he had succeeded in
cracking the code that encrypted the smart cards used by the satellite
television station Digiturk. This was a lucrative skill. Digiturk had
recently won the rights to broadcast the Süper Lig, the wildly popular
top flight of Turkish football. To decrypt the channel, subscribers had
to buy a smart card from Digiturk and slip it into the satellite receiver
before being ushered into soccer heaven.

Once Mert had worked out how to crack these cards, he set about
reproducing them for illegal sale on the streets of Istanbul, pulling in
significant sums of money in the process. No sooner were the Turkish
lire filling up one pocket than they were pouring out of the other. Mert
would throw parties for friends whom he would invite up from Ankara,
paying for their travel and accommodation once they reached Istanbul.

He was never able to control his spending, even later on when he was making considerable sums of money from his carding activities.

Mert's friends were very important to him, in part because he sometimes found affection hard to come by. Whether he was aware of it or not, he used the Digiturk money to buy friendship – and there were plenty of twenty-somethings in Istanbul who were prepared to become pals with a young man apparently willing to underwrite expensive partying. Of course, whenever the money ran out, most of those characters went missing.

He was also desperate to prove that he was something special (which, given his computer talents, he undoubtedly was). And so he would systematically exaggerate his achievements. As this tendency developed, so did Mert's consciousness start to float permanently between reality and fantasy. He seemed to lose the ability to distinguish between the two at an early stage. So complete was this meshing that, were he ever to take a lie-detector test, it would probably either go off the scale or not register a blip. Of course, in one respect this meant that he adapted to the culture of the Internet – the valley of lies – with ease.

Following a series of jobs in IT for various companies, Mert was taken on, in June 2006, by the local concession of Toshiba, whose personnel department failed to spot that he was under criminal investigation for the Digiturk fraud. Nonetheless, it did not take long for Mert's colleagues at Toshiba to start wondering at some of his behaviour. They were also a touch suspicious of the certificate which purported to show that he had a degree in the Science of Cryptology from the University of Cambridge.

The trustees, so read the certificate, 'have granted this diploma as evidence thereof given in the city of London in the Cambridge at the twenty-second day of june two thousand four'.

Perhaps they conferred the diploma in the Cambridge Arms in the City of London? Wherever the fictitious ceremony had taken place, the certificate was so crude that it hardly merited the epithet 'counterfeit'.

One of his colleagues at Toshiba's IT department was struck by how often Mert boasted about his relationship with National Intelligence. He, too, had offered occasional assistance to the spooks, especially in the late 1990s when the Agency had yet to develop its own effective cyber division. But one did not brag about such matters. Mert's constant mutterings about his close relationship with intelligence really did jar.

However, Toshiba kept him for six months because whenever his bosses there asked him to come up with a solution to a problem, he invariably delivered the goods. He struck them as smart, but something told them to keep a close eye on him.

Of an evening, Mert would be called in by his control at the Intelligence Agency and asked to give a forensic assessment of various hard disks and computers, which they had conjured up seemingly from nowhere. He was supposed to gut the files, crack passwords where possible and deliver any incriminating materials. The Agency's primary responsibility was for Turkey's domestic security and it was tasked with monitoring the wide range of organisations that the government deemed were engaged in terrorism.

Towards the end of 2006 Toshiba sacked Mert – his attitude was not right, he boasted a little too much about his dubious exploits with credit cards, and yet he was also constantly asking his colleagues for loans or bonus payments.

Mert claimed that he left Toshiba on the instructions of his handlers at National Intelligence. They were working on finding him another cover job, he said.

Just before he began work at his new post, his handler brought him a hard disk that formed part of a highly sensitive investigation. Control wanted to know everything about each file on the disk, whether visible or hidden, accessible or encrypted. The disk belonged to a senior member of a left-wing underground organisation known by its acronym, the DHKP/C.

During the 1990s and early 2000s the DHKP/C had been one of the most violent and effective left-wing organisations committed to armed struggle in Turkey. The Revolutionary People's Liberation Party/ Front (the Party was the political wing and the Front, in theory, the military wing) was a splinter group from Dev Yol, the larger revolutionary movement, which bore the brunt of military repression during the 1970s and 1980s.

This group was no tinpot outfit – it took its politics and its terrorism seriously, concentrating primarily on attacking the collaboration between what it denounced as NATO imperialism and the Turkish military establishment. It carried out successful assassinations against Turkish, American and British citizens who were either influential businessmen or linked to the military. In contrast to most leftist armed outfits, it boasted a sophisticated counter-intelligence capacity and, as such, was one of National Intelligence's trickiest surveillance targets.

On one raid agents had picked up a laptop, and it was handed to Mert in the guesthouse where he was first interviewed and where he now always worked. His handler explained that the user had been accessing a website called DarkMarket. The handler was also a geek and told Mert that he had followed DarkMarket's connections as far as a server in Singapore, which looked to him like a proxy. After that, he said, he lost the digital trail. He knew nothing about who was behind this site, although the evidence strongly suggested to him that the DHKP/C was involved in carding as a way of maximising its revenue and perhaps also investigating the use of botnets and whether this might assist the DHKP/C in achieving its goals.

Suddenly DarkMarket was no longer just a criminal website: it was helping to fund a designated terrorist organisation.

Did Mert, the handler asked, know anything about this site?

Mert did not. He, too, tracked DarkMarket's server back to Singapore, but try as he might he could not trace it any further. This was in fact thanks to Grendel's sterling efforts. Nonetheless, Mert told his handler he knew somebody who might be better acquainted with DarkMarket.

Mert was tired. National Intelligence invariably expected him to complete these assignments overnight. His new job was working for the Turkish concession of Fox TV. Fox Turkey was not wholly owned by Rupert Murdoch's News International because, according to Turkish law, a local citizen had to control 51 per cent of the stock. This majority shareholder was a former diplomat who was known to have links to the police and secret service. At Fox, Mert's colleagues noticed that he was frequently, if not always, distracted. And that he would find it difficult to finish even simple jobs – not because he couldn't do them, but because he was up to something else at the same time.

One of Mert's contacts had asked the young man to keep an eye out for a certain Sadun Özkaya, a middle-class teenager whose parents were worried that he was straying. He had just been extracted from jail, where he was under investigation for fraud. The contact asked Mert to keep Sadun on the straight and narrow – which was like engaging a wolf to preach the benefits of veganism to another wolf, as the two of them lick their chops over the remains of a juicy young lamb.

Mert knew about cryptography and programming; Sadun knew about credit cards. Before long the two were pooling their skills. And, to Mert's astonishment, Sadun told him that he was a member of Dark-Market, which he visited using two nicknames, Cryptos and PilotM. Within hours Mert Ortaç was logging in as the latter.

O, wonder! thought Mert as he espied the innards of DarkMarket for the first time:

> How many goodly creatures are there here!
> How beauteous mankind is! O brave new world,
> That has such people in't!

Mert was transfixed. He explored every nook and cranny of the website, looking into its forums, learning to imitate its argot and then trying to uncover its secrets through slightly more devious means. Until now, Mert's criminal aspirations had been focused on the area of smart-card decryption and selling cloned cards once he had cracked their coding system. Let loose on DarkMarket, he was quickly picking up new tips about credit-card fraud. The combination of these skills would lead him and Sadun into some very murky, if financially nutritious, waters.

Before that, however, he started to map everything about DarkMarket as if it were an underground maze with hidden traps and treasures. His bosses at National Intelligence of course wanted to uncover anything that related to DHKP/C, the terrorist organisation they were investigating. But Mert was more interested in everything else that was going on across the boards.

He very quickly understood that Cha0, Master Splyntr, Shtirlitz and Lord Cyric were key members of the site. By the time Mert started playing on DarkMarket, JiLsi and Matrix001 had already been taken down.

It took him only seconds to figure out that Cha0 was Turkish, although this was entirely by accident and had nothing to do with his hacking skills. He was browsing the advertisements for Cha0's skimming machines when he spotted a Turkish sign for a doner kebab in the background. On another photo a skimmer for sale was standing next to some Turkish washing powder.

He relayed the news about the heavy Turkish influence on the website to his supervisor at the Intelligence Agency, who became even more interested in DarkMarket: not only were there left-wing terrorists active on the site, but it was actually run by Turks! This could be something major, so it required further investigation. Mert was given the authority to make contact with Cha0 and any other Turks that he found loitering around the DarkMarket board. It was not long before he thought he had identified another – Lord Cyric.

Mert started searching the archives of the early 1990s, when many geeks were using something called the BBS, or Bulletin Board Service, a bridge between an electronic messaging system and the Internet. As he was looking through the logs, his jaw dropped when he came across two familiar nicknames, sitting side by side: Cha0 and Lord Cyric! It would appear, he deduced, that these two masterminds of DarkMarket had known each other for a very long time.

31

A SERVANT OF
TWO MASTERS

The fictional Lord Cyric had become popular among gamers and geeks in the 1980s and early 1990s. He was a self-appointed deity who haunted The Forgotten Realms, a godforsaken fantasy world where warriors roamed to seek out treasure and dark secrets while vanquishing creatures with magical powers and destructive urges. The Realms became a favourite territory for gamers to explore once they had assumed a fantasy role in a team of adventurers playing Dungeons and Dragons. Subsequently, these Badlands of a sub-Tolkienian world appeared in a variety of computer games, including the hugely popular Baldur's Gate.

They were also described in many novels that were inspired in equal measure by Dungeons and Dragons and the Lord of the Rings. The figure of Lord Cyric had a crucial part to play in the mythology of the Forgotten Realms – in addition to being a god, he was thoroughly evil. More importantly for the world of carding and DarkMarket, Cyric was known *inter alia* as the Prince of Lies, whose satanic powers included a mastery of deception and illusion as well as the ability to promote strife and intrigue.

Whoever lay behind the avatar in CardersMarket, DarkMarket and elsewhere, he or she wanted to project the concept of what Dungeons and Dragons gamers refer to as 'chaotic evil', implying that the character scatters the seeds of mayhem and despair arbitrarily wherever he or she may roam. That certainly fitted DarkMarket's Lord Cyric as snugly as his penchant for deception, illusion, strife and intrigue. Few carders generated as much hostility in the community as this character did. His speciality was to spread accusations through rumour and innuendo.

For reasons never understood, Cyric would pick a target, like RedBrigade, who had exploited Shadowcrew to such lucrative effect in New York. Then he would set out to destroy his reputation among fellow carders with a thousand cuts. A little hint here or a little insinuation there that RedBrigade was not all he appeared, or coded drop-ins to suggest that RedBrigade was in fact working for law and order. His language was snarky and childish, yet carefully designed to cause maximum distress to the target of his attacks.

Yet Cyric had his champions, too – none more stalwart than Cha0. With an oversized brain and a superiority complex to match, Cha0 only ever recognised two computer users as his equal. His contempt for the FBI's cyber division was boundless, but he warmly acknowledged the hacking skills of Max Vision, aka Iceman, even though the two had often found themselves at loggerheads due to Iceman's attacks on DarkMarket. And when talking of Lord Cyric, Cha0 almost went so far as to recognise his old friend as being even more elevated in the hackers' pantheon than he himself was.

In a short space of time, Lord Cyric had succeeded in positioning himself as a key moderator and administrator on boards like The Grifters, CardersMarket and finally DarkMarket. Nobody understood what his game was or what he was trying to achieve, although those whom he targeted immediately assumed that he was working for law enforcement either as an officer or as a confidential informant.

In Pittsburgh, FBI Agent Keith Mularski had no idea. Like many others, he believed that the person behind Lord Cyric lived in Montreal, Canada, but his enquiries of the Royal Canadian Mounted Police cyber division brought him no joy. In fact, although Cyric's IP addresses could be traced to Montreal, they would occasionally show up as being located in Toronto, which is where some sleuths suspected he really lived.

Several carders picked up and ran with the rumour that Lord Cyric was in reality Brian Krebs, a journalist writing on cyber security who at the time worked for *The Washington Post*. There was no evidence for this – indeed, quite the contrary, for Krebs is far too serious a writer to risk ruining his reputation by becoming involved with the people he is actually investigating. There followed a slew of rumours, but nobody ever got to the bottom of who Lord Cyric really was or what he was doing.

While exhorting others to indulge in all manner of dubious activities, Lord Cyric never engaged in criminal transactions himself, which reinforced the thesis that he was working for law enforcement or an intelligence agency.

Everybody believed, however, that Lord Cyric had a voluminous knowledge of the carding community and how it worked. And that is why he was much sought after. Carders wanted him to put them in touch with peers whom he could vouch for, or because they wanted to know what he had on them. And the police in the US and Western Europe were still searching for him in the hope of recruiting him as part of their crusade against cybercrime.

Cyric was the quintessential figure of the cyber underground – he appeared as if from nowhere; he displayed boundless, if unappealing arrogance; but above all his motivation for spending endless hours posting messages, engaging in often-futile debate and agitating his peers was obscure.

Until Mert Ortaç revealed that two of the most prominent posters on Turkey's embryonic Internet, the Bulletin Board Service, were nicknamed Cha0 and Lord Cyric, nobody had even begun to pull the threads together.

Using his trademark mixture of charm and duplicity, Mert – posting as PilotM in the late spring of 2007 – introduced himself to Lord Cyric as a third person, a mutual acquaintance of them both. 'Hey, old boy!' he messaged him, 'what are you doing on a board like this?' Cyric was keen to ask the man masquerading as his old friend exactly the same question! Soon, however, they were chatting happily, especially about encryption issues. Mert noticed that Lord Cyric was an extremely gifted computer engineer, confirming his suspicions about the character's real identity. After some days or weeks of exchanging ideas and information, Cyric agreed to facilitate a virtual meeting between Cha0 and Mert (still pretending to be somebody else). Using encrypted icq exchanges, Mert started chatting to Cha0 (in Turkish of course).

'Look,' Cha0 told Mert, 'I don't spend much time in Turkey. I prefer to be abroad.' He went on that he didn't much like his compatriots and avoided dealing with them whenever possible. 'My name,' he said, 'is Şahin and I will only speak Turkish if I absolutely have to.' He was prepared to talk Turkish with Mert because they were introduced by Lord Cyric. 'He and I are very old friends,' Cha0 said.

In April 2007 Cha0 had expelled Dron from DarkMarket, and with him went Dron's ability to fix the microprocessors on his skimming machines. He asked Mert if he would be able to do this and Mert agreed. He was now becoming seriously involved with Cha0's criminal business, which meant that he was garnering a most precious commodity – trust.

Only Mert has claimed an intimacy between himself, Cha0 and Cyric. Of course, the latter two cannot say with any certainty whether they exchanged messages with Mert because he was masquerading as somebody else. Cha0 explicitly denied ever having met or communicated with him until the fateful day when he abducted him and placed his photograph, via Haber 7, on the Internet.

More importantly, nobody else in Turkey or elsewhere has ever acknowledged the existence of the mysterious Şahin. Beyond Mert's word, there is no evidence that Şahin exists, including when the two eventually met. But Mert did prove correct in one important fact: the friendship between Lord Cyric and Cha0 went back a very long way.

Mert, of course, was also still working for Turkey's Intelligence Agency. And so most evenings after he had spent much of the day pretending to work at Fox Turkey, playing around on DarkMarket or fashioning microprocessors for Cha0's illegal skimming industry, Mert would report back to his handlers on his day's findings. He told them about a Polish spammer called Master Splyntr, about the security genius Grendel, about Lord Cyric and Cha0, about the backup servers that the DarkMarket administrators managed in different European countries, and about the activities of the DHKP/C.

What else was he up to? His boss at Fox Turkey began to grow very suspicious of him. He noted that Mert now almost never completed the tasks that were given to him, providing instead a litany of excuses as to why he was absent from his work station. He claimed he had a serious medical condition and repeatedly tried to borrow money from his colleagues. If he was so successful, his boss wondered, how come he was always short of cash?

One day the boss discovered that Mert had asked for all his co-workers' passwords. He allegedly needed them to install a major upgrade of the system. Just in time, the boss put a stop to this plan as he suspected that Mert wanted the passwords for less honourable reasons.

On another day, while quietly keeping an eye on Mert, he spotted a stack of credit cards on his table. Later he came across two ID cards for Mert, neither of which had his correct name, date or place of birth on them. Finally, he noticed Mert surfing a website with detailed instructions on how to crack open an ATM machine. The longer Mert stayed, the greater his need for money – and large sums of money at that.

Mert had met Sanem – a dream woman with whom he was besotted. Sanem is the one person in the world who can confirm whether or not Mert's extraordinary story is true. And Sanem isn't talking.

32

TURKISH DELIGHT

The Şükrü Saracoğlu Stadium in the bustling Asian district of Kadıköy was packed to the rafters for Fenerbahçe's final home game of the season. Fenerbahçe had already won the Süper Lig title and so this game on a gorgeous Sunday in late May was a noisy celebration for some of the most fanatical football supporters in the world.

And into it stepped Mert Ortaç. Perhaps for real; perhaps just in his own mind.

Up in the executive boxes there was an expectant and convivial atmosphere. Şahin and his trusted lieutenant, Çağatay Evyapan, were awaiting the kick off at 5 p.m. The football fans of Istanbul were regarded as among the most fanatical in Europe and they were divided into three camps. Two were on the European side of the city, Galatasaray and Beşiktaş, while the yellow and navy-blue shirts of Fenerbahçe lay across the straits in Asia. Şahin and Çağatay were both committed Fenerbahçe supporters and the former's visits to his home city usually coincided with a game – indeed, he had an executive box at the stadium.

Among the friends invited to this game was Mert, who, Şahin told Çağatay, was one of the new boys working on his skimming trade. Mert also introduced his new girlfriend, Sanem. She dazzled Mert, while the ostentatious wealth of his companions dazzled her.

Sanem already knew the profiles of some of the people in the executive box. It was not difficult wheedling secrets out of Mert. Not only was he a chatterbox by nature, but he was desperate to impress his young paramour, whom he considered way out of his league. Seeing powerful men like Şahin and his well-built sidekick Çağatay strut around the executive box must have been confirmation for Sanem that little Mert really did have some impressive contacts. If, that is, the Fenerbahçe game was not an episode from Mert's dream.

Life had been good for Mert. He and Sadun were starting to make serious money from the Akbank scam. As an active informant for National Intelligence, he enjoyed wide-ranging protection and he was highly regarded by Cha0, the key player on DarkMarket. But above all else, he was spending every day and night with a fabulous, beautiful young woman who seemed to be similarly smitten.

Summer had arrived and Mert decided to capitalise on his good fortune by taking a holiday in Antalya at the coveted Adam & Eve Hotel, where designers had successfully mated a high budget with singularly poor taste. Huge infinity pools lapped at an atrium with ever-changing light shows, while the rooms were known for the countless mirrors, conducive to much high-energy sex. None of this came cheaply. Rooms started at $400 a night, while visitors noted that one could quickly rack up huge bills with the extras. But for Turkey's young, beautiful or rich, it was the holiday destination of the season.

As soon as Mert and Sanem had checked in, they ran into Çağatay, who had also flown south for the summer. Çağatay explained to a tubby bespectacled gentleman accompanying him that Mert had been assisting the Cha0 team with 'administrative matters'. The tubby gentleman squinted at Mert before exclaiming, 'Wait a minute? I've known this guy since he was a kid in shorts! What the hell are you doing in this business?' And Mert responded as he always did by giggling and smiling mischievously.

As he and Sanem headed to their bedroom, Mert leaned over and said, 'The second guy? That was Lord Cyric.' Sanem wanted to know whether Cyric was more powerful than Cha0. Mert assured her that he wasn't, but he remembered that she was interested in power first and money second.

Mert was in heaven and in love. He was a moneyed man, respected by criminals and the intelligence service alike, and to the outside world he had an impressive job running the IT department at Fox Turkey. Furthermore, he was spending his summer lounging around the Adam & Eve Hotel with his hot new girlfriend. It couldn't get any better.

And it didn't – in retrospect, August 2007 represented the brief golden age of Mert Ortaç's dream world, in which his fantasy projections coincided for once with reality. Almost as soon as he returned to

Istanbul, matters began slipping out of his control and, as summer turned to autumn, dark shadows started to spread. Sanem and Mert were wont to take expensive shopping trips to places like the island of Mykonos in neighbouring Greece. The pair would drop thousands of euros in a day, which placed a strain even on Mert's well-stuffed treasure chest. His resentment at what he regarded as her profligacy was matched by her growing irritation with his secrets and lies.

In a typically convoluted episode, Mert was detained for having allegedly stolen €5,000 from a friend of Sanem's brother. His detention proved to be the last straw for Fox Turkey, which dismissed him. More ominously, National Intelligence finally decided that he had become a liability who was no longer worth protecting. Out of the blue, he felt suddenly very exposed, as well as being deprived of two important sources of income.

On remand, he stepped up his carding activities with Sadun, thanks to the continuing vulnerability of the Akbank's systems. Desperation translated into nervousness, compounded by the miserable discovery that Sanem was having an affair. The subsequent bust-up was a tempestuous business and bitter accusations were hurled back and forth. Mert believed that she had stolen large sums of money from him. She must have thought he was quite simply insane.

With his world suddenly falling apart, Mert travelled south for the New Year to consider his next move. On the road, he received further bad tidings – Sadun had been arrested and the police had already raided Mert's flat, brandishing a warrant for his detention. Had he stayed in Istanbul he would already be under lock and key. As so often when faced with a tough situation, Mert's decision was to keep digging until he was well and truly underground.

Returning under an assumed name to Istanbul, he started to plot an escape strategy. Using one of his many false IDs, he applied for and received a new passport, before bribing a consular official at the French Embassy in order to secure a visa. He then embarked on a tortuous journey via the French Caribbean territory of Martinique and Paris to Alès, a sleepy town lying fifty miles north of France's Mediterranean coast.

Mert was isolated. He possessed limited funds, barely spoke a word of French and, even more unsettling, he had no ready access to the Internet. At least he was able to console himself with the knowledge that he was safe. And so, with nothing else to do, Mert sunk into an extended period of rest and relaxation.

After the harum-scarum experience of being a fugitive from Turkish justice while feuding with his ex-lover, he soon regarded Alès as a welcome refuge. For the first time in months, maybe years, he could dispense with the half-truths, the deception, the thieving and the prevarications. He could cease the extreme compartmentalisation that his multiple online and offline personalities demanded and seek his real essence – provided, of course, he still had a recognisable essence. Perhaps the time had come to make a break from the madness: time to go straight, find a proper job and settle down with a decent woman. If he played his cards wisely, all this lay within his grasp.

Then one morning at around eight o'clock there was the knock on the door.

Mert was lying in bed sipping some coffee. He had never received visitors here in Alès and was not expecting them. Throwing on his dressing gown, he shuffled towards the door and opened it to two men who were carrying backpacks. 'Hello, Mert! How are you?' said the first one in Turkish. In return, Mert muttered feebly, '*Je ne comprends pas . . .*' 'Come on, Mert,' said the second man in English, 'we know who you are. It would be in your interest to invite us in.'

As they sat with mugs of coffee around the kitchen table, one of the men pulled out a folder and put it on the table. Mert had the first man down as a second-generation immigrant to America from Turkey because he spoke colloquial Turkish, but with an accent and occasional grammatical errors. The second guy, who did most of the talking, was American.

Mert was presented with alternatives: 'Either you help us unconditionally or we are giving this folder to the Sécurité.' Mert flicked through the pages of French credit cards, which he and Sadun had skimmed after they had wormed their way into the innards of the Akbank's computer system. The two men reminded him that in France he could receive up to eight years for just one credit-card fraud.

This was Hobson's choice, but before he consented, Mert demanded to know who the two men represented. American law enforcement came the reply. 'And what,' Mert continued, 'do you want from me?'

'Go on, Mert, have a wild guess!'

Mert, irritated and frightened, shook his head.

'We want you to give us Cha0.'

33

RETURN TO HADES

As the three men discussed Cha0 and his possible whereabouts, Mert could tell from their questions and comments that they knew neither Cha0's identity nor Lord Cyric's. The two agents told Mert that he would have to return to Turkey, re-establish himself on DarkMarket and flush out Cha0 and his colleagues. They surprised him even more by telling him that one of their people controlled the DarkMarket server. Thus they could easily help to get him back on the boards.

As far as Mert could ascertain, the FBI now wanted to move in on all the remaining central players on DarkMarket: Cha0, Lord Cyric, Master Splyntr, Shtirlitz and Grendel. They had not told him how exactly, but he was evidently supposed to be instrumental in all this. It was not a prospect he relished, but then neither was a spell inside one of France's prisons, which were rumoured to be among the most unforgiving in Western Europe.

The American agents offered Mert some vague promises and armed him with a phone number and email address for Lucy Hoover, the Assistant Legal Attaché at the US Embassy in Istanbul. He was also given an email account, *sadinsider@gmail.com* (Mert chose the name), through which he could leave messages for her.

Mert's sojourn in the Languedoc is the second episode from his dream world that is not verifiable. But he did establish contact with Lucy Hoover of the FBI, who was in Turkey at the time.

Mert had been away for two months when he arrived back on 2nd March 2008. The first thing he had to do was devise a plan of action. He decided to approach the news organisation and TV station, Haber 7, offering them an interview in which he promised to reveal the secrets of the carding world and DarkMarket. His aim, perhaps unwisely, was to put the frighteners on Cha0, to let him know that information about his operation was leaking out and that the police might well be investigating him.

In his innocence – which, despite everything, was still an integral part of his character – Mert assumed that Cha0 would not be able to establish who this mystery hacker offering interviews to the press actually was. But Mert had not reckoned with Haber 7 taking a sneaky photograph of him at the McDonald's in Kadıköy where he and their journalist met. Once that was published, Cha0 knew who had been blabbing. Mert was firmly in the big man's sights.

With a warrant out for his arrest and Sadun under lock and key, Cha0, Lord Cyric et al. would have known that Mert was vulnerable to pressure from law enforcement. The interview reinforced those suspicions. So instead of returning to the DarkMarket board directly, Mert made contact with a young hacker friend of his called Mustafa, who was also known to Cha0. Mustafa was, by all accounts, keen to develop his skills in the easy money culture of carding and cybercrime.

Mustafa's family came from Antalya, which also gave Mert an excuse to get out of Istanbul where he felt insecure. He stayed in the south for more than a month, back in his favourite part of the country.

Mustafa worked on DarkMarket using the nickname MYD, and he developed a good working relationship with Cha0. What Mert did not know, however, was that Mustafa had warned Cha0 that Mert appeared to be stalking him.

Mustafa arranged to meet Cha0 up in Istanbul, and so he and Mert headed back north. Mert had kept Lucy Hoover informed of his movements and alerted her that he was preparing to meet Cha0. The Americans needed to get a sighting of Cha0 and to establish both his coordinates and his communications infrastructure. Mert, for once, was keeping a promise – leading the Americans to their quarry. Cha0 had instructed Mustafa to meet his people outside a Burger King not far from Göztepe suburban rail station, which is on the Asian side of Istanbul, a couple of miles from Fenerbahçe's stadium.

When they reached Göztepe, they found Hakan Öztan, a big bull of man who had acted as Çağatay's minder when the two were in prison together and now offered the same services to Şahin as well. The bodyguard took them both to a house named Sözdener Apartments in the wealthy middle-class district of Suadiye, some two miles away. The rooms were sparsely furnished and not especially welcoming. Hakan told the two men to stay put and that somebody would be in touch with them.

No longer under the protection of open spaces, still less of National Intelligence, Mert was now worried that Çağatay was on his way to sort him out. Unbeknownst to him, Mustafa had placed a trojan virus on Mert's laptop on the instructions of Cha0, and that infection was now revealing to Cha0 all of Mert's secrets, a dense jungle of duplicity. Cha0 was not only a master criminal; he was also an unforgiving one. He now had solid evidence that Mert was working for the police. Mert assumed (and certainly hoped) that Lucy Hoover had somehow organised surveillance of the apartment, but he could not see any signs of it. So if Çağatay, Şahin, Hakan or any combination of the three turned up, he was in serious trouble.

At ten o'clock on Sunday morning, 18th May 2008, Mert was alone when the doorbell rang at Sözdener Apartments. He opened up to find Hakan standing in front of him. His visitor didn't speak, but strode brusquely past Mert, closing the door behind him. Mert said cheerfully that he had been expecting him. Hakan glared at him. 'One minute,' he said. Then he opened the door and in walked Çağatay. Mert's colour changed from red to purple to white.

Çağatay pushed Mert into a chair and started slowly pacing up and down in front of him, ritually intoning, 'Mert . . . Namert . . . Mert . . . Namert' – a play on words in Turkish in which the antonym of the word *mert* (courageous) is *namert* (cowardly).

Then Mert found himself on the floor being kicked in his stomach, chest and legs. Two more heavies walked in, threw a blanket over his head so that he could not recognise them and joined in the beating. Occasionally Mert caught a glimpse of a gun being pointed at his head.

He blacked out. When he came to, he was still on the floor, but he noticed a video camera filming everything that was going on. By placing the trojan on Mert's laptop, Cha0 had not only been able to access information about the relationship with Lucy Hoover, but would also have discovered that National Intelligence had been running Mert (albeit with only partial success).

'Right,' said Çağatay, who, acting as master of ceremonies, switched on the record button. 'Now you are going to tell us the whole story from beginning to end.' And so Mert went through his *Looking Glass* tale, finishing at about three o'clock in the morning. They wanted to know everything – about the spooks, the carding with Sadun, the DarkMarket exploration, the girlfriend – and not one detail was left out.

The thugs finally went to sleep, except that one was always awake to ensure that whenever Mert nodded off, they could rouse him with a shower of kicks and punches.

At midday on Monday, Şahin called, and Çağatay placed him on speaker phone. By this time Mert's will had been broken. He assumed he was going to be killed. He was not surprised when Şahin told him to repeat everything he had already said. It was all filmed. At the end, Şahin spoke. 'Okay, now is the time for your punishment,' he said without irony, 'I want you to do everything that Çağatay tells you to do and I will judge the outcome.'

Çağatay told Mert to stand up and strip. Fearing that he was about to be gang-raped, Mert finally snapped. 'Oh, for God's sake, just put a bullet through my head,' he pleaded. 'What the hell do you think you are doing with me?'

'Shut up,' Çağatay retorted. 'You've got nothing to worry about. We're not a bunch of shirt-lifters. Keep your boxers on and accept your punishment!' On the phone to Şahin, Çağatay now scrawled the infamous piece of paper that branded Kier or Mert Ortaç a traitor and a snitch. This is how the myth of Kier was established. The journalist from Haber 7 had found Mert's name on a website alongside the nickname 'Kier'. In fact, Mert had never, and would never, use this name – his real nick was SLayraCkEr. But after Çağatay took the photograph, journalists, police and carders around the world would refer to Mert Ortaç as Kier, even though he had never been called that in his life.

After the photo session, Mert was thrown down onto the floor again and the blanket was tossed over him. 'Stay here for half an hour and then you can leave,' Çağatay said. 'We are leaving you your clothes and we won't touch your money. You can also have one ID. From now on – for the rest of your life – don't even think of writing the name Cha0, because if you do, I'll have my hands round your neck before you take another breath.' Finally Çağatay could not resist adding a personal note, 'If it had been up to me, I would have killed you here and now. But the man likes you. Be grateful and keep your mouth shut.' (Çağatay himself considered any idea that he might want to murder someone like Mert – a little squit in his eyes – laughable.)

Half an hour later the battered Mert Ortaç, with just fifty dollars in his pocket, stumbled out of the apartment and headed for the national bus station, from where he caught a ride to the town of Izmir. Here he would lick his wounds and wonder what on earth he should do next. It was obvious: he would go underground. Mert disappeared for the last time – until he was arrested many months later while applying for a passport under a different name in November 2008.

Further strange tales inhabit Mert's dream world – neither reality nor fantasy – but, for our purposes, this is where it ends.

34

TURKEY SHOOT

Before Mert was finally arrested, Inspector Bilal Şen had no idea whether the hacker was on the run, still a prisoner or simply dead. He did know, however, that time was not on his side. The only option open to the officer was to continue to track down Cha0 as efficiently and patiently as possible. At least he now had a photograph and a number for the man sending the skimmer, and he was convinced that this would eventually lead him to Cha0. Because the henchman who had delivered the skimmer was using one of the phone numbers that he had registered with the shipping company, the police were able to 'triangulate' the suspect – in other words, they could spot which cell-phone masts the device was accessing. They soon had an accurate idea both of where he was and of the pattern of his movements.

Before long they had a second sighting and were able to put a tail on him. Sure enough, within a matter of days the man had led them to a villa in Tuzla, a distant suburb of Istanbul that lay about fifteen miles down the Asian coast. Home to one of Turkey's largest naval bases, this area, once famous for its fishing, was one of only a handful in the city that had not been completely dominated by new buildings. With its spacious houses with their colourful exteriors, it was a highly sought-after neighbourhood, peopled largely by wealthy families.

The suspect led them to a luxury villa complete with outdoor swimming pool. After days of observation, the surveillance team had ascertained that several men were living in the villa. But it did not take Bilal long to establish who was giving orders to the team. Going through criminal records, he soon identified him as one Çağatay Evyapan.

At college a gifted student of electrical engineering, Çağatay now had real form. He had first been arrested on fraud charges in 1998. Two years later came his biggest miscalculation when he and his collaborators were caught red-handed using cloned white plastic credit cards to extract cash from ATMs in the port of Izmir. After having served five years of a twenty-seven-year sentence, the prospect of further incarceration was too much for him. And so one day in May 2005 Çağatay went over the top of his prison walls and off the radar. He was less a fugitive and more a ghost.

He blamed his arrest in 2000 on the men with whom he was working – something he was determined not to allow again. If you want something done properly, ran Çağatay's basic philosophy, do it yourself.

Naturally he understood that during his five years in prison the cyber world had undergone significant changes. He knew all about Moore's Law, which predicts that the number of transistors that may be placed inexpensively onto an integrated circuit will continue to double every two years until roughly 2015. Translated into real life, that law means that every year gadgets get funkier, computer programs more complex, hacking tools more devious and the rewards correspondingly more juicy. And so he set about adapting to the new circumstances.

First, he needed a new cyber identity. Çağatay disappeared for almost four years, his name being replaced on his passport with the name of one his subordinates, the bodyguard Hakan Öztan, and in the ether by Cha0 (pronounced like the Italian greeting). He had been using the first syllable of his name and the figure zero since he first graced the BBS boards in the early 1990s. At that time, Cha0's exceptional security system had ensured that nobody could identify him. In public forums like CrimeEnforcers and DarkMarket, Cha0 sold skimmers. In private, he sold impenetrable security systems for computer users who really did not want their identity revealed.

But now Bilal had stumbled upon him. However, it was one thing spotting Cha0's location. It was quite another gathering the requisite evidence to build a case against him. Turkey's judges and prosecutors are even less acquainted with the Internet than their equivalents in Western Europe or America, and already the city had spawned several high-profile, expensive defence lawyers who were quickly learning how to exploit that ignorance for the benefit of their clients and their own bank balances.

Çağatay was enjoying his summer – he was a convivial chap who liked to step out with his friends. He often escorted beautiful women, including, it was rumoured, one daring member of the Saudi royal family. He liked expensive drinks, fine dining and attending parties on yachts, and over the years had put on some weight. Money appeared to be no object in the pursuit of his fancy lifestyle.

Bilal put tails on Çağatay's various co-workers – the evidence was mounting that Cha0 was not just Çağatay Evyapan, but a well-oiled criminal syndicate. This was organised crime, not some script-kiddy hacking servers for the first time. As such, it was evidence of a growing trend around the world. For a long time traditional organised-crime syndicates regarded fraud on the Web as crime-lite and scarcely worthy of their attention. That was now beginning to change. Cybercrime was becoming more systematic, more efficient and more security-conscious as it moved out of its original incubator, where mischievous geeks giggle and play, and into the more adult realm of real mafia structures. By implication, Bilal's quarry would have correspondingly greater resources and so building the case required close care and attention, if the Inspector were to avoid being tripped up in court.

The cops duly gathered evidence, and of course Keith Mularski and Cha0 were still fellow administrators on DarkMarket. The operation lasted a full five months, as Bilal stored tiny scraps of evidence day by day. He ascertained that Çağatay's group of intimates was relatively small and that his security was military in its precision. But along with those scraps, which might link Çağatay with any crime, Bilal had a second agenda: he was still trying to establish whether Çağatay had someone on the inside – while praying that he didn't.

In late August Çağatay disappeared. Panic spread throughout the team that had been tracking him. Nonetheless, the journalist with Haber 7 continued to receive messages, not from Cha0, but from a certain Yarris, who seemed to have an intimate knowledge of Cha0's activities. Mercifully for Bilal, Cha0 turned up in Istanbul as unexpectedly as he had departed. Nonetheless it was a warning as to how precarious the situation was, and Bilal made the decision to move on him in early September.

Back at the villa in Tuzla, surveillance had identified that one of the residents would go out every few days or so to fetch provisions. On 8th September out he came. Bilal Şen was back in Ankara, biting his nails as the SWAT team surrounding the building relayed to him all the events minute by minute over the phone. Then, as the shopper returned, they swooped – crashing into the villa and pinning down four other men on the floor. Around them were countless computers and dozens upon dozens of skimmers, moulds, PIN pads, POS devices and lots of cash. The raid was a triumph – nobody was hurt and all the suspects were arrested.

Strangely Cha0's arrest had been anticipated a few days earlier on the message boards of *Wired* magazine after one of the journal's writers had posted a story about DarkMarket on *Wired*'s website. One of the comments placed at the bottom came from somebody purporting to be Lord Cyric, the DM administrator. He claimed to be in direct touch with Cha0. And he added cryptically that some of Cha0's subordinates might see the inside of a jail, but Cha0 never would.

Farewell, Cha0?

35

THE DEATH OF
DARKMARKET

Whoever Cha0 really was, the unexpected arrest of Çağatay Evyapan appeared to sow panic among his fellow administrators on DarkMarket. On 16th September 2008, less than a week after the bust in Istanbul, Master Splyntr announced on the DM website that the police successes were fraying his and his fellow administrators' nerves. It was a burden they no longer felt able to shoulder:

> It is apparent that this forum . . . is attracting too much attention from a lot of the world services (agents of FBI, SS, and Interpol). I guess it was only time before this would happen. It is very unfortunate that we have come to this situation, because . . . we have established DM as the premier English speaking forum for conducting business. Such is life. When you are on top, people try to bring you down.

In the space of a week the premier criminal website of the English-speaking world was dead. Its followers were distraught. 'DarkMarket was our bridge to business, and if that bridge is broken . . .' lamented a member named Iceburg, posting on *Wired* magazine's website. 'Long live cashing and carding. Short live all the RATS and FBI and all stupid secret agencies who are not just ruining our lives and families, but are destroying everything we left behind.'

It seemed as though the cybercops had won. This being DarkMarket, though, the story wasn't quite so simple.

Part IV

36

DOUBLE JEOPARDY

Stuttgart, September 2007

Officer Dietmar Lingel was pleased with his work. A week earlier his boss had given him the logs from the Canadian webmail provider, hushmail. This email system was supposedly watertight – nobody could read your correspondence if you were using hushmail. This was largely true, but by 2007 the company had caved in to pressure from the Canadian police and afforded the cops access to log records. These revealed to an investigator which IP address had been logging on to a particular email account. And the RCMP had passed the logs for two accounts, *auto432221@hushmail.com* and *auto496064@hushmail.com*, to Agent Mularski of the FBI.

Back in May 2007 Matrix001 had sent Keith Mularski a redacted version of the anonymous email he had received warning him that he was under surveillance by the German police. Mularski's initial reaction was to assume that his colleagues at the US Secret Service were responsible for the leak. At the time, the Feds and the Secret Service were running competing operations into DarkMarket, multiplying the possibility of a security breach out of either incompetence or malice. But at least three overseas police forces knew about Matrix: the British, the French and, of course, the Germans.

Nobody from the police underestimated the importance of the emails. Along with the possible existence of a mole was the equally disturbing idea that someone had hacked into the computers belonging to one of the investigating units. Operation DarkMarket had begun in earnest, but the busts of Matrix001 and JiLsi were just the start – the plan was to expand it over several years. The emails jeopardised the whole strategy built up over two years of painstaking work. The leak had to be stopped. The need to find the source became the topmost priority for the international investigation.

The arrival of the hushmail logs on Lingel's desk meant that a detailed examination of the evidence could begin. As the technical specialist on the team who had investigated Matrix001, it was Lingel's job to establish who had attempted to access those accounts at around the time that Matrix was sent them.

Lingel identified that one IP address trying to access the anonymous hushmail accounts came from the Stuttgart area. He discounted that one immediately – it was his own. After Keith Mularski had first alerted Stuttgart to the existence of the emails, Lingel had attempted to log onto the hushmail account using some standard passwords (such as *admin* or *password*) and others belonging to prominent DarkMarketeers that were already known to law enforcement. The other login attempts came from IP addresses in Berlin and elsewhere in Germany. On the morning of 12th September during a discussion with his head of department Gert Wolf, Lingel explained that they did not have a suspect yet, but they had succeeded in narrowing down the possibilities.

After lunch Wolf put his head round Lingel's door and said they had to go and see their divisional chief. Lingel walked into the room to find a panel of senior policemen awaiting him, including an officer from the sinister-sounding Dezernat 3.5, the Stuttgart department for internal police investigations. Lingel was baffled and rather nervous. The officer suddenly announced, 'Mr Lingel, we are placing you under investigation on suspicion of having informed a suspect that he was under surveillance.'

Lingel was speechless. Gradually shock gave way to anger. 'There I was,' he thought, 'working all week with my boss to resolve this mess, and then he pops his head round the door after lunch one day and sinks a knife straight into my back.'

'Look, Mr Lingel,' the officer continued, 'you've got two choices. Either you cooperate with us in this investigation or we are going to place you right now in investigative custody.'

Lingel agreed to cooperate. His chief explained that he must now take all his remaining leave, after which he would be suspended until further notice.

In his mid-forties, Lingel had an unconventional history. He was born in Windhoek, the capital of Namibia, which, as South-West Africa, had been one of the few outposts of imperial Germany during the colonial period. As a five-year-old he then moved with his parents to Cape Town, so he grew up speaking fluent English as well as German. He returned to his parents' homeland to study, and after graduating joined the police. Here he progressed well through the ranks of the motorway force, while never finding the work particularly challenging.

As an amateur geek, he leaped at the chance to apply for a post in the Baden-Württemberg police in 2001. The Stuttgart headquarters needed somebody with experience of the open-source operating system Linux, to provide network security. Five years later he was permitted to migrate with his computer skills to the criminal-investigations department, where he was assigned to work under Frank Eissmann.

Matrix001 was not the only German identified by Keith Mularski as an active member of DarkMarket. The other two were Soulfly, real name Michael Artamonow, and Fake, real name Bilge Ülusoy. Initially, the State Prosecutor sought to indict Matrix001 on charges of forming a criminal conspiracy, but this required proof that he was working in cahoots with the other two.

For some reason, however, no investigation was ever launched into Fake and Soulfly, and this was partly responsible for a judge in October 2007 forcing the State Prosecutor to drop the accusation of conspiracy in favour of the lesser charges of credit-card fraud. Why they dropped the investigation into the presumed co-conspirators was just the first of several unanswered questions, which were to undermine confidence in the ability of the Provincial and Federal Police in Germany to investigate the case.

And the Baden-Württemberg police in Stuttgart had a lot riding on the investigation into Matrix001. Usually all communication in international cases like this would be filtered through Wiesbaden, but the chief investigator, Frank Eissmann, had persuaded his superiors that he should be allowed to talk directly to Keith Mularski, the FBI's key man.

There were thus jitters aplenty when Mularski heard from Matrix001 that the German hacker had received a message from an anonymous hushmail account warning him that he was about to be busted. And police in London, Pittsburgh and Stuttgart were all praying that the source was not too close to their own home.

After Lingel's arrest, relief spread among the investigators – it seemed as though they had their man. But in December 2007 Dezernat 3.5 sent Lingel a letter saying that there was no further evidence linking him with the email breach and that he could return to work the following month, at the beginning of 2008. However, he did not return to Department IV, which was handling the Matrix001 investigation. Lingel felt extremely bitter towards his immediate boss, Frank Eissmann, who had, it seemed, been partially responsible for pointing the finger at his subordinate.

As the trial of Matrix approached in the late spring, the atmosphere in the Stuttgart police headquarters was gloomy and riven with discord. Unable to press charges of conspiracy against Matrix, the prosecution knew that they were unlikely to get a custodial sentence. Furthermore, they were back to square one in trying to ascertain who the source of the leak was.

Although Lingel was resentful at what had happened to him, his reassignment to Department I turned out to be perfectly palatable and his new colleagues' behaviour towards him was exemplary. It was a relief and a welcome change after months of being viewed with suspicion.

Then, in May 2008, Lingel was placed under arrest again. But this time he was not accused of having written the emails to Matrix. Lingel was charged with having jeopardised the undercover identity of the FBI Agent, Keith J. Mularski.

37

ZORRO UNMASKED

Just as Matrix was standing trial in June 2008, a radio reporter, Kai Laufen, was flicking through a copy of the MIT's* Technology Review when he spotted an article on cybercrime. Until this moment the investigative journalist from Karlsruhe in south-west Germany had no idea that it was becoming such a problem. He was intrigued and decided to discover the extent to which cybercrime was affecting Germany.

Cautious but thorough, Laufen began by researching the clauses in Germany's penal code relating to computer crime. Once he had found them, he dispatched emails to about fifty district and municipal courts around the country asking whether they were dealing with any such cases.

He received only a couple of replies, but conveniently one of them referred to a case of credit-card fraud at a local court in Göppingen, a small backwater in Baden-Württemberg, just a short drive from where Laufen lived. A young man, Detlef Hartmann, was awaiting sentencing on thirteen charges of having used cloned credit cards.

The story didn't sound particularly interesting, but Laufen decided nonetheless to contact the provincial police in Stuttgart, and before long the basics of cybercrime were being explained to him by Inspector Frank Eissmann. In passing he said that the FBI had assisted his Department IV in the investigation of Hartmann.

The day after Detlef received a nineteen-month suspended sentence on 2nd July, Kai wrote to him requesting an interview, sent quaintly

---

* Massachusetts Institute of Technology, not to be confused with the acronym of Turkey's National Intelligence Agency.

by post rather than email. Detlef and his parents resisted the journalist's first few attempts to talk to him, but after three months they
relented, so in early October Kai found himself sitting opposite the
young man over a cup of coffee.

Kai Laufen was no novice. Born in northern Germany, he was
brought up partly in Brazil and spoke fluent Portuguese, Spanish and
English. He had worked throughout South America and knew a thing
or two about organised crime and gangsters. But now he could scarcely
believe his ears as Detlef regaled him with the tale of Matrix001 and
his adventures in a virtual world where everyone boasted peculiar
names and communicated in a hybrid English – part gangster, part
anarchist and part Tolkien – as they bought and sold stolen financial
details.

Kai readily grasped the implications of this new style of wrongdoing.
With the aid of the Internet, the perpetrators could commit crimes
thousands of miles away, on a multitude of unknown victims who
might or might not discover that their privacy had been violated and
their money or identity stolen.

Yet if it was so foolproof, Kai wondered, how did Detlef manage to
get himself arrested? 'Simple,' he replied, 'one of my fellow administrators, who I worked with over many months, was an FBI agent. He
was tracking me and he alerted the German police.' The journalist
thought the young man was perhaps exaggerating his own importance,
so he asked him whether he had any documentary evidence to support
that. 'Yes,' said Detlef, 'I'll send it to you.'

A few days later Detlef sent Laufen the prosecutor's statement
outlining the state's case against the young man, written in the German
language's inimitable legalese:

As evidenced by the investigation dossier, this administrator who
in the final analysis had complete control over all arrangements
at least from June 2006 onwards was the FBI Agent, Keith
Mularski, who had offered to host the server in order to gather
more accurate information about the buyers and sellers. I refer
here to the Case Document 148, File 1, in which Mr Keith Mularski
informs the investigating officer of the Regional Police, Frank
Eismann [sic], as follows: *Master Splynter* [sic] *is me*. That the user
Master Splynter [sic] ran the server is proven by Case Document

190, Email from Keith Mularski dated 09.03.2007: *He paid me for the Server.*

Kai was startled. He read the key sentence again. *Master Splynter is me.* Not only was Detlef Hartmann correct that the FBI had been on his cyber tail, but the prosecutor's office had named the agent *and* his alias. The game was up and he, Kai Laufen, had uncovered the truth about one of the world's most prominent cybercops. Three months earlier he had barely heard of cybercrime.

When Kai called the National Cyber Forensics Training Alliance in Pittsburgh, he was put straight through to Keith Mularski, whose manner was, as always, most accommodating. But as the journalist read the sentence from the email – *Master Splynter is me* – there was total silence on the other end of the line. Keith knew he had been nailed. On the bright side, he had been nailed by a radio journalist in south-western Germany and there was an outside chance, even in the age of the Internet, that the news might not get much further than the borders of Baden-Württemberg. In his heart, however, he knew that it really was an outside chance.

Was this the famous leak again?

Kai Laufen was unaware that Stuttgart's police Commissioner had for a second time sanctioned the suspension of Dietmar Lingel from the force. On this occasion, however, they suspected the officer of having intentionally fed Mularski's name and alias to the prosecutor for inclusion in his outline of the case. Lingel's aim, it was alleged, was to bring Mularski's identity into the public domain as a way of discrediting the FBI. The motivation, the Commissioner claimed, lay in Lingel's dissatisfaction with some of the policing methods involved in the Hartmann investigation.

The allegations against Lingel served to highlight fundamental differences in the philosophy of law enforcement in Europe and the United States. Europeans tend to shun sting operations as risky, as well as morally and legally questionable. The Americans by contrast use them frequently. There is an intense debate in America as to where a sting ends and entrapment begins. In Europe some police officers regarded the DarkMarket operation as verging on entrapment, especially as the Secret Service, in particular, seemed to encourage members to engage in criminal activity (in the case of Dron) during their investigation.

The FBI and Keith Mularski vigorously defended their actions, emphasising that the presence of Mularski and his team on DarkMarket
enabled intelligence-gathering – notably about the intended expansion
of Cha0's US operation – which prevented, so Mularski claimed, $70
million in potential losses.

Just as he was putting the finishing touches to his radio feature on
this peculiar, yet important story, Kai Laufen suffered a slipped disc.
Almost completely unable to move, the journalist was forced to brood
in bed for two weeks. He arrived at the conclusion that nobody in
Germany would care about the fact that the FBI had busted a German
carder and that he, Kai, had uncovered the agent's identity. On the
other hand, the DarkMarket story had attracted considerable attention
in the US tech media. Led by the San Francisco-based *Wired* magazine,
a fair amount had already been published on the subject, especially
after the dramatic kidnapping of Mert Ortaç in April that year and then
the arrest of Cha0 in September.

Kai felt strongly that he should disseminate the proof that Dark-
Market was in part an FBI sting operation. But just as the Atlantic
divides the culture of policing, so it does the ethical standards of German
journalists and their Anglo-American counterparts. (Britain's police are
more European than American, but their newshounds have even fewer
scruples than America's do.)

In Germany it is considered bad form to publish the full names of
alleged criminals while they are still on trial, and in many cases the
German media desist from doing so even if the criminals are subsequently found guilty. The same goes for undercover police agents. For
anybody familiar with the Anglo-American media, the notion is, of
course, as foreign as can possibly be.

So when Kai Laufen spoke by phone to Kevin Poulsen, *Wired* magazine's Security Editor, in early October 2008, he said that he would
provide Mr Poulsen with documentary evidence which proved that law
enforcement had penetrated DarkMarket. He would include Keith
Mularski's email admission of his role as Master Splyntr, but only on
the strict condition that Poulsen did not publish Mularski's name.
Reiterating the point, Laufen ended his email, which included the
document scans, with the exhortation: 'Burn after reading!'

Poulsen remembers it differently: he only agreed to keep Matrix's
name out of the paper. Over the years he and his team had done an

impressive job in tracking most cybercrime stories, including Dark-Market. Indeed, he brought the same ruthless zeal to the job that he did to his previous occupation as a hacker – a career that ended in a criminal conviction. And so Poulsen did not burn after reading. On Monday 13th October he published. Master Splyntr was dead.

For his part, Keith Mularski was furious when *Wired* published his name – the trust that he had built up with so many carders was instantly lost. He had closed the DarkMarket board a couple of weeks earlier because JiLsi's registration of the domain name was about to expire. Had Master Splyntr attempted to re-register it, a curious hacker might have used the opportunity to uncover his identity.

The DarkMarket operation was the opening phase in a long-term plan by law enforcement to infiltrate the world of cyber criminality. In fifteen months, prior to the publication of Mularski's name in *Wired* magazine, the FBI, SOCA and the other police agencies involved had been careful to pick off individuals here and there. They had deliberately decided not to go for a large-scale sweep of DarkMarket members, in contrast to the tactics used by the Secret Service in 2004 with Shadow-crew. Master Splyntr fully intended to return with his reputation enhanced, armed with his large database of carders and their activities. That plan was now blown out of the water.

Not that Mularski's efforts had been in vain – in a remarkable example of cross-border cooperation among disparate police forces, they had caught one of the biggest fish in the carding world, Cha0, and had arrested dozens of others, some of whom were already convicted, most of whom were awaiting trial.

But neither Agent Mularski nor anybody else was in a position to blame Dietmar Lingel. He had not allowed the identity of Master Splyntr to slip into the court papers for the Matrix case, as the officer from Dezernat 3.5 had alleged.

That distinction belonged to Detective Frank Eissmann, Lingel's boss, who later confessed that he had 'made a big mistake' in submit-ting the document to the State Prosecutor as part of the police evidence against Matrix. It was Eissmann's error that led to Kai Laufen identifying Mularski, which in turn triggered the collapse of the long-term opera-tion against the carders.

Dietmar Lingel, however, remained suspended and heard nothing from his employers until Dezernat 3.5 informed him in September

2010 that he was to stand trial. The prosecutor had dropped the unsub-
stantiated claim that Lingel had intentionally leaked Mularski's name.
Instead, the original charge was resurrected: he was accused of having
informed a suspect that he was under surveillance.

Lingel opted to contest the charges and later that month the longest
trial anywhere related to the DarkMarket case began in Stuttgart. Ironically, it did not involve any actual cyber criminals (except that Matrix001
and Fake testified as witnesses), but pitted the Baden-Württemberg
police against one of its own. It was a fascinating event played out in
front of a handful of people in a clean, small, anonymous court in Bad
Cannstatt, Stuttgart's spa district. The testimony of almost a dozen
actors in the drama was startling, revealing many of the errors and
misfortunes that plagued the policing operation in both Europe and
the United States.

38

WHO ARE YOU?

Istanbul, October 2008

Çağatay Evyapan appeared relaxed in jail. Now and then a member of the Istanbul force would whisper something about a supercop flying in from Ankara to conduct the main interrogation of Çağatay. In Turkey the longest you can hold someone suspected of involvement in organised criminal activity is four days. The prisoner was intrigued to see if this Mr Big from the capital would turn up.

Finally, Inspector Şen arrived. He needed to know only one thing.

'Who is the little bird? Who are you talking to inside? This is all I want to know from you.'

The prisoner hesitated and then looked desperate.

'There is nobody.'

39

ON THE ROAD
TO NOWHERE

Inspector Şen's work was done. After the arrest, the case was handed over to the prosecution service, as required by Turkish law. But if Çağatay Evyapan was Cha0, then who was this character Şahin, whom Mert Ortaç insisted was the real Cha0. Was Şahin a mere figment of Mert's imagination? After all, Mert did have a history as a fantasist and embellisher.

Fond though he was of spinning a yarn, the fundamental aspects of Mert's story were true. He did work for various official organisations, including the Intelligence Agency; he was a highly gifted programmer with a particular skill for decrypting smart cards; he did make huge sums of money from selling fake Digiturk cards, for which he was later investigated; he did lavish money and entertainment on people he wanted to impress; he did tread the DarkMarket boards using Sadun's nicknames, Cryptos and PilotM; he did holiday with his girlfriend at the Adam & Eve Hotel in Antalya; and he was most definitely kidnapped and humiliated by Çağatay Evyapan.

However, he was unable to offer any proof for his central claim that Cha0's real identity was the mysterious Şahin. Mert demonstrated such a detailed knowledge of the inner workings of DarkMarket that, if he was lying, somebody or some organisation must have furnished him with some or all of these details. The question is – and it remains stubbornly unanswered – why? And who were they trying to frame or discredit by throwing the extraordinary Mr Ortaç into the mix? Certainly not Çağatay Evyapan as he emerges from Mert's story as a lesser criminal? The police? Or was it perhaps the man who Mert claims was Lord Cyric, a prominent member of the Turkish and global internet scene?

Even so, Mert's truth remains no less plausible than Inspector Şen's truth. The key lies not in the identity of Şahin or Çağatay. It is hidden within the character of Cha0. There is no doubt that the man who masterminded the skimming factory and acted as administrator on DarkMarket was Çağatay Evyapan. The issue is whether Evyapan controlled the entire operation or whether he was working on behalf of a bigger criminal syndicate.

All in all, Turkish police arrested some two dozen people who, the evidence suggests, were connected to Cha0's operation either as an inner core or as satellites. The virtual criminal was just that – he was not a real character, but an amalgam of individuals with different skills working as a unit. In the same way the Ukrainian founder of Carder-Planet, Script, had recognised that the generic term 'carder' in fact hid a multitude of different skills: some were real hackers; some were graphic designers; some were electronic engineers building skimmers; some skimmed ATMs; some cashed out; some provided security; some gathered intelligence, sometimes on behalf of the criminals and some-times on behalf of the police.

Thus both men, Cha0 and Script, anticipated the world of cybercrime post-DarkMarket – a move away from a loosely bound community of individuals engaged in opportunistic criminal activity towards a much more systematic criminal organisation in which its members fulfilled specialist tasks: spamming, virus-writing, money-laundering, operating botnets and other essential criminal activities of the virtual world.

So maybe 'Cha0' was just such an operation – the whole caboodle rolled into one. Cha0 was a collective name that sought in the first instance to gain at least a partial monopoly in the new industry of credit-card fraud through skimming. It was an audacious plan, which came very close to succeeding, had it not been for the combined efforts of Keith Mularski and Bilal Şen, as well as the backup provided by other police agencies and by certain other individuals.

The degree to which Cha0, the entity, was organised hints strongly at something else. Traditional criminal fraternities have until recently 'tended to regard cyber criminals as second-class citizens', as one of SOCA's leading cybercops described them. But during the existence of DarkMarket police forces across the world started observing how traditional organised-crime groups were making unexpected appear-ances during investigations into cybercrime.

Within DarkMarket itself there were three quite well-defined circles involved in the project. The first were the administrators, moderators and others holding senior 'bureaucratic' positions on the site. These tended to be men with advanced hacking skills and certainly fluent computer skills. Furthermore, with the exception of Cha0, they were either not making large sums of money or were working directly as police agents or as confidential informants.

Beyond this, the second circle mostly comprised skilful experienced criminals who worked largely on their own – like Freddybb and RedBrigade. They demonstrated varying degrees of computing ability and, if they themselves were unable to solve a technical problem, they always knew people who could. These individuals were less conspicuous on boards like DarkMarket than the administrators and their crew. Their aim was to make as much money as possible without drawing attention to themselves, although they, too, would occasionally engage in banter and chat about the carding community as a whole.

The third circle was home to highly professional criminals who were virtually invisible – unknown except by myth and reputation to the police and their fellow carders. These were people even beyond major wholesalers of credit cards and malware – such as the Ukrainian Maksik, arrested by Turkey's cybercrime team in Antalya in 2007. The most famous one (who, it is believed, supplied Maksik with much of his material) is the Russian known simply as Sim, who, police assume, is actually another very efficient syndicate. These are people who never emerge from the shadows.

Cha0 was fascinating and important because this was the first time that an outfit resembling traditional organised crime had involved itself in large-scale cybercrime and sought to influence the workings of a website like DarkMarket. This was the first real proof that cybercrime was no longer the domain of second-class citizens alone – it was beginning to attract some bigger figures.

Organised crime has traditionally played a huge role in Turkey. For example, in combination with Kurdish and some other Balkan groups, Turkish gangs dominate the wholesale heroin trade throughout Western Europe.

In late 1996 an armoured Mercedes was involved in a spectacular road accident in the small town of Susurluk. Among the dead were the Chief of the Police Academy and the leader of the right-wing terror group, the Grey Wolves, who also happened to be on Interpol's most-wanted list as one of Europe's major heroin-traffickers and a recognised assassin. The one person who survived was an MP for the then-ruling party.

This event enabled journalists and opposition politicians to start untangling the web of violent deceit that implicated Turkey's Deep State with the most influential members of organised criminal groups. For years they had been enjoying one another's friendship, hospitality and protection. Not only did the stories shock ordinary Turks, but they gave an important fillip to emerging forces in Turkish politics – like the organisation that would eventually become the AK Party, which made the fight against crime and corruption a central part of its political platform.

Turkey has moved on somewhat since then. But when the roots of corruption and organised crime extend as deeply as they did in Turkey during the 1980s and 1990s, it takes several decades before they can be eradicated from the body politic. This explains Bilal Şen's fears when he was first told that Cha0 might live under the protective wing of powerful establishment figures. It is also credible, as some of Bilal's law-enforcement collaborators outside Turkey believe, that the Cha0 who inhabited DarkMarket was part of a much larger organisation. Crime groups in Turkey straddle various sectors – along with heroin-trafficking, Turkey is a major centre for people-trafficking (again because of the proximity of the European Union). And in the last two decades a huge money-laundering trade has grown up there as well.

So Çağatay Evyapan, their theory goes, was actually just a lieutenant for the real CEO of Cha0 Criminal Holdings. Çağatay would be the Vice President for the cybercrime division and he was content to return to jail because he is, speaking metaphorically, 'taking a bullet for the boss'. Perhaps Şahin is the CEO of the whole company. Were that the case, Mert's 'Şahin' might exist, but Inspector Şen would still have arrested the correct man.

DarkMarket was closed down in October 2008, but nobody – whether from law enforcement or among the criminals themselves – has a grasp on what its real history was and its real significance is. Three years on and only a tiny proportion of the nearly 100 arrests carried out around the world have made it to trial.

Legal systems are finding it extremely hard to come to terms with the highly technical nature of evidence in cybercrime, but the pattern that sees most crimes committed in third countries also creates tremendous barriers to the detection and prosecution of the offences. Ambiguity, doubt, illusion and dissemblance have always played an important role in fathoming the ways and means of organised crime. And the Internet magnifies their power severalfold.

40

MIDDAY EXPRESS

Tekirdağ Prison, Western Turkey, March 2011

A vaguely handsome man in an elegant black suit and black tie scrutinised me carefully as he entered the small, oblong room. His black eyes under a slightly receding hairline accentuated the hypnotic stare and, momentarily, I was tongue-tied. Here was the man I had been reading about, talking about, thinking about for nearly two years. Now, when I finally met him, I was suddenly unable to think of anything appropriate to say.

He may have been wasting in prison for two and a half years, but he had lost neither his poise nor his careful self-control. Throughout our three hours of discussion I was keenly aware that he was interviewing me just as much as I was interviewing him.

My first brief stay in Tekirdağ occurred in 1976, just before publication of the book *Midnight Express*, which was later made into a successful film by Alan Parker. It tells the story of Billy Hayes, a young American who was caught smuggling drugs out of Turkey. The hideous ordeal he suffered at the hands of a sadistic prison officer shocked audiences throughout Europe and the United States. Turkey had a reputation as a brutal and unforgiving country at the time; indeed, while I was there I had been attacked, while sleeping in a tent, by a group of hoodlums, to the accompaniment of demands for foreigners to go home.

Thirty-five years later I approached Tekirdağ prison. Like the one where Hayes had been kept, it was a top-security facility. Lying a mile or so up a moderate incline, it was surrounded by barren fields as far as the eye could see. Behind a thick curtain of heavy snow I spotted the prison's high, faded cream walls and watchtowers manned by silhouetted machine-gunners. My first impression suggested that nothing had changed since Parker's movie.

Inside, however, I was relieved to learn that in this part of the country at least prison conditions had improved beyond recognition. All inmates had a television, shower and toilet in their cell. The food was a touch spartan, but undoubtedly nutritious and reasonably tasty, while the guards acted with courtesy, not just towards me, but towards the prisoners as well. In several respects conditions here were preferable to those found in many British prisons.

There were some notorious convicts in Tekirdağ, including the instigator of the murder of Hrant Dink, the ethnic Armenian writer assassinated by extremists for, well, being an ethnic Armenian writer. It was also no surprise that the prison contained some of Turkey's most notorious drug lords.

And among the terrorists and mafia dons there was a representative of the most state-of-the-art form of malfeasance – cybercrime. It had taken me more than a year to get an audience with Çağatay Evyapan: I had needed to convince both the Turkish authorities and Evyapan himself. For months, this seemed completely impossible. My astonishment was boundless when I received a message one Monday in early March 2011 from the Prison Directorate in Ankara informing me that, if Çağatay was willing, I would be permitted to see him that very Wednesday. After that, I was told, Çağatay would be moved and my window of opportunity would be slammed shut.

What the Turkish authorities did not know, nor would they have cared, was that my passport was deep in the bowels of the consular section of the Chinese Embassy in London, having a visa processed. My attempts to extract the passport in order to fly to Istanbul on Tuesday were dismissed robotically by the Chinese officials. Instead, I contacted Tekirdağ prison directly and begged them to allow me to postpone the interview for one day. I was informed that if they received the order to move Cha0 before Thursday, then regardless of whether or not I travelled there, I would not be permitted to see him. The hunt would be over.

So I was extremely agitated as I battled my way through the snow-storm from Istanbul to Tekirdağ on Thursday morning, a day late. It was quite possible that I would arrive only to be told that I had lost the chance to meet Cha0 in person. After a long wait I was taken through three thick revolving steel gates whose mechanism had a biometric print of my hand, and was introduced to the Director of the prison. Far from the ogre one might have expected, he was charming and affable. He said that they had not received any directive from Ankara and that after lunch in the canteen I would be able to talk to Mr Evyapan.

Eventually I was led through to the small, oblong room. Çağatay Evyapan is cautious but self-confident. Just as Bilal Şen had told me, his instincts would detect immediately if I was trying to ferret out some snippet of information in a devious way. He reminded me of Julian Assange, the mastermind behind WikiLeaks – super-smart, but with an iron conviction in his own intellectual superiority, which at times might be taken for extreme narcissism.

When I suggested to him that Lord Cyric was Tony – the tubby, bespectacled businessman named by Mert Ortaç – he emitted a snort of the deepest contempt. 'You've been talking to Turkish intelligence, haven't you?' he said sharply. In a manner of speaking Cha0 was correct: if Mert was lying (let's face it, a real possibility), then the bespectacled man must have been planted in his story by MIT, Turkish intelligence.

But as we talked Çağatay confirmed some very important aspects of Mert's story, including the location of the apartment where Mert was kidnapped and the existence of exchanges between Mert and the local American Embassy worker, Lucy Hoover. He also conceded that once again his own arrest had been prompted by a real-world error.

For all his self-possessed intelligence, Cha0 indicated he had one great fear – ironically the same unspoken worry that stalked his nemesis from the Turkish police. He claimed that during his questioning one of his interrogators offered him the opportunity to go into witness protection. In exchange, he would be asked to testify in the Ergenekon investigation. They demanded that he admit to having established a secret cyber network for the Deep State conspiracy among the military, intelligence services and media. The police flatly deny that any such offer was made.

Cha0 refused – the last thing he would want, like Inspector Şen, is to come under the wheels of a struggle between the Deep State and the government. They do things differently in cyberspace.

Throughout our chat Çağatay suggested that he and a narrow group of hackers possessed a far greater grasp of what was happening on the darkside of the Web than anybody from the authorities. He implied that his aim was merely to demonstrate the hopelessness of the attempts by the forces of law and order to police the Internet – he contended that there will always be people like him who are ahead of the game.

Remarkably, he seemed unperturbed by his incarceration and the fact that he may have to serve the remaining twenty-two years on his earlier conviction from 2000, not to mention any additional charges that may be preferred against him as a consequence of his activity on DarkMarket.

When we broached the subject of the FBI and Keith Mularski, a withering look spread slowly across his face. 'The FBI have nothing on me. If they did, why did not Master Splyntr send information which the Turkish police could use to charge me?' he asked. 'Instead all they can do is use this small-time nobody, Ortaç, to try and trap me.' Çağatay then claimed that he had hacked into Mularski's database and extracted the information gathered by the FBI on all the DarkMarket members, including the material on himself.

Being in prison, Çağatay was of course unable to document his claims. He said he knew that Splyntr was FBI from the beginning (although Çağatay joined DarkMarket at JiLsi's invitation in February 2006 when Master Splyntr was quite well established on the board) and that his strategy was 'to keep my friends close and my enemies even closer' – hence his willingness to work with Splyntr as an administrator.

It was an appropriate topic on which to end. At its heart, the story of DarkMarket was about two men – Çağatay Evyapan and Keith Mularski, both supported by impressive teams and contacts. Cha0 was no ordinary criminal. While making money was the primary purpose of the enterprise, Çağatay seemed to regard the struggle between himself and law enforcement as having a deeper significance, almost as though he was seeking to demonstrate his superior ability and, by implication, the futility of law enforcement's attempts to police cyberspace. In this lay a strong element of the original anarchism of geek culture – behavioural patterns and moral codes undergo a shift as we move from the real to the virtual. The rules of the game are different and new.

The FBI agent ran out the winner, but it was a narrow victory and by no means complete. Three years after DarkMarket closed down, the echoes of this extraordinary criminal venture can be heard in prisons and courts in several parts of the world. And, of course, many Dark-Marketeers are still stalking cyberspace.

The Internet is a transcendental invention that has seeped into every part of our lives and into every room in our homes. But beware – Lord Cyric might be hiding in a virtual cupboard somewhere.

EPILOGUE

At first glance the demise of DarkMarket appeared to deal a major blow to crime on the Internet. But it didn't. It did, however, temporarily place a spanner in the works of some major carding networks, including Cha0's operation in Turkey, Maksik's in Ukraine and Freddybb's in England. But the primary message that other serious cyber criminals took from the whole affair was simple: engagement in carding forums like Shadowcrew and DarkMarket, especially those English-language sites with large memberships, now entailed an unacceptable level of risk.

There was already some evidence that members whose main aim was to make money rather than enhance their reputation were far less present on DarkMarket than they had been on Shadowcrew. The number of posts made by people like Freddybb declined dramatically from one to the other. On Shadowcrew he posted fifty public messages and 200 private. On DarkMarket this stood at fifteen and twelve respectively. The US Secret Service's takedown of Shadowcrew clearly demonstrated the vulnerability of these sites and Freddybb had learned the lesson: lower your visibility.

Alongside the dangers of being busted, the carding forums had in any event outlived their use. It was via these websites that criminals had, over almost a decade of activity, established global networks of people they could trust. Whether as buyers or sellers of illegally procured data and documents, they had found their markets.

But the exposure of Keith Mularski as Master Splyntr, and the revelation that DarkMarket was in part a law-enforcement sting operation, undoubtedly hastened the demise of the carding forums. This wrecked the long-term strategy of the FBI and its partner agencies in

Western Europe. The plan had been for Master Splyntr to re-emerge as the one honest carder who had foiled the FBI's attempts at capture, who was hence deserving of even greater levels of trust within the carding fraternity.

Instead, in response to the DarkMarket affair, hackers, crackers and cyber criminals are burrowing deeper into the digital underground. There is also increasing specialisation in the business. Hackers and malware coders are developing designer programs that target specific systems or seek out particular information. They then sell this to a group that actually supervises the penetration of a financial institution or its customers. Once they have access to the money, they will contact a 'mule herder', a person or group who employs 'money mules' across the world. There are countless advertisements on websites offering work to people using their computers at home. A number of these are placed by mule herders. The herder asks potential mules to place their bank accounts at the herder's disposal in exchange for a percentage of the sums flowing through them.

The breaking down of criminal activity into these distinct entities makes it more difficult for law enforcement to identify what is actually going on and who is cooperating with whom. The proliferation of mobile devices and apps also offers huge opportunities to cyber criminals.

The rapid expansion of Internet users presents another major problem. Police in Western Europe have noted that the size of the Chinese criminal hacking community is growing apace. Until recently, the 419 or Advanced Fraud Fee scam was the preserve of West African criminal groups, especially Nigerians, the proud creators of those bizarre emails urgently entreating the recipient to assist in the movement of millions of dollars of a deceased dictator.

419, named after the relevant paragraph in Nigeria's penal code, is a very old trick – it forms the heart of *The Alchemist*, a comedy by the Elizabethan playwright Ben Jonson. In essence, the fraudster persuades the victim to advance a small sum of money on the promise that this will lead to the victim receiving a much greater amount later on. He then either milks his victim for more money or simply disappears with the first tranche. While possible in Elizabethan times, it was a laborious business. The Internet has made it extremely lucrative because, using spam emails, the criminal can reach an audience of tens of millions. The chances of finding a sucker are very greatly enhanced.

The 419 scam comes in many shapes and sizes. It sometimes arrives as an appeal to rich Westerners to come to the aid of an impoverished African child. Letters, faxes and emails beseeching Americans in particular for funds to erect a new church or bolster a congregation are frequent – in these cases, the motivation of the victims is well intentioned and charitable. Another lucrative prey of the 419 scammers are the lovelorn, in particular middle-aged widows and divorcees who develop virtual relationships with West African toy boys, who slowly leech them of their savings as an advance on sexual dalliance that never comes to pass.

419s are now being dispatched from China in both Chinese and English. This complements a second Chinese hacking speciality, which is the theft of items from MMORPG, an awkward acronym for the awkwardly named Massively Multiple Online Role-Playing Games, such as World of Warcraft, or the 'real life' games, Second Life or Habbo Hotel. These all have digital currencies that can be exchanged for genuine money. This in turn invests value in the virtual goods and services, which players can purchase to add to the pleasure of their gaming experience. Although they are not alone, Chinese hackers have learned to 'steal' these digital items or monies, which they can convert to actual real-world cash. China's monumental computing potential remains largely untapped at the moment, yet it is already regarded in most sectors relating to computer security in civilian and military life as second in the global pecking order after the United States. As China begins to realise that potential, the nature of the Internet will change.

To combat these growing threats, governments and industry are now pouring hundreds of billions of dollars into cyber security, whether in law enforcement, the protection of intellectual copyright or the military domain. Almost all of these funds are invested in technology, the idea being that this will be sufficient to protect the Internet from all the bad code, malware and viruses that are prowling around cyberspace looking for unprotected computer networks to attack.

By contrast, there is virtually no investment in trying to ascertain who is hacking and why. Nobody differentiates between the hackers from WikiLeaks, from the American or Chinese military, from criminal syndicates and from the simply curious.

But hackers are a rare and very special breed. Their psychological and social profiles differ, on the whole, from those of traditional criminals, above all the ones who are key to unlocking the criminal business opportunities on the Web, but are not very interested in money – in other words, the geeks. Understanding their abilities and their motivation in engaging in specific activities, whether criminal or otherwise, would enormously benefit a security industry that is over-dependent on technical solutions. On those rare occasions when law enforcement or the private sector tracks down hackers, leading to their prosecution and conviction, little is done to engage with the wrongdoers. Instead, the criminal-justice systems of Europe and the United States seek to impose heavy jail sentences on them and thereafter to restrict their access to computers.

Given their peculiar psycho-sociological profile, this is a big error. First, one should take their age into consideration: most hackers engage at a very early age in activity that one might best describe as legally ambiguous. Like Detlef Hartmann, they can be seduced into illegal work on the Web before their moral compass has properly evolved and before they fully understand the implications of what they are doing.

In real life they are often psychologically vulnerable, which means that locking them away among real criminals can be very counterproductive, as was the case with Max Vision. While he has an unpredictable ego, all officials agree that Vision has a planet-sized brain with an unparalleled understanding of computer security. In a world where there is a dearth of computer security specialists and where the threats are proliferating, it seems unwise to incarcerate a phenomenal asset. This is not to argue that hackers who have engaged in criminal activity should escape punishment, but that the need for rehabilitation is not only a moral imperative for the state, but potentially of considerable practical value.

Raoul Chiesa, a former hacker, runs a small academic centre called the Hacker Profiling Unit based in Turin and funded by the United Nations. His research is grounded in his intimate knowledge of the hacking community and on hackers' answers to the extensive questionnaires that he sends out to them. The early results from his work offer important clues as to the make-up of the hacker.

Most striking is the gender imbalance that pervades not just the illicit domains of cyber, but also the organisation and operation of the

Internet as a whole. It is a subject only alluded to in the pages of this book, but deserves detailed study. While men still dominate politics and the economy the world over, this domination is extreme when it comes to new technology. There are, of course, many very dynamic women engaged in new technology and new media, but statistically they comprise a tiny percentage: according to Chiesa, just 5 per cent. Hackers are almost invariably men.

A second finding in Chiesa's study is that the average hacker is either smart or very smart. Furthermore he has noted that there is a high incidence, close to 100 per cent, among hackers of advanced ability in science – physics, maths and chemisty. This is combined with a relatively low level of ability in the humanities.

Finally, there is the critical issue of hackers' relationships. Most – but not all – hackers find it much easier to form relationships in the impersonal environment of the Internet than they do in real life. The interesting question is why.

Hackers usually enter the fray as adolescents, exactly at the time when a great majority find it difficult to establish relationships, especially with the opposite sex. So, at least in part, their difficulties in this area are entirely natural. But Chiesa has also identified that an abnormally high number of hackers have described problems in communicating with family, above all with their parents.

Reading Chiesa's research and having spent a great deal of time interviewing different types of hackers put me in mind of the work of Simon Baron-Cohen, Professor of Developmental Psychopathology at Cambridge University. His pioneering work on autism has led to a deeper understanding of the spectrum of male/female behavioural patterns. In essence, typical males show an enhanced ability to 'systematise' the external world, whereas typical females show a greater skill at 'empathising'. This is not to say that all women are poor map-readers and that all men are hopeless listeners, merely that there is a pronounced tendency in each gender towards either 'systematising' among men or 'empathising' among women.

Baron-Cohen's subsequent research led to him uncovering a link between the extreme male mind, which in certain circumstances could be described as 'autistic', and high levels of testosterone to which a foetus may be exposed in the womb. His thesis is controversial, but in many respects convincing, and without question of value when considering hackers and their behavioural patterns. Hackers are not, of course, all autistic; in fact very few of them are (although some celebrated ones, such as Gary McKinnon, wanted in the United States for hacking into the Pentagon, have been diagnosed with Asperger's syndrome). But they do appear to conform to many of the clinical observations recorded by Professor Baron-Cohen of personalities who sit quite far down the 'male' end of the spectrum.

With further research, this could mean that it will be possible to identify hacker personality types among children who are still at school. In this way, peers and mentors could encourage their skills while, at the same time, offering them ethical guidance so that their abilities can be channelled in positive directions. The word 'hacker' tends to carry pejorative overtones. But the capacity to hack is in fact an asset, both personal and societal. Computers and networks will never be safe if they are not protected by advanced hackers. Some such individuals are already working to that end. In my experience, 90 per cent of the hackers involved in criminal activities expressed a powerful desire to work within the licit security industry – and, even with a criminal conviction, they should surely be given the chance.

Adewale Taiwo, aka Freddybb

On 1st January 2009 Adewale Taiwo was sentenced to four years' imprisonment by Hull Crown Court for conspiracy to defraud between June 2004 and February 2008. He had pleaded guilty the previous November to one count, having already admitted to defrauding just under £600,000 from bank accounts around the world. The judge recommended that, on completion of his sentence, he be deported to Nigeria.

With time discounted for good behaviour, Taiwo was due for release on 29th August 2010. Two weeks earlier he had appeared in court in Grimsby, across the Humber estuary from Hull. This was a hearing stipulated by Britain's Proceeds of Crime Act, one of Tony Blair's rare sensible amendments to the criminal-justice system, which enables the state to recover assets from criminals. It was a farcical end to a serious case. The prosecutor had mislaid a key file, triggering an unexpected reaction from the bearded Judge Graham Robinson, whose initial good humour quickly turned sour. He announced that he was not going to reschedule the hearing and so the two sides should therefore come to an agreement more or less immediately. This placed Adewale in a very strong position. The judge finally accepted a figure of just over £53,000, which had been whittled down from the initial assessment of £353,067. Taiwo announced that he would not be paying, which meant that he would have to serve an extra year in prison. In fact, on 7th April 2011 he was deported to Nigeria. One of the most intelligent characters to grace the carding boards, Taiwo almost succeeded in sustaining his dual life as a gifted chemical engineer and a cyber criminal.

Detective Sergeant Chris Dawson

DS Chris Dawson had worked on Freddybb's case with exceptional diligence, putting in many of his own hours to ensure that the jumble of figures, dates and technological detail was comprehensible to any lay person when it reached court. In a break for consultations during Taiwo's Proceeds of Crime hearing, Dawson thought he heard Taiwo say, 'Fuck it, I'm not paying.' When the judge left the courtroom, the detective stormed out in a fury caused by the incompetence of the English judicial system.

He continues to work as a senior homicide officer in Hull.

Dimitry Golubov

Following his arrest in Odessa, the hacker Dimitry Golubov spent five and a half months in prison, during which time he was interrogated by American law-enforcement officials, including Greg Crabb of the US Postal Inspection Service. However, on the intervention of two Ukrainian MPs, he was released and finally exonerated of any wrongdoing by a court in Kiev in 2009.

Six foot two, with a charismatic blue-eyed gaze, Golubov denies any relationship with Script although there are inconsistencies in his version of events, and the digital evidence in the hands of American law enforcement tells a very different story (this included data uncovered on Roman Vega's computer that Script was Golubov).

Script faded away after his release from custody, but Golubov returned with a renewed commitment to social change and enterprise by forming

The Internet Party of Ukraine. Still based in Odessa, Golubov has developed a political programme that aims at fighting corruption, pornography and drug-dealing on the Internet. He is confident that within a decade he will be elected either Prime Minister or President of the Ukraine, and although at the moment that looks like an outside bet, his drive and ambition should be taken seriously. The Internet Party has fielded dozens of candidates at local council elections in Odessa, and although, so far, it has only won a single seat, there is no question that the movement is growing throughout the country.

Strangely, though, despite his organisation's fierce moral stands on some criminal issues, such as child pornography, Golubov has launched a campaign to secure the release of the notorious carder Maksik from his thirty-year jail sentence in Turkey.

Roman Vega

Roman Vega has been incarcerated since his arrest in Nicosia in February 2003. Transferred to California in June 2004 at the request of the United States, he has been in custody ever since, but has never been tried. At the time of writing he is a prisoner in the Metropolitan Detention Center, Brooklyn, a dour facility near Gowanus Bay. During this entire period Vega has had no visitors except for his legal representatives.

In August 2007 a hearing was scheduled in front of Judge Charles R. Breyer in the Northern District of California. Prosecution and defence were ready to sign off on a plea bargain, which would have seen Vega released, having already served the forty-six months' sentence that the lawyers had agreed. On the afternoon before his release a prosecutor from the Eastern District of New York filed a whole new set of charges, requesting Vega's transfer to Brooklyn. The charges were in substance identical to the Californian ones. The prosecuting counsel in New York, however, chose a different statute under which to file the charges, to avoid a double-jeopardy ruling.

The transcript of the court hearing makes it clear that Judge Breyer, a brother of the Supreme Court member Stephen Breyer, was embarrassed and angered by the tactics of New York's Eastern District. The new indictment was based on information furnished by agents of the US Secret Service.

After Vega arrived in Brooklyn, the Secret Service offered him a deal: if he were to testify against Dimitry Golubov and other members of Ukraine's establishment (not hackers, but senior political figures), then they would drop the charges. But if he refused, they would bring further charges against him filed in different states of the Union. They would continue until he agreed to cooperate.

Regardless of what Vega has or has not done, he has already spent three times longer in jail than those sentenced for their activity in Shadowcrew, with two unresolved cases still hanging over him and the threat of more in the wings. Vega has been suffering from advanced dental decay for several years and is in constant pain, often unable to eat properly. He has been refused medical assistance by the Bureau of Prisons and the US Marshall Service.

There is no prospect of Vega being released in the foreseeable future.

Maksym Kovalchuk, aka Blade

Kovalchuk was arrested in May 2003 in Thailand and extradited to the United States, where he served four years in jail. The FBI consented to a negotiated plea agreement and he was released in late 2007, after which he returned to anonymity in the Ukraine. The FBI's decision to release him contrasts starkly with the Secret Service's tactic of holding onto Roman Vega.

Renukanth Subramaniam, aka JiLsi

On 26th February 2010 Subramaniam pleaded guilty to one charge of credit-card fraud and four charges of mortgage fraud, for which the judge at Blackfriars Crown Court sentenced him to four years' imprisonment. At the time of writing he is an inmate at West London's Wormwood Scrubs prison, whose alumni include the composer Sir Michael Tippett and the Rolling Stones guitarist, Keith Richards.

With time off for good behaviour, Subramaniam is expected to be released in late July 2012. The bulk of his case relates not to DarkMarket but to mortgage fraud. The prosecution included five such instances (although three of these applications were turned down by the financial institutions). While mortgage fraud is a crime in its own right, the prosecution suggested a link between Subramaniam's earnings from

DarkMarket and his ability to pay the mortgages. In fact, Subramaniam argues that he was not responsible for the mortgage payments, as he applied for the loans on behalf of friends who were not eligible to do so themselves. Additionally, Subramaniam is awaiting the outcome of his Proceeds of Crime hearing to see whether he is liable to further forfeiture of funds. Under the terms of his Prevention of Crime Order, he will have no unsupervised access to computers for five years following his release from prison.

Detlef Hartmann, aka Matrix001

On 9th October 2007 the Regional Court in Stuttgart ruled that Hartmann should stand trial on thirteen counts of credit-card fraud. However, the same court announced that the motion to prosecute him on a charge of Forming a Criminal Conspiracy was rejected. With the more serious charge dropped, Hartmann was released from Stammheim prison, where he had spent the previous four months. The key decision preventing his prosecution on the charge of conspiracy lay in the court's interpretation of Germany's Basic Law, its constitution, which states that a member of a conspiracy must feel part of a 'unified group' in which there is presumed 'the subordination of the individual to the will of the collective'. The judge argued that the fluid nature of the Internet and the membership structures of DarkMarket did not meet these criteria – a ruling that, of course, has important implications for the development of laws relating to crime on the Internet in Germany.

In July 2008 Hartmann received a suspended sentence of twenty-one months for the fraud charges. He has since taken up his studies in graphic design again and has completely broken any links with the underground.

RedBrigade

He has largely gone straight and is currently in Europe.

Max Vision, aka Max Butler, aka Iceman

On 12th February 2010 Max Vision was sentenced by a court in Pittsburgh to thirteen years behind bars, the longest jail term ever handed down by an American court for hacking. The prosecution calculated that his hacking resulted in credit-card losses of more than $85 million. He is now an inmate at the low-security Federal Correctional Institution Lompoc in southern California, where he is allowed no access to computers of any sort.

Vision's hacking ability is unparalleled – he is unquestionably one of the smartest men serving time in the United States. At a closed conference in the autumn of 2010 I discussed his case with one of the most senior officials from the Department of Homeland Security to deal with cyber threats. He agreed with me that having a computer user of Vision's ability languishing in jail was probably a misuse of the US's human assets, but pointed out that Vision's ego – almost as large as his intellect – had also played a major part in the affair.

Nicholas Joehle, aka Dron

Joehle has been released from prison, having served his sentence for credit-card fraud and the illegal manufacture of skimming machines.

Hakim B, aka Lord Kaisersose

Lord Kaisersose is in Marseilles still awaiting trial, but on bail. France is another country where the wheels of justice could use a spot of grease.

Cha0

Cha0 is either running his businesses in Slovenia or in jail, depending on whether the real Cha0 is Şahin or Çağatay Evyapan. The latter is on remand at one of Turkey's highest-security facilities in Tekirdağ. His trial is due to begin this year, but the prosecutor has dropped the more serious charges relating to organised crime.

Mert Ortaç, aka SLayraCkEr

Mert was on remand in an Istanbul prison facing charges relating to the Akbank case when he was released on a technicality in March 2010. He was rearrested in November 2010 and, at the time of writing, is still on remand. Of all those involved in DarkMarket, Mert was one of the most gifted, if wayward and unpredictable, characters.

Keith Mularski and Bilal Şen

They are both back out patrolling the mean streets of cyber.

Lord Cyric

Who is he? The hunt continues . . .

A NOTE ON SOURCES

The bulk of the information in this book is provided by roughly 200 hours of interviews which I conducted between 2009 and 2011. Leonida Krushelnycky also undertook several hours of interviews.

In addition to this, I have relied on two main documentary sources. The first are the court records from a number of trials related to the websites CarderPlanet, Shadowcrew and DarkMarket. The second are the archives of the websites themselves, in particular the former two which are readily available on the web. Unfortunately, the DarkMarket archive is less accessible. I know of only one and that is in the possession of the FBI who, for operational reasons, are not at liberty to share it.

There is a considerable amount of literature on the issues of cyber crime, cyber industrial espionage and cyber warfare, much of it found on the Internet. For thoroughness, I would highlight the work of Kevin Poulsen and his team whose blog, *Threat Level*, is both well-written and properly researched. I would recommend two books dealing specifically with cyber crime, Kevin Poulsen's *Kingpin* and Joseph Menn's *Fatal System Error*. For a broader introduction into some of the challenges emerging as a consequence of Internet technology, Jonathan Zittrain's *The Future of the Internet: And How to Stop It* should be the first port of call.

Other blogs of real value include *Krebsonsecurity* by Brian Krebs; Bruce Schneier's newsletter, *Crypto-gram*; the blog of F-Secure, the Finnish Computer Security company; and, finally, Dancho Danchev and Ryan Naraine's *Zero Day* blog on Znet.

ACKNOWLEDGEMENTS

Writing this book presented many challenges which I could never have met had it not been for the generous assistance I received from a number of friends and colleagues around the world.

In Britain, two people played a vital role. Leonida Krushelnycky has proved to be an indefatigable researcher, often uncovering vital material long after I had given up any hope of finding it. But for her efforts, the book would have been considerably poorer. Vesna Vucenovic ensured that the administration of this project was as painless as one could hope.

On my travels, I had the fortune to encounter two journalists whose patience and cheerfulness matched their professionalism and skill which were of the highest order. Kai Laufen helped me understand the complexities of German justice. But his contribution was still greater because of the contacts he helped me make and the hospitality he offered. Equally, I would have been completely lost in Istanbul, and Turkey, were it not for Şebnem Arsu. Tenacious, unfailingly polite and able to conjure up a solution when all appeared lost, I owe her a considerable debt.

From the various police forces around the world who have discussed DarkMarket with me, I must highlight Agent Keith J. Mularski of the FBI, Inspector Bilal Şen of the Anti-Smuggling and Organized Crime Department of the Turkish Police, and Detective Sergeant Chris Dawson of the Humberside police. All three have given up much of their valuable time to talk to me in the most illuminating fashion and were always happy to clarify anything I had not fully grasped. I would also like to thank the officers from the Serious Organised Crime Agency in London and Christian Aghroum, formerly of OCLCTIC in Paris.

From a rather different perspective, RioRita in Ukraine was a mine of information about CarderPlanet and beyond – my special thanks to him. I learned as much about the nuts and bolts of cyber crime from RedBrigade, I owe him a great deal for his friendliness and good-natured response to my countless requests for information and analysis.

Matrix001 and JiLsi were always willing to share their knowledge about the details of DarkMarket and their assessment of specific events. In Pittsburgh, I found Max Vision to be a brilliant and helpful interlocutor. All three have my sincere thanks.

Çağatay Evyapan and Mert Ortaç were two of the most interesting personalities I have met in the past three years even if they don't see eye to eye themselves. I would like to convey my gratitude to both of them despite the difficulty of their current situations.

In Estonia, Madis Tüür was an exemplary guide to the politics and history of the country, not to mention an ever entertaining host.

Thanks also to Brooks Decillia from CBC in Calgary for his selfless research. Likewise, Daniel Goldberg and Linus Larsson came to my rescue in Stockholm.

Two people have helped me in the background with technical issues. In Helsinki, Mikko Hyppönen, Chief Research Officer of F-Secure and Vicente Diaz of Kaspersky Labs in Barcelona were always available to help me get my head round things I simply could not understand. I also received much wise advice regarding more general cyber security issues from Rex Hughes at Wolfson College, Cambridge.

I also want to thank the following people who helped me in a variety of different ways: Allison Culliford, Luke Dembosky, Sophie Devonshire, Joris Evers, Detective Spencer Frizzell, Tamara Glenny, Camino Kavanagh, Suat Kınıklıoğlu, Dirk Kolberg, Darryl Leaning, Melissa Llewelyn-Davies, Jane McClellan Q.C., Mark Medish, Steve Milner, Jaan Prisaalu, Colin Robinson, Anya Stiglitz and Eneken Tikk.

My agents and publishers have been unstinting in their support. Clare Conville in London is as good an agent as one can imagine, backed by a wonderful team. Michael Carlisle provides an equally dynamic service in New York. I am fortunate to have a trio of editors, Will Sulkin at The Bodley Head, Dan Frank at Knopf and Sarah MacLachlan at Anansi Press, who have both made the writing experience more manageable while greatly enhancing the final product. If errors have crept in, I, naturally, bear full responsibility for them. I would also like to thank two others who have had a significant impact on the book, Kay Peddle at The Bodley Head and Janie Yoon at Anansi.

My three children to whom this work is dedicated have maintained a healthy interest in the book despite the fact that I have been frequently both absent and absent-minded while writing. They have never been anything less than cheerful and supportive.

And finally my thanks and love to Kirsty Lang, my wife, who has commented, critiqued, cajoled and kept me afloat throughout. Not for the first time, I could not have done it without her.

June 2011

INDEX